JSON at Work
Practical Data Integration for the Web

Tom Marrs

Beijing · Boston · Farnham · Sebastopol · Tokyo

JSON at Work

by Tom Marrs

Printed in the United States of America.

Published by O'Reilly Media, Inc., 1005 Gravenstein Highway North, Sebastopol, CA 95472.

O'Reilly books may be purchased for educational, business, or sales promotional use. Online editions are also available for most titles (*http://oreilly.com/safari*). For more information, contact our corporate/institutional sales department: 800-998-9938 or *corporate@oreilly.com*.

Editor: Meg Foley
Production Editor: Nicholas Adams
Copyeditor: Sharon Wilkey
Proofreader: Charles Roumeliotis

Indexer: Ellen Troutman-Zaig
Interior Designer: David Futato
Cover Designer: Randy Comer
Illustrator: Rebecca Demarest

July 2017:   First Edition

Revision History for the First Edition
2017-06-16:   First Release

See *http://oreilly.com/catalog/errata.csp?isbn=9781449358327* for release details.

978-1-449-35832-7

[LSI]

To everyone who produces or consumes JSON data with web/mobile applications, REST APIs, and messaging systems—I hope this makes your job easier.

To the unsung JSON community that produces JSON-based tools and libraries for the rest of us—thank you for all your hard work to make JSON useful and meaningful.

Table of Contents

Part II. The JSON Ecosystem

Preface

JavaScript Object Notation (JSON) has become the de facto standard for RESTful interfaces, but an ecosystem of little-known standards, tools, and technologies is available that architects and developers can start using today to build well-designed applications. JSON is more than just a simple replacement for XML when you make an AJAX call. It is becoming the backbone of any serious data interchange over the internet. Solid standards and best practices can be used to harness the energy and enthusiasm around JSON to build truly elegant, useful, and efficient applications.

The only thing missing is a book to pull everything together. This book aims to help developers leverage JSON so that they can build enterprise-class applications and services. My goals are to promote the use of JSON tooling and the concept of message/document design as a first-class citizen in the fast-growing API community.

My journey into JSON began in 2007 when I was leading a large web portal project, and we had to populate a drop-down list with several thousand entries. At that time, I was reading *Head First AJAX* by Rebecca Riordan (O'Reilly), so I had a decent architectural approach. AJAX would solve overall latency and page load issues, but what about the data? I had been using XML successfully for several years, but it seemed like overkill for the task at hand—moving data from the backend of a web application to the View. *Head First AJAX* mentioned a new data format called JSON, and it looked like the way to go. My team began looking into APIs that would convert our Java objects into JSON, and chose the one that had the simplest and shortest JUnit tests—the goal was to do the simplest thing that could possibly work. We put the application under rigorous load testing, and the Java-to-JSON conversion was never a performance issue. The application scaled up in production, and the users saw their drop-down list in a timely manner.

Along my journey, I considered the use of JSON with web applications, RESTful APIs, and messaging. As of 2009, I was still working with XML because XML Schema provided the semantic validation needed for meaningful data interchange. So, my position at that time was to use JSON for web user interfaces, or UIs (for speed), and

XML for Web Services and Messaging (for integration). But then I heard about JSON Schema in 2010, and found that I had no further need for XML. The JSON Schema specification is still under development, but it's sufficiently mature enough now to use for enterprise-class integration.

At this point, I was hooked on or, more accurately, obsessed with JSON. I began looking around the internet to see what else JSON could do, and I found copious APIs, online tools, search capabilities, and more. In short, anything that has been done with XML can (and should) now be done with JSON.

I then began to look for JSON in books, and was disappointed when I could find only a chapter or two on the topic in a JavaScript or RESTful Web Services book. I saw a growing JSON community along with lots of tool support and articles and blogs, but there was no single place—other than Douglas Crockford's JSON site (*http://www.json.org*)—that pulled everything together.

Audience, Assumptions, and Approach

This book is for architects and developers who design/implement web and mobile applications, RESTful APIs, and messaging applications. Code examples are in JavaScript, Node.js, Ruby on Rails, and Java. If you're a Groovy, Go, Scala, Perl, Python, Clojure, or C# developer, you'll need to follow along with the code examples provided. But rest assured that most major/modern languages provide excellent JSON support. For the architect, I've provided guidelines, best practices, and architecture and design diagrams where appropriate. But in addition to providing visionary leadership, real architects prove their ideas with working code. While I love working with JSON and writing code, it's entirely meaningless without use cases, and a business and technical context. For developers, this book is packed with code examples, tooling, and Unit Tests, along with a GitHub repository (see "Code Examples" on page xvii).

Chapters 5–10 only have code examples only in Node.js to keep things simple and focused. But it's not hard to translate these examples into your platform of choice.

What Does "At Work" Mean?

When I wrote *JBoss at Work* with Scott Davis back in the mid-2000s, our vision was to write a book that developers could use at work on their daily jobs. In the same manner, the purpose of *JSON at Work* is to provide practical examples to developers based on my real-world integration experience with JSON. To that end, I've baked Unit Testing (wherever feasible) into every chapter. It's simple: if there's no test for a piece of code, then that code doesn't exist. Period.

Expect to roll up your sleeves and look at code. Whether you're an architect or developer, you'll find something here to help you on your job.

What You'll Learn

By reading and following this book's examples, you'll learn how to do the following:

- JSON basics and how to model JSON data
- Use JSON with Node.js, Ruby on Rails, and Java
- Structure JSON documents with JSON Schema to design and test APIs
- Search the contents of JSON documents with JSON Search tools
- Convert JSON documents to other data formats with JSON Transform tools
- Use JSON as part of an enterprise architecture
- Compare JSON-based Hypermedia formats, including HAL and `json:api`
- Leverage MongoDB to store and access JSON documents
- Use Apache Kafka to exchange JSON-based messages between services
- Use freely available JSON tools and utilities to simplify testing
- Invoke APIs in your favorite programming language with simple utilities and libraries

What You'll Work With

Here's a sample of the JSON tooling you'll use in this book:

- JSON editors/modelers
- Unit-Testing tools (e.g., Mocha/Chai, Minitest, JUnit)
- JSON Validators
- A JSON Schema Generator
- JSON Search tools
- JSON Transform (templating) tools

Who This Book Is Not For

This book is not for you if your only interest in JSON is to make AJAX calls from JavaScript. Although I cover this topic, it's just the tip of the iceberg. Plenty of JavaScript books have the chapter you're looking for.

Developers looking for a deep reference on REST, Ruby on Rails, Java, JavaScript, etc. won't find it here. This book relies on these technologies, but focuses on how to use JSON with these languages and technologies.

Organization

This book consists of the following parts:

- Part I, *JSON Overview and Platforms*
- Part II, *The JSON Ecosystem*
- Part III, *JSON in the Enterprise*
- Appendices

Part I, JSON Overview and Platforms

- Chapter 1, *JSON Overview*, starts with an overview of the JSON data format, describes best practices in JSON usage, and introduces the tools used throughout the book.
- Chapter 2, *JSON in JavaScript*, shows how to use JSON with JavaScript, Node.js, and Mocha/Chai Unit Tests.
- Chapter 3, *JSON in Ruby on Rails*, describes how to convert between Ruby objects and JSON, and integrate with Rails.
- Chapter 4, *JSON in Java*, tells you how to use JSON with Java and Sprint Boot.

Part II, The JSON Ecosystem

- Chapter 5, *JSON Schema*, helps you structure JSON documents with JSON Schema. Along the way, you'll generate a JSON Schema and design an API with it.
- Chapter 6, *JSON Search*, shows how to search JSON documents with jq and JSONPath.
- Chapter 7, *JSON Transform*, provides the tools you'll need transform a poorly designed JSON document to a better designed/more useful JSON document. Plus, it shows how to convert between JSON and other formats such as XML and HTML.

Part III, JSON in the Enterprise

- Chapter 8, *JSON and Hypermedia*, looks at how to use JSON with several well-known Hypermedia formats (e.g., HAL and `jsonapi`).

- Chapter 9, *JSON and MongoDB*, shows how to leverage MongoDB to store and access JSON documents.

- Chapter 10, *JSON Messaging with Kafka*, describes how to use Apache Kafka to exchange JSON-based messages between services.

Appendices

- Appendix A, *Installation Guides*, shows how to install the applications you'll need to run the code examples in this book.

- Appendix B, *JSON Community*, provides further information and links to connect you to the JSON community (e.g., standards and tutorials) and to help you go further with JSON.

Code Examples

All code examples for this book are freely available from the *JSON at Work* examples GitHub repository (*https://github.com/tmarrs/json-at-work-examples*).

This book is here to help you get your job done. In general, if example code is offered with this book, you may use it in your programs and documentation. You do not need to contact us for permission unless you're reproducing a significant portion of the code. For example, writing a program that uses several chunks of code from this book does not require permission. Selling or distributing a CD-ROM of examples from O'Reilly books does require permission. Answering a question by citing this book and quoting example code does not require permission. Incorporating a significant amount of example code from this book into your product's documentation does require permission.

We appreciate, but do not require, attribution. An attribution usually includes the title, author, publisher, and ISBN. For example: "*JSON at Work* by Tom Marrs (O'Reilly). Copyright 2017 Vertical Slice, Inc., 978-1-449-35832-7."

If you feel your use of code examples falls outside fair use or the permission given above, feel free to contact us at *permissions@oreilly.com*.

O'Reilly Safari

 *Safari* (formerly Safari Books Online) is a membership-based training and reference platform for enterprise, government, educators, and individuals.

Members have access to thousands of books, training videos, Learning Paths, interactive tutorials, and curated playlists from over 250 publishers, including O'Reilly Media, Harvard Business Review, Prentice Hall Professional, Addison-Wesley Professional, Microsoft Press, Sams, Que, Peachpit Press, Adobe, Focal Press, Cisco Press, John Wiley & Sons, Syngress, Morgan Kaufmann, IBM Redbooks, Packt, Adobe Press, FT Press, Apress, Manning, New Riders, McGraw-Hill, Jones & Bartlett, and Course Technology, among others.

For more information, please visit *http://oreilly.com/safari.*

How to Contact Us

Please address comments and questions concerning this book to the publisher:

O'Reilly Media, Inc.
1005 Gravenstein Highway North
Sebastopol, CA 95472
800-998-9938 (in the United States or Canada)
707-829-0515 (international or local)
707-829-0104 (fax)

We have a web page for this book, where we list errata, examples, and any additional information. You can access this page at *http://bit.ly/json-at-work.*

To comment or ask technical questions about this book, send email to *bookquestions@oreilly.com.*

For more information about our books, courses, conferences, and news, see our website at *http://www.oreilly.com.*

Find us on Facebook: *http://facebook.com/oreilly*

Follow us on Twitter: *http://twitter.com/oreillymedia*

Watch us on YouTube: *http://www.youtube.com/oreillymedia*

Acknowledgments

First of all, I'd like to acknowledge Douglas Crockford for creating and standardizing the JSON data format. JSON is the data language of REST and Microservices, and the overall community is indebted to his vision and efforts.

I appreciate my O'Reilly editor, Megan Foley, and my former editor, Simon St. Laurent, for believing in this book and for their patience and guidance on the project. Thanks for sticking with me and helping me throughout the project. I would also like to thank my O'Reilly copy edit team, Nick Adams and Sharon Wilkey, whose diligent work improved the quality of this manuscript.

Thanks to Matthew McCullough and Rachel Roumeliotis from the O'Reilly Open Source Convention (OSCON), Jay Zimmerman from No Fluff Just Stuff (NFJS), and Dilip Thomas from the Great Indian Developer Summit (GIDS) for giving me the chance to speak about JSON and REST at your conferences. It's always fun to speak at conferences, and I hope to continue doing this well into the future.

I'm grateful to my technical reviewers who provided valuable feedback on this book: Joe McIntyre, David Bock, Greg Ostravich, and Zettie Chinfong. I would also like to thank the following people who helped shape and mold my ideas on how to talk about JSON: Matthew McCullough, Scott Davis, Cristian Vyhmeister, Senthil Kumar, Sean Pettersen, John Gray, Doug Clark, Will Daniels, Dan Carda, and Peter Piper.

The Colorado Front Range technical community is world class, and I've had fun presenting at the following user groups to help refine my material:

- HTML5 Denver
- Denver Open Source User Group (DOSUG)
- Colorado Springs Open Source User Group (CS OSUG)
- Denver Java User Group (DJUG)
- Boulder Java User Group (BJUG)
- BoulderJS Meetup

Thanks to my friends in the Toastmasters (*http://www.toastmasters.org*) community who encouraged me, believed in me, and pushed me to finish the book: Darryle Brown, Deborah Frauenfelder, Elinora Reynolds, Betty Funderburke, Tom Hobbs, Marcy Brock, and many, many others. You have inspired me to communicate clearly, to "Lift as You Climb," and to "Travel Beyond."

There is an amazing JSON community on the internet. Much of this book is based on the great work that you've done and continue to do. You've inspired me to tell your story and to connect the dots.

To my late parents, Al and Dorene Marrs, who loved me and always believed in me and supported me—I know you're in a better place. You inspired me to be adaptable, to innovate, and to work hard. You always encouraged me to do my very best. Thank you for everything you did for me.

Finally, to my beautiful wife, Linda, and my daughter, Abby—I love you. Thanks for your patience with me while I spent my evenings and weekends on the manuscript and code.

PART I

JSON Overview and Platforms

CHAPTER 1

JSON Overview

The *JavaScript Object Notation* (JSON) data format enables applications to communicate over a network, typically through RESTful APIs. JSON is technology-agnostic, nonproprietary, and portable. All modern languages (e.g., Java, JavaScript, Ruby, C#, PHP, Python, and Groovy) and platforms provide excellent support for producing (serializing) and consuming (deserializing) JSON data. JSON is simple: it consists of developer-friendly constructs such as Objects, Arrays, and name/value pairs. JSON is not limited to Representational State Transfer (REST); it also works with the following:

- Node.js (which stores project metadata in *package.json*)
- NoSQL databases such as MongoDB (see Chapter 9)
- Messaging platforms such as Kafka (see Chapter 10)

JSON Is a Standard

In the early days, REST's detractors derided RESTful Web Services as being non-standard, but (just like HTTP) JSON is in fact a standard. Both the Internet Engineering Task Force (IETF) and Ecma International (formerly the European Computer Manufacturers Association, or ECMA) have recognized JSON as a standard. Douglas Crockford originally created JSON in 2001, and initially standardized it in 2006 under RFC 4627 through the IETF; see the JSON specification (*http://tools.ietf.org/html/rfc4627*). In the fall of 2013, Ecma International also standardized JSON under ECMA 404; see their JSON specification (*http://bit.ly/2skDdEV*). With Ecma recognition (per Douglas Crockford; see his Google+ page (*http://bit.ly/2thZmkj*)), JSON is now considered a formal international data processing standard.

In March 2014, Tim Bray published an updated version of Douglas Crockford's original standard as IETF RFC 7158 (*http://tools.ietf.org/html/rfc7158*) and RFC 7159 (*http://tools.ietf.org/html/rfc7159*) to correct errata with the original IETF 4627 standard (thus rendering it obsolete).

A Brief Sample

Before we go further, let's look at a small JSON sample. Example 1-1 shows a simple JSON document.

Example 1-1. firstValidObject.json

```
{ "thisIs": "My first JSON document" }
```

A valid JSON document can be either of the following:

- An Object surrounded by curly braces, { and }
- An Array enclosed by brackets, [and]

The preceding example shows an Object that contains a single key/value pair, where the key, "thisIs", has a value of "My first JSON document".

Just to keep us honest, let's validate this document by using JSONLint (*https://json lint.com/*). Just paste the text into the text area, click the Validate button, and you should see the page in Figure 1-1.

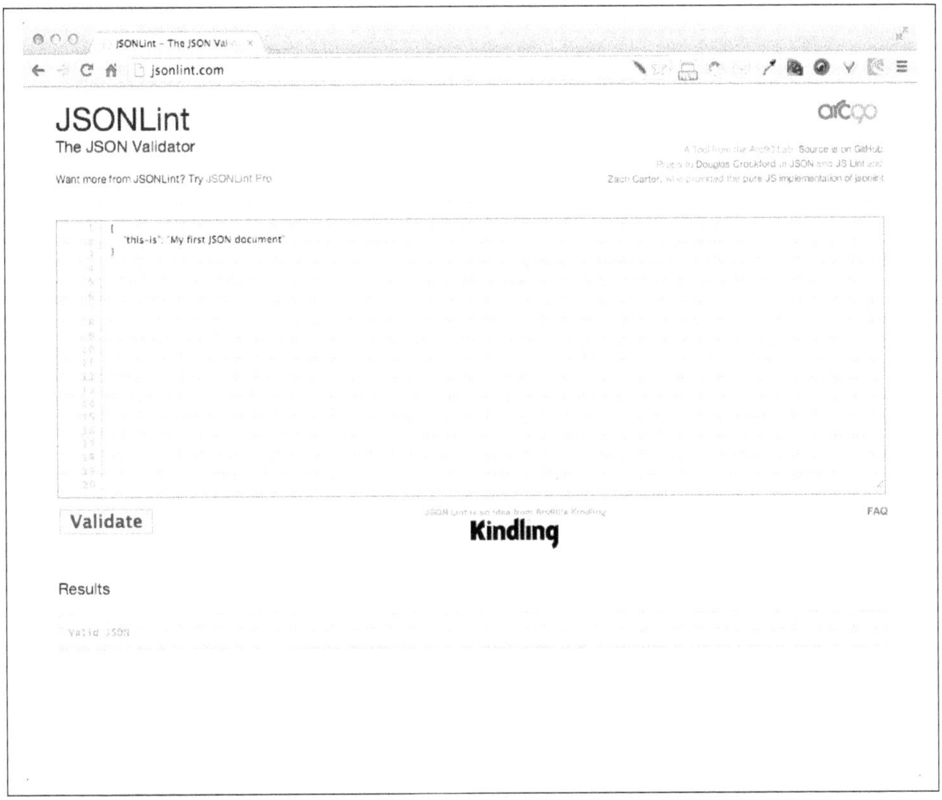

Figure 1-1. Simple/valid JSON document in JSONLint

Example 1-2 presents a simple JSON Array.

Example 1-2. firstValidArray.json

```
[
  "also",
  "a",
  "valid",
  "JSON",
  "doc"
]
```

In JSONLint, paste the JSON Array into the text area, and click the Validate button, and you should get the result shown in Figure 1-2.

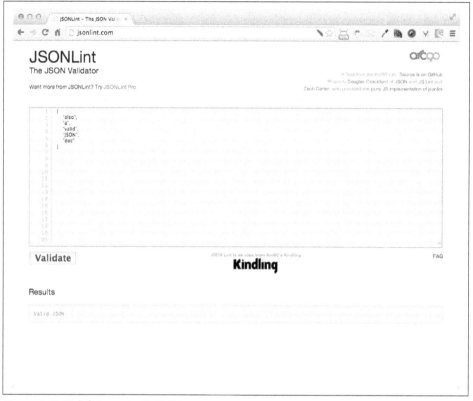

Figure 1-2. Valid Array in JSONLint

But we're getting ahead of ourselves. We'll cover JSON syntax more thoroughly in "Core JSON" on page 8.

Why JSON?

Although standardization through Ecma International and the IETF has helped JSON gain industry acceptance, other factors have popularized JSON:

- The explosive growth of RESTful APIs based on JSON
- The simplicity of JSON's basic data structures
- The increasing popularity of JavaScript

JavaScript's resurgence is boosting JSON's popularity. Over the past several years, we have seen the rise of JavaScript as a first-class development language and environment. This ecosystem includes platforms such as Node.js, and Mode/View/Controller (MVC) frameworks such as AngularJS, React, Backbone, and Ember. There has also been a tremendous increase in the number of books and websites showing best practices in JavaScript Objects and Patterns. According to Douglas Crockford, JSON is a subset of JavaScript's Object Literal notation, and fits seamlessly into JavaScript development.

Thousands of RESTful APIs leverage JSON. A sample list of popular JSON-based RESTful APIs includes the following:

- LinkedIn
- Twitter
- Facebook
- Salesforce
- GitHub
- DropBox
- Tumblr
- Amazon Web Services (AWS)

To see the thousands of available JSON-based REST APIs available, visit ProgrammableWeb (*http://www.programmableweb.com*), and do a search on *REST* and *JSON*. Then, take several weeks to review the results.

JSON is simple and is gradually replacing XML as the primary data interchange format on the internet. JSON is easy to read, and its structures easily translate to concepts well understood by software developers—Arrays, Objects, and name/value pairs. We don't have to scratch our heads or argue anymore about what should be an Element or an Attribute. Objects and their data members are a much better fit for Object-Oriented (OO) design and development. A document formatted in JSON is usually smaller than its XML equivalent, because JSON has less overhead and is more compact. This is due to the lack of begin and end tags surrounding each data element. So, at an enterprise level, JSON is more efficient to process than XML, because JSON documents can be transmitted over a network and processed faster than their XML counterparts.

Although Douglas Crockford initially intended JSON to be a data interchange format (typically with REST), JSON is now finding a home in configuration files for widely used products such as Node.js and Sublime Text. Node.js has a *package.json* file that it uses to define its standard npm package structure; we'll cover this in Chapter 2. Sublime Text, a popular IDE in the web development community, uses JSON to configure its appearance along with its package managers.

Core JSON

The Core JSON data format includes JSON Data and Value Types. We'll also cover versions, comments, and File/MIME Types.

JSON Data Types

JSON has the following core Data Types:

Name (or Key)/value pair
    Consists of a key (a data attribute) and a value.

Object
    An unordered collection of name/value pairs.

Array
    A collection of ordered values.

Now that we've covered basic definitions, let's dig deeper into each Data Type.

Name/value pairs

Example 1-3 shows some sample name/value pairs.

Example 1-3. nameValue.json

```
{
  "conference": "OSCON",
  "speechTitle": "JSON at Work",
  "track": "Web APIs"
}
```

Name/value pairs have the following characteristics:

- Each name (e.g., `"conference"`)
  - Is on the left side of the colon (`:`)
  - Is a String, and must be surrounded by double quotes
- The value (e.g., `"OSCON"`) is to the right of the colon. In the preceding example, the value type is a String, but there are several other Value Types.

We'll cover Strings and other valid Value Types further in "JSON Value Types" on page 11.

Objects

Objects consist of name/value pairs. Example 1-4 shows a sample Object that represents an address.

Example 1-4. simpleJsonObject.json

```
{
  "address" : {
    "line1" : "555 Any Street",
    "city" : "Denver",
    "stateOrProvince" : "CO",
    "zipOrPostalCode" : "80202",
    "country" : "USA"
  }
}
```

Example 1-5 shows an Object with a nested Array.

Example 1-5. jsonObjectNestedArray.json

```
{
  "speaker" : {
    "firstName": "Larson",
    "lastName": "Richard",
    "topics": [ "JSON", "REST", "SOA" ]
  }
}
```

Example 1-6 shows an Object that contains another Object.

Example 1-6. jsonObjectNestedObject.json

```
{
  "speaker" : {
    "firstName": "Larson",
    "lastName": "Richard",
    "topics": [ "JSON", "REST", "SOA" ],
    "address" : {
      "line1" : "555 Any Street",
      "city" : "Denver",
      "stateOrProvince" : "CO",
      "zipOrPostalCode" : "80202",
      "country" : "USA"
    }
  }
}
```

Objects have the following characteristics:

- Are enclosed within a beginning left curly brace ({) and an ending right curly brace (})
- Consist of comma-separated, unordered, name/value pairs
- Can be empty, { }
- Can be nested within other Objects or Arrays

Arrays

Example 1-7 shows an Array (containing nested Objects and Arrays) that describes conference presentations, including title, length, and abstract.

Example 1-7. jsonArray.json

```
{
  "presentations": [
    {
      "title": "JSON at Work: Overview and Ecosystem",
      "length": "90 minutes",
      "abstract": [ "JSON is more than just a simple replacement for XML when",
                    "you make an AJAX call."
                  ],
      "track": "Web APIs"
    },
    {
      "title": "RESTful Security at Work",
      "length": "90 minutes",
      "abstract": [ "You've been working with RESTful Web Services for a few years",
                    "now, and you'd like to know if your services are secure."
                  ],
      "track": "Web APIs"
    }
  ]
}
```

Arrays have the following characteristics:

- Are enclosed within a beginning left brace ([) and an ending right brace (])
- Consist of comma-separated, ordered values (see the next section)
- Can be empty, [ ]
- Can be nested within other Arrays or Objects
- Have indexing that begins at 0 or 1

JSON Value Types

JSON Value Types represent the Data Types that occur on the righthand side of the colon (:) of a Name/Value Pair. JSON Value Types include the following:

- object
- array
- string
- number
- boolean
- null

We've already covered Objects and Arrays; now let's focus on the remaining Value Types: string, number, boolean, and null.

String

Example 1-8 shows valid JSON Strings.

Example 1-8. jsonStrings.json

```
[
  "fred",
  "fred\t",
  "\b",
  "",
  "\t",
  "\u004A"
]
```

Strings have the following properties:

- Strings consist of zero or more Unicode characters enclosed in quotation marks (""). Please see the following list for additional valid characters.
- Strings wrapped in single quotes (') are not valid.

Additionally, JSON Strings can contain the following backslash-escaped characters:

\"
 Double quote

\\
 Backslash

\/

Forward slash

\b

Backspace

\f

Form feed

\n

Newline

\r

Carriage return

\t

Tab

\u

Trailed by four hex digits

Number

Example 1-9 shows valid numbers in JSON.

Example 1-9. jsonNumbers.json

```
{
  "age": 29,
  "cost": 299.99,
  "temperature": -10.5,
  "unitCost": 0.2,
  "speedOfLight": 1.23e11,
  "speedOfLight2": 1.23e+11,
  "avogadro": 6.023E23,
  "avogadro2": 6.023E+23,
  "oneHundredth": 10e-3,
  "oneTenth": 10E-2
}
```

Numbers follow JavaScript's double-precision floating-point format and have the following properties:

- Numbers are always in base 10 (only digits 0–9 are allowed) with no leading zeros.

- Numbers can have a fractional part that starts with a decimal pont (.).

- Numbers can have an exponent of 10, which is represented with the e or E notation with a plus or minus sign to indicate positive or negative exponentiation.

- Octal and hexadecimal formats are not supported.

- Unlike JavaScript, numbers can't have a value of NaN (*not a number* for invalid numbers) or Infinity.

Boolean

Example 1-10 shows a Boolean value in JSON.

Example 1-10. jsonBoolean.json

```
{
  "isRegistered": true,
  "emailValidated": false
}
```

Booleans have the following properties:

- Booleans can have a value of only true or false.

- The true or false value on the righthand side of the colon(:) is not surrounded by quotes.

null

Although technically not a Value Type, null is a special value in JSON. Example 1-11 shows a null value for the line2 key/property.

Example 1-11. jsonNull.json

```
{
  "address": {
    "line1": "555 Any Street",
    "line2": null,
     "city": "Denver",
        "stateOrProvince": "CO",
        "zipOrPostalCode": "80202",
        "country": "USA"
    }
}
```

null values have the following characteristics:

- Are not not surrounded by quotes

- Indicate that a key/property has no value
- Act as a placeholder

JSON Versions

According to Douglas Crockford, there will never be another version of the core JSON standard. This isn't because JSON is perfect; nothing is perfect. The purpose of a sole JSON version is to avoid the pitfalls of having to support backward compatibility with previous versions. Crockford believes that a new data format should replace JSON when the need arises within the development community.

But as you'll see in subsequent chapters, this "no versions" philosophy applies only to the core JSON data format. For example, in Chapter 5, that specification is currently at version 0.5 as of this writing. Please note that these JSON-related specifications were created by others in the JSON community.

JSON Comments

There are no comments in a JSON document. Period.

According to his postings on the Yahoo! JSON group (*https://yhoo.it/2sp7za1*) and Google+ (*http://bit.ly/2sp83gw*), Crockford initially allowed comments, but removed them early on for the following reasons:

- He believed that comments weren't useful.
- JSON parsers had difficulties supporting comments.
- People were abusing comments. For example, he noticed that comments were being used for parsing directives, which would have destroyed interoperability.
- Removing comments simplified and enabled cross-platform JSON support.

JSON File and MIME Type

According to the core JSON specification, *.json* is the standard JSON file type when storing JSON data on filesystems. JSON's Internet Assigned Numbers Authority (IANA) media (or MIME) type is `application/json`, which can be found at the IANA Media Types site (*http://bit.ly/1cogNWM*). RESTful Web Service Producers and Consumers use a technique known as *content negotiation* (which leverages the JSON MIME type in HTTP Headers) to indicate that they are exchanging JSON data.

JSON Style Guidelines

JSON is all about interoperability, and it's important to provide JSON data feeds in a way that Consumers expect. Google has published a JSON Style Guide (*https:// google.github.io/styleguide/jsoncstyleguide.xml*) to support maintainability and best practices.

The Google JSON Style Guide is extensive, and here are the most important things for an API designer and developer:

- Property Names
- Date Property Values
- Enum Values

Property Names

Property Names (in Google parlance) are on the left side of the colon in a name/value pair (and Property Values are on the righthand side of the hyphen). Two main styles can be used to format a JSON Property Name:

- `lowerCamelCase`
- `snake_case`

With `lowerCamelCase`, a name is created by joining one or more words to look like a single word, and the first letter in each word is capitalized (except for the first word). Both the Java and JavaScript communities use `lowerCamelCase` in their coding guides. With `snake_case`, all letters are lowercase, and words are separated with an underscore (_). But the Ruby on Rails community prefers `snake_case`.

Google, along with the majority of RESTful APIs, uses `lowerCamelCase` for its Property Names, as shown in Example 1-12.

Example 1-12. jsonPropertyName.json

```
{
  "firstName": "John Smith"
}
```

Date Property Values

You may think that Date formats aren't that important, but they are. Imagine exchanging date information between a Producer and Consumer who come from different countries or continents. Even within a single enterprise, two development groups will likely use different date formatting conventions. It is important to consider the semantics of how to interpret timestamps so that we have consistent date/time processing and interoperability across all time zones. The Google JSON Style Guide prefers that dates follow the RFC 3339 (*http://www.ietf.org/rfc/rfc3339.txt*) format, as shown in Example 1-13.

Example 1-13. jsonDateFormat.json

```
{
  "dateRegistered": "2014-03-01T23:46:11-05:00"
}
```

The preceding date provides a Coordinated Universal Time (UTC) offset (from UTC/GMT—Greenwich Mean Time) of -5 hours, which is US Eastern Standard Time. Note that RFC 3339 is a profile of ISO 8601. The main difference is notably that the International Standards Organization's ISO 8601 (*http://www.iso.org/iso/home/standards/iso8601.htm*) allows the replacement of the T (which separates the date and time) with a space, and RFC 3339 does not allow this.

Latitude/Longitude Values

Geographical APIs (e.g., Google Maps) and APIs related to a geographical information system (GIS) use latitude/longitude data. To support consistency, the Google JSON Style Guide recommends that latitude/longitude data follows the ISO 6709 (*http://en.wikipedia.org/wiki/ISO_6709*) standard. According to Google Maps, the coordinates for the Empire State Building in New York City are 40.748747° N, 73.985547° W, and would be represented in JSON as shown in Example 1-14.

Example 1-14. jsonLatLon.json

```
{
  "empireStateBuilding": "40.748747-73.985547"
}
```

This example follows the ±DD.DDDD±DDD.DDDD format, with the following conventions:

- Latitude comes first.
- North (of the equator) latitude is positive.
- East (of the prime meridian) longitude is positive.
- The latitude/longitude is represented as a String. It can't be a Number because of the minus sign.

Indentation

Although the Google JSON Style Guide is silent on this topic, here are a few rules of thumb:

- JSON is a serialization format, not a presentation format. So, indentation is meaningless to an API Producer or Consumer.
- Many JSON Formatters let the user choose between two, three, or four spaces when beautifying a JSON document.
- JSON originated from JavaScript (as part of the ECMA 262 standard), but unfortunately there is no single consensus throughout the JavaScript community. Many people and coding style guides prefer two spaces, so this is the convention used in this book for consistency. It's OK if you prefer another style here, but be consistent.

Our Example—MyConference

Our examples throughout this book cover conference-related data, including the following:

- Speakers
- Sessions

Our Technical Stack

We'll start by creating a simple JSON data store for speakers and publishing it to a Stub RESTful API by taking the following steps:

1. Model JSON data with JSON Editor Online
2. Generate sample JSON data with JSON Generator
3. Create and deploy a Stub API (for future testing)

Our Architectural Style—noBackEnd

Our architectural style is based on the concept of noBackend (*http://nobackend.org/*). With noBackend, the developer doesn't have to worry about the nuts and bolts of application servers or databases at the early stages of application development.

The first seven chapters of this book use noBackEnd architecture to maintain focus on our application from a business perspective (services and data first) so that we can support not only UI-based (e.g., mobile, tablet, and web) clients, but APIs and non-web-based client applications as well. We'll deploy JSON data with simple tools such as `json-server` to emulate a RESTful API.

By using this approach, we take an interface-first approach to designing and building an API, which provides the following:

- More Agile, rapid, iterative frontend development due to the decoupling from the backend.
- Faster feedback on the API itself. Get the data and URI out there quickly for rapid review.
- A cleaner interface between the API and its Consumers.
- A separation of concerns between the Resource (e.g., speakers as JSON data) exposed by the API and its (eventual) internal implementation (e.g., application server, business logic, and data store). This makes it easier to change implementation in the future. If you create and deploy a real API with Node.js/Rails/Java (or other framework) too early, you've already made design decisions at a very early stage that will make it difficult to change after you start working with API Consumers.

A Stub API does the following:

- Eliminates the initial need to work with servers and databases
- Allows API Producers (those developers who write the API) to focus on API Design, how best to present the data to the Consumers, and initial testing
- Enables API Consumers (e.g., UI developers) to work with the API at an early stage and provide feedback to the API development team

By using the lightweight tools in this book, you'll see that you can go a long way before writing code and deploying it on a server. Of course, you'll eventually need to implement an API, and we'll show how to do that when we cover JavaScript, Ruby on Rails, and Java in Chapters 2–4.

Model JSON Data with JSON Editor Online

Creating a valid JSON document of any real size or complexity is tedious and error-prone. JSON Editor Online (*http://www.jsoneditoronline.org*) is a great web-based tool that does the following:

- Enables you to model your JSON document as Objects, Arrays, and name/value pairs

- Makes it easier to rapidly generate the text for a JSON document in an iterative manner

JSONmate (*http://jsonmate.com*) is another solid editor on the web, but we don't cover it further in this book.

JSON Editor Online features

In addition to JSON modeling and text generation, JSON Editor Online provides the following features:

JSON validation
Validation occurs as you type JSON data in the JSON text area on the left side of the page. If you forget a closing double quote for a value (e.g., `"firstName":` `"Ester,`), an X will show next to the following line of JSON text along with hover text that explains the validation error.

JSON pretty-printing
Click the Indent button at the upper-left corner of the JSON text area.

Full roundtrip engineering between the model and JSON text
After creating some Objects and key/value pairs (with the Append (+) button) in the JSON model on the right side of the page, generate JSON text by clicking the left-arrow button (in the upper-middle portion of the page). You should see the changes reflected in the JSON text area on the left side of the page.

Modify some data in the JSON text area and click the right-arrow button, and you should see the changes in the JSON model on the righthand side of the page.

Save JSON document to disk
You can save a JSON document to your local machine by selecting the Save to Disk option under the Save menu.

Import JSON document
You can import a JSON document from your computer by choosing the Open from Disk option from the Open menu.

Please remember that JSON Editor Online is publicly available, which means that any data you paste into this app is visible to others. So don't use this tool with sensitive information (personal, proprietary, and so forth).

Speaker data in JSON Editor Online

After you're finished modeling Speaker data, click the right-arrow button to generate a pretty-printed (indented) JSON document that represents the model. Figure 1-3 shows JSON Editor Online with our initial Speakers model.

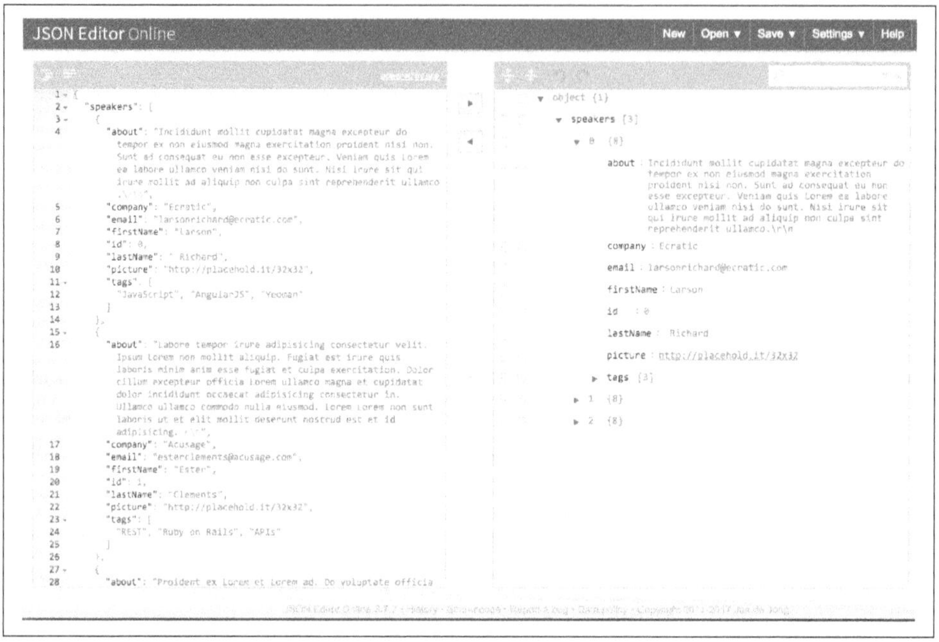

Figure 1-3. Speaker data model in JSON Editor Online

This is just a rough model, but this initial sketch is a decent starting point. Use the initial model to visualize JSON data, get early feedback, and iterate quickly on the design. This approach enables you to refine the JSON data structure throughout the development life cycle without investing heavily in implementation and infrastructure.

Generate Sample JSON Data with JSON Generator

JSON Editor Online provides a decent start, but we want to generate *lots* of test data quickly. Test data can be problematic because of the sensitivity of the data, and the data volume needed to do any meaningful testing. Even with JSON Editor Online, it will take a great deal of effort to create the volume of test data we're looking for. We need another tool to help create the data we need to create our first version of the API, and that's where JSON Generator (*http://www.json-generator.com*) comes in. This excellent tool was used to create our *speakers.json* test data file (*https:// github.com/tmarrs/json-at-work-examples/blob/master/chapter-1/speakers.json*). The template used to generate the *speakers.json* file is available on GitHub (*https:// github.com/tmarrs/json-at-work-examples/blob/master/chapter-1/jsonGeneratorTem plate.js*). Chapter 5 covers JSON Generator in more detail.

Create and Deploy a Stub API

To create the Stub API, we'll use the Speaker data we just created and deploy it as a RESTful API. We'll leverage the `json-server` Node.js module to serve up the *speakers.json* file as a Web API; this enables us to prototype quickly. You can find more information on the `json-server` GitHub page (*https://github.com/typicode/json-server*).

Before going further, please set up your development environment. Refer to Appendix A to do the following:

1. Install Node.js. `json-server` is a Node.js module, so you need to install Node.js first. Refer to "Install Node.js" on page 320.

2. Install `json-server`. See "Install npm Modules" on page 325.

3. Install JSONView and Postman. See "Install JSON Tools in the Browser" on page 319. JSONView pretty-prints JSON in Chrome and Firefox. Postman can also run as a standalone GUI application on most major operating systems.

Open a terminal session and run `json-server` on port 5000 from your command line:

```
cd chapter-1

json-server -p 5000 ./speakers.json
```

You should see the following:

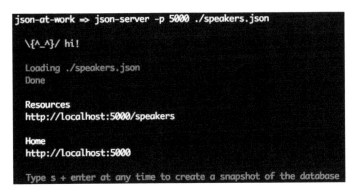

Visit *http://localhost:5000/speakers* in your browser, and (with JSON pretty-printing provided by JSONView) you should see all the speakers from our Stub API as shown in Figure 1-4.

Figure 1-4. Speakers on json-server viewed from the browser with JSONView

You can also get a single speaker by adding the id to the URI as follows: *http://local-host:5000/speakers/0*.

This is a good start, but a web browser has limited testing functionality; it can only send HTTP GET requests. Postman provides the ability to fully test a RESTful API. It can send HTTP GET, POST, PUT, and DELETE requests and set HTTP Headers.

Let's use Postman to delete the first speaker in the API as follows:

1. Enter the *http://localhost:5000/speakers/0* URL.

2. Choose DELETE as the HTTP verb.

3. Click the Send button.

You should see that the DELETE ran properly in Postman with a 200 (OK) HTTP Status, as shown in Figure 1-5.

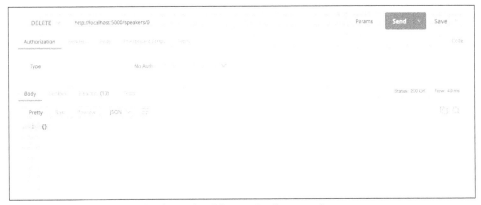

Figure 1-5. Postman: results from the deleting the first speaker

Now, ensure that the first speaker has truly been deleted by revisiting *http://localhost:5000/speakers/0* in your browser. You should now see the empty response shown in Figure 1-6.

Figure 1-6. Verify the results of deleting the first speaker

You can stop `json-server` by pressing Ctrl-C at the command line.

With the Stub API in place, we can now invoke it from any HTTP client (e.g., JavaScript, Ruby, or Java) to consume the data from an external application. Although most of our examples in subsequent chapters use an HTTP `GET`, rest assured that `json-server` can handle all the core HTTP verbs (`GET`, `POST`, `PUT`, `DELETE`). Although not covered in this book, Mountebank (*http://www.mbtest.org*) is an alternative server that provides more robust functionality for stubbing and mocking APIs and protocols.

The main point here is that an API Producer can use JSON-based tools to prototype a testable RESTful API without having to write any code. This technique is powerful because it enables the API Consumer to test without having to wait for the API to be 100 percent complete. At the same time, the API development team can iteratively upgrade the design and prototype.

What We Covered?

We started by covering the basics of JSON. We modeled JSON data with JSON Editor Online, and deployed it with a Stub API.

What's Next?

The next three chapters show how to use JSON with the following core platforms:

- JavaScript
- Ruby on Rails
- Java

In Chapter 2, you'll learn how to use JSON in JavaScript with the Stub API we just created with `json-server`.

JSON in JavaScript

We've covered the basics of the JSON data interchange format, and in this chapter we'll begin to develop applications with JSON. JSON began as a subset of the Java-Script definition for Objects and Arrays, but rest assured that JSON is now decoupled from JavaScript. JSON is language-agnostic and works across multiple platforms. Because JSON has its roots in JavaScript, this is where we begin our journey.

Here's what we'll cover:

- Using JavaScript serialization/deserialization with `JSON.stringify()` and `JSON.parse()`
- Working with JavaScript Objects and JSON
- Making RESTful API calls and testing the results with Mocha/Chai Unit Tests
- Building a small JSON-based web application

In our examples, we'll leverage Node.js, scaffold a web application with Yeoman, and make RESTful API calls to pull in the data we created on `json-server` in the previous chapter. That's a lot of moving pieces and parts, so we'll iteratively build on each concept. But before we develop our web app, we need to start with the basics of Java-Script serialization/deserialization and Objects.

Node.js Setup

Before we go any further, let's start building our development environment by installing Node.js. Please go to Appendix A, and follow the instructions in "Install Node.js" on page 320.

JSON Serialization/Deserialization with JSON.stringify() and JSON.parse()

Applications need to *serialize* (or flatten) their information into JSON in order to produce data for other applications in a platform-neutral manner. An application must also be able to *deserialize* (or unflatten) JSON data consumed from external sources into data structures for use by that application.

The JSON Stringifier/Parser Object

The JSON stringifier/parser Object was originally developed by Douglas Crockford, has been part of the JavaScript library as of ECMAScript 5 in 2009 (*http://bit.ly/2sIwlyZ*), and provides the following methods:

- JSON.stringify() serializes to JSON
- JSON.parse() deserializes from JSON

Additionally, the JSON Object

- Was originally developed by Crockford
- Can't be instantiated
- Has no other functionality

JSON Serialization with Simple JavaScript Data Types

We'll start by serializing some basic JavaScript Data Types:

- Number
- String
- Array
- Boolean
- Object (Literal)

Example 2-1 shows how to use JSON.stringify() to serialize simple Data Types.

Example 2-1. js/basic-data-types-stringify.js

```
var age = 39; // Integer
console.log('age = ' + JSON.stringify(age) + '\n');

var fullName = 'Larson Richard'; // String
console.log('fullName = ' + JSON.stringify(fullName) + '\n');
```

```
var tags = ['json', 'rest', 'api', 'oauth']; // Array
console.log('tags = ' + JSON.stringify(tags) + '\n');

var reqistered = true; // Boolean
console.log('registered = ' + JSON.stringify(reqistered) + '\n');

var speaker = {
  firstName: 'Larson',
  lastName: 'Richard',
  email: 'larsonrichard@ecratic.com',
  about: 'Incididunt mollit cupidatat magna excepteur do tempor ex non ...',
  company: 'Ecratic',
  tags: ['json', 'rest', 'api', 'oauth'],
  registered: true
};

console.log('speaker = ' + JSON.stringify(speaker));
```

When you run the preceding file with node from the command line, you should get the following:

`JSON.stringify()` doesn't do anything too interesting with the scalar types (Number, String, Boolean). Things begin to get interesting with the **speaker** Object Literal because here `JSON.stringify()` initially generates a valid, yet unattractive, JSON String. `JSON.stringify()` has other parameters that enhance serialization. According to the Mozilla Developer Network (MDN) JavaScript Guide (*https://mzl.la/ 2s8UCRU*), here is the method signature:

```
JSON.stringify(value[, replacer [, space]])
```

The parameter list is as follows:

value *(required)*
   The JavaScript value to serialize.

replacer *(optional)*
   Either a function or an array. If a function is provided, the `stringify()` method invokes the `replacer` function for each key/value pair in an Object.

space *(optional)*

> Indentation—either a Number or String. If a Number is used, this value specifies the number of spaces used for each indentation level.

Let's leverage the `replacer` and `space` parameters to pretty-print the `speaker` Object and filter out some data elements, as shown in Example 2-2.

Example 2-2. js/obj-literal-stringify-params.js

```
var speaker = {
  firstName: 'Larson',
  lastName: 'Richard',
  email: 'larsonrichard@ecratic.com',
  about: 'Incididunt mollit cupidatat magna excepteur do tempor ex non ...',
  company: 'Ecratic',
  tags: ['json', 'rest', 'api', 'oauth'],
  registered: true
};

function serializeSpeaker(key, value) {
  return (typeof value === 'string' || Array.isArray(value)) ? undefined : value;
}

// Pretty Print.
console.log('Speaker (pretty print):\n' + JSON.stringify(speaker, null, 2) + '\n');


// Pretty print and filter out Strings and Arrays.
console.log('Speaker without Strings and Arrays:\n' +
  JSON.stringify(speaker, serializeSpeaker, 2));
```

Running the preceding file yields the following:

```
json-at-work => node obj-literal-stringify-params.js
Speaker (pretty print):
{
    "firstName": "Larson",
    "lastName": "Richard",
    "email": "larsonrichard@ecratic.com",
    "about": "Incididunt mollit cupidatat magna excepteur do tempor ex non ...",
    "company": "Ecratic",
    "tags": [
        "json",
        "rest",
        "api",
        "oauth"
    ],
    "registered": true
}

Speaker without Strings and Arrays:
{
    "registered": true
}
json-at-work =>
```

The first `JSON.stringify()` call pretty-prints the JSON output with an indentation level of 2. The second call uses the `serializeSpeaker()` function as a replacer (Java-Script functions are treated as expressions and can be passed as parameters). `serializeSpeaker()` checks the type of each value and returns `undefined` for Strings and Arrays. Otherwise, this function returns the value "as is."

`JSON.stringify()` does one of the following with an `undefined` value:

- Omits the value if it's part of an Object
- Converts the value to `null` if that value belongs to an Array

JSON Serialization with an Object and toJSON()

As you've seen, JSON serialization makes the most sense with Objects. Let's customize `JSON.stringify()`'s output by adding a `toJSON()` method to our `speaker` Object, as shown in Example 2-3.

Example 2-3. js/obj-literal-stringify-tojson.js

```
var speaker = {
  firstName: 'Larson',
  lastName: 'Richard',
  email: 'larsonrichard@ecratic.com',
  about: 'Incididunt mollit cupidatat magna excepteur do tempor ex non ...',
  company: 'Ecratic',
  tags: ['json', 'rest', 'api', 'oauth'],
  registered: true
};

speaker.toJSON = function() {
  return "Hi there!";
}

console.log('speaker.toJSON(): ' + JSON.stringify(speaker, null, 2));
```

Serialization works as follows:

```
json-at-work => node obj-literal-stringify-tojson.js
speaker.toJSON(): "Hi there!"
json-at-work => ▮
```

If an Object has a `toJSON()` method, `JSON.stringify()` outputs the value returned by the Object's `toJSON()` method rather than stringifying the Object. Although the use of `toJSON()` is legal, it's probably a bad idea. `toJSON()` defeats the whole purpose of `JSON.stringify()`, because the developer is now responsible for serializing the entire Object structure. This could work with simple Objects such as speaker (as currently defined), but you'll end up writing lots of code to serialize more complex Objects that contain other Objects.

JSON Deserialization Using eval()

Originally, JavaScript developers used the eval() function to parse JSON. eval() takes a String parameter that could be a JavaScript expression, a statement, or a sequence of statements. Consider Example 2-4.

Example 2-4. js/eval-parse.js

```
var x = '{ "sessionDate": "2014-10-06T13:30:00.000Z" }';

console.log('Parse with eval(): ' + eval('(' + x + ')').sessionDate + '\n');

console.log('Parse with JSON.parse(): ' + JSON.parse(x).sessionDate);
```

Running the preceding file yields the following:

```
json-at-work => node eval-parse.js
Parse with eval(): 2014-10-06T13:30:00.000Z

Parse with JSON.parse(): 2014-10-06T13:30:00.000Z
json-at-work =>
```

In this case, both eval() and JSON.parse() work the same and parse the date properly. So what's the problem? Let's look at another example with a JavaScript statement embedded in the String; see Example 2-5.

Example 2-5. js/eval-parse-2.js

```
var x = '{ "sessionDate": new Date() }';

console.log('Parse with eval(): ' + eval('(' + x + ')').sessionDate + '\n');

console.log('Parse with JSON.parse(): ' + JSON.parse(x).sessionDate);
```

When we run this, we now see the following:

```
tmarrs => node eval-parse-2.js
Mon Oct 06 2014 20:54:18 GMT-0600 (MDT)

undefined:1
{ "sessionDate": new Date() }
                 ^
SyntaxError: Unexpected token e
    at Object.parse (native)
    at Object.<anonymous> (/Users/tmarrs/projects/json-at-work/chapter-2/js/eval-parse-2.js:5:18)
    at Module._compile (module.js:456:26)
    at Object.Module._extensions..js (module.js:474:10)
    at Module.load (module.js:356:32)
    at Function.Module._load (module.js:312:12)
    at Function.Module.runMain (module.js:497:10)
    at startup (node.js:119:16)
    at node.js:906:3
tmarrs => ▮
```

We passed in text that contains a JavaScript statement, new Date(), and eval() executes that statement. Meanwhile, JSON.parse() correctly rejects the text as invalid JSON. Although we passed in only a fairly innocuous statement to create a Date, someone else could pass in malicious code and eval() would still execute it. Even though eval() *can* be used to parse JSON, it is considered a bad/unsafe practice because it opens the door to any valid JavaScript expression, leaving your application vulnerable to attacks. Because of this security issue, the eval() function has been deprecated (for parsing JSON) in favor of JSON.parse().

JSON Deserialization with an Object and JSON.parse()

Let's return to our Speaker example, and use JSON.parse() to deserialize a JSON String into a speaker Object, as shown in Example 2-6.

Example 2-6. js/obj-literal-parse.js

```
var json = '{' +  // Multi-line JSON string.
  '"firstName": "Larson",' +
  '"lastName": "Richard",' +
  '"email": "larsonrichard@ecratic.com",' +
  '"about": "Incididunt mollit cupidatat magna excepteur do tempor ex non ...",' +
  '"company": "Ecratic",' +
  '"tags": [' +
    '"json",' +
    '"rest",' +
    '"api",' +
    '"oauth"' +
  '],' +
  '"registered": true' +
'}';

// Deserialize JSON string into speaker object.
```

```
var speaker = JSON.parse(json);

// Print 2nd speaker object.
console.log('speaker.firstName = ' + speaker.firstName);
```

When we run this file, we get the following:

```
json-at-work => node obj-literal-parse.js
speaker.firstName = Larson
json-at-work => ▮
```

`JSON.parse()` takes a JSON String as input and parses it into a fully functional Java-Script Object. We're now able to access the `speaker` Object's data members.

JavaScript Objects and JSON

So far, we've shown how core JavaScript Data Types and simple Object Literal–style JavaScript Objects interact with JSON. But we've glossed over some details, and now it's time to go a bit deeper. There are several ways to create (or *instantiate*) JavaScript Objects, and we'll focus on Object Literal form because this type of Object is the one that is the closest match to a JSON Object.

We've already shown the `speaker` Object in Object Literal form, but we'll show it again in Example 2-7 for reference.

Example 2-7. js/obj-literal.js

```
var speaker = {
  firstName: 'Larson',
  lastName: 'Richard',
  email: 'larsonrichard@ecratic.com',
  about: 'Incididunt mollit cupidatat magna excepteur do tempor ex non ...',
  company: 'Ecratic',
  tags: ['json', 'rest', 'api', 'oauth'],
  registered: true,
  name: function() {
    return (this.firstName + ' ' + this.lastName);
  }
};
```

With Object Literal syntax, you define an Object's properties (both data and func-tions) inside the curly braces. In the preceding example, the `speaker` Object is instan-tiated and populated with data. If you never need to create another instance of the `speaker` Object in your application, Object Literal is a good approach because it pro-vides a simple yet modular way to group an Object's data and functionality. The real drawback to the Object Literal approach is that you can create only one instance of speaker, and you can't reuse the name( ) method.

Node REPL

So far we've been using Node.js from the command line to execute JavaScript files. Let's change things up a bit and start using Node.js's interpreter, the Request-Eval-Print-Loop (REPL), instead. The REPL is really great because it provides instant feedback on your code, and enables you to iteratively debug and improve your application. You can find in-depth coverage of the REPL in the Node.js documentation (*http://nodejs.org/api/repl.html*). But nothing is perfect, and neither is the REPL. One of my pet annoyances is the following:

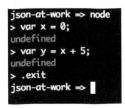

For each statement that doesn't produce output, the interpreter outputs undefined. Many people find this distracting, and there's a way to turn it off. See Appendix A ("Taming the REPL—mynode" on page 321) to configure a command alias I affectionately call mynode that I find easier to work with than the standard Node.js REPL.

Without further ado, let's work with our speaker Object by using the mynode REPL:

```
json-at-work => mynode
> var speaker = {
...     firstName: 'Larson',
...     lastName: 'Richard',
...     email: 'larsonrichard@ecratic.com',
...     about: 'Incididunt mollit cupidatat magna excepteur do tempor ex non ...',
...     company: 'Ecratic',
...     tags: ['json', 'rest', 'api', 'oauth'],
...     registered: true,
...     name: function() {
.....         return (this.firstName + ' ' + this.lastName);
.....     }
... };
>
> speaker
{ firstName: 'Larson',
  lastName: 'Richard',
  email: 'larsonrichard@ecratic.com',
  about: 'Incididunt mollit cupidatat magna excepteur do tempor ex non ...',
  company: 'Ecratic',
  tags:
   [ 'json',
     'rest',
     'api',
     'oauth' ],
  registered: true,
  name: [Function] }
>
> speaker.name();
'Larson Richard'
> .exit
json-at-work =>
```

In this run, you'll notice that we can interact with the speaker Object by calling its methods and viewing the results in the interpreter.

Here are some of the commands you'll need to use the REPL:

.clear
   Clear the context of the REPL session.

.break
   Go back to the REPL prompt. Use this to break out of a multiline statement.

.exit
   Exit the REPL session.

.save
   Save the REPL session to a file.

Where to Learn More About JavaScript Objects

We've glossed over many details of Object-Oriented JavaScript, and there are several other ways to interact with objects. We've shown just enough OO here so that we can work with JavaScript Objects and JSON in a meaningful way within an application. Complete, in-depth coverage of JavaScript Objects is far beyond the scope of this book. To gain a deeper understanding, here are a few excellent resources:

- *Learn JavaScript Next* by JD Isaacks (Manning).
- *The Principles of Object-Oriented JavaScript* by Nicholas K. Zakas (O'Reilly).
- *Learning JavaScript Design Patterns* by Addy Osmani (O'Reilly).

Unit Testing with a Stub API

Now that you know how to serialize/deserialize JSON to/from a `speaker` Object, we're ready to run a simple server-side Unit Test against a Stub API provided by `json-server`. We'll also use this Stub API when we later create a small web application.

Unit Test Style—TDD and BDD

Test-Driven Development (TDD) is an approach that uses Unit Testing to drive development. Here's a typical flow:

1. Write some tests.
2. Run the tests, which fail because there isn't any code.
3. Write just enough code to make the tests pass.
4. Refactor the code to improve design and flexibility.
5. Rerun tests and fix code until all tests pass.

TDD-style Unit Tests tend to be procedural.

Behavior-Driven Development (BDD) is an approach that tests a User Story based on acceptance criteria and expected outcomes. BDD-style tests read like English sentences; for example: "Speakers should receive their payment from the Conference within 30 days." For more information on BDD, please see Dan North's excellent article, "Introducing BDD" (*http://dannorth.net/introducing-bdd*). Some people see BDD as a refinement to TDD, and I tend to agree because a developer would follow the same workflow as TDD.

Both BDD and TDD are solid approaches, and can be combined to form a robust test suite for an application. The Unit Tests in this chapter use a BDD-style approach for assertions.

Just Enough Unit Testing with Mocha and Chai

Here are the tools for our server-side Unit Test:

Mocha
>   Mocha is a JavaScript Unit Test framework that runs in both Node.js and a browser. We'll leverage Mocha from the command line within a Node.js project, and add a few features to support JSON-based API testing. You can find more details at the Mocha website (*https://mochajs.org/*).

Chai
>   Chai is an assertion library that complements JavaScript testing frameworks and adds a richer set of assertions, in this case to Mocha. Chai enables developers to write TDD or BDD style tests. The tests in this chapter use the expect (BDD) assertion style, but you're free to experiment with the should (BDD) or assert (TDD) assertion styles. Use the approach that makes you comfortable. For more details on Chai, visit the Chai Asssertion Library website (*http://chaijs.com*).

Setting Up the Unit Test

Before going further, please be sure to set up your test environment. If you haven't installed Node.js yet, see Appendix A, and install Node.js (see "Install Node.js" on page 320 and "Install npm Modules" on page 325). If you want to follow along with the Node.js project provided in the code examples, cd to *chapter-2/speakers-test* and do the following to install all dependencies for the project:

```
npm install
```

If you'd like to set up the Node.js project yourself, follow the instructions in the book's GitHub repository (*https://github.com/tmarrs/json-at-work-examples/tree/master/chapter-2/Project-Setup.md*).

Unirest

Our Unit Test will invoke an API with HTTP, so we'll include Unirest in our testing repertoire. Unirest is an open source cross-platform REST client provided by the Mashape team. There are implementations in JS, Node.js, Ruby on Rails (RoR) and Java. Unirest is simple and works well in any client code that makes HTTP calls to REST APIs, but it's also great for Unit Testing. Unirest enables cleaner Unit Tests because you can do a one-time setup (e.g., URI, Headers) and then make multiple

HTTP calls throughout the test suite. For detailed documentation, visit the Unirest website (*http://unirest.io*).

Unirest is great because it's cross-platform, and the concepts and method signatures are similar regardless of the language implementation. There are other excellent Java-based HTTP libraries (e.g., Apache Commons HTTPComponents HttpClient (*http://hc.apache.org/httpcomponents-client-ga*), but as a polyglot (multilanguage) developer, I prefer Unirest. Please note that Unirest is not just for Unit Tests. It's widely used as an HTTP client wrapper by APIs (which invoke other APIs), and by web and mobile client applications.

Test Data

We'll use the Speaker data from Chapter 1 as our test data and deploy it as a RESTful API. Again, we'll leverage the `json-server` Node.js module to serve up the *data/speakers.json* file as a Web API. If you need to install `json-server`, please refer to "Install npm Modules" on page 325 section of Appendix A.

Here's how to run `json-server` on port 5000 from your local machine:

```
cd chapter-2/data

json-server -p 5000 ./speakers.json
```

Speakers Unit Test

The Unit Test in Example 2-8 shows how to use Unirest to make an API call to the Speaker Stub API provided by `json-server`.

Example 2-8. speakers-test/speakers-spec.js

```
'use strict';

var expect = require('chai').expect;
var unirest = require('unirest');

var SPEAKERS_ALL_URI = 'http://localhost:5000/speakers';


describe('speakers', function() {
  var req;

  beforeEach(function() {
    req = unirest.get(SPEAKERS_ALL_URI)
      .header('Accept', 'application/json');
  });

  it('should return a 200 response', function(done) {
    req.end(function(res) {
```

```
      expect(res.statusCode).to.eql(200);
      expect(res.headers['content-type']).to.eql(
        'application/json; charset=utf-8');

      done();
    });
  });

  it('should return all speakers', function(done) {
    req.end(function(res) {
      var speakers = res.body;
      var speaker3 = speakers[2];

      expect(speakers.length).to.eql(3);
      expect(speaker3.company).to.eql('Talkola');
      expect(speaker3.firstName).to.eql('Christensen');
      expect(speaker3.lastName).to.eql('Fisher');
      expect(speaker3.tags).to.eql([
        'Java', 'Spring',
        'Maven', 'REST'
      ]);

      done();
    });
  });

});
```

In this Unit Test, the following occurs:

- The test sets up the URI and Accept Header for unirest by using Mocha's befor
  eEach() method, so that setup occurs in only one place in the code. Mocha executes beforeEach() before running each test (i.e., it) within the context of the
  describe.

- The should return all speakers test is the most interesting, and it works as
  follows:

  — req.end() executes the Unirest GET request asynchronously, and the anony-
    mous (unnamed) function processes the HTTP response (res) from the API
    call.

  — We populate the speakers object with the HTTP Response Body (res.body).
    At this point, the JSON from the API has already been parsed by Unirest and
    converted to a corresponding JavaScript Object (in Object Literal form).

  — We use Chai's BDD-style expect assertions to check for expected results:

    — We have three speakers.

— The third `speaker`'s company, `firstName`, `lastName`, and `tags` match the values in the *speakers.json* file.

To run this test from the command line (in a second terminal session), do the following:

```
cd chapter-2/speakers-test

npm test
```

You should see the following results:

```
json-at-work => npm test

...

> mocha test

...

  speakers
    ✓ should return a 200 response
    ✓ should return all speakers


  2 passing
```

Building a Small Web Application

Now that you know how to serialize/deserialize JSON to/from a `speaker` Object and how to do a Unit Test with the Speaker Stub API (on `json-server`), we're ready to build a simple web application that leverages the API data and presents it to a user.

We'll develop the web application in three iterations:

- Iteration 1—generate a basic web application with Yeoman.
- Iteration 2—make an HTTP call with jQuery.
- Iteration 3—consume Speaker data from a Stub API (with `json-server`) and use a template.

Yeoman

Yeoman (*http://yeoman.io*) provides an easy way to create (i.e., scaffold) a web application and simplify developer workflow, and is similar to Gradle and Maven (from the Java community), and Ruby on Rails. We'll use Yeoman to set up, develop, and run the example application. To install Yeoman (which depends on Node.js), refer to Appendix A, and follow the instructions in "Install Yeoman" on page 324.

Yeoman provides the following functionality:

- Creates the development environment
- Runs the application
- Automatically reloads the browser when changes are saved
- Manages package dependencies
- Minifies the application's code and packages it for deployment

Yeoman follows the philosophy of convention over configuration:

- Automates setup
- Just works
- Uses standardized directory structures
- Provides Dependency Management
- Assumes reasonable defaults
- Encourages best practices
- Enables tool-based developer workflow (e.g., test, lint, run, and package)

Please review the following Yeoman tutorials for more information:

- Let's Scaffold a Web App with Yeoman (*http://yeoman.io/codelab/*)
- Building Apps with the Yeoman Workflow (*http://bit.ly/2r9XKNh*)

The Yeoman toolset

Yeoman consists of the following tools:

Scaffolding
> Yo (*https://github.com/yeoman/yo*) generates the directory structure and Grunt/Gulp/Bower configuration files for an application.

Build
> You can use either Gulp (*http://gulpjs.com*) or Grunt (*http://gruntjs.com*) to build, run, test, and package an application.

Package Management
> Either Bower (*http://bower.io*) or npm (*https://www.npmjs.org*) can be used to manage and download package dependencies.

Although Grunt is a solid build tool, and npm is an excellent package manager, we'll use Gulp and Bower for our examples because the Yeoman generator for the web application uses these tools.

Yeoman generators

Yeoman leverages generators to build and scaffold a project. Each generator creates a default preconfigured boilerplate application. There are over 1,000 generators, and Yeoman provides a complete official list (*http://yeoman.io/generators*).

Iteration 1—Generate a Web Application with Yeoman

Let's start with a simple application that has no real functionality, and hardcode the Speaker data into a table. We'll add the speaker functionality in Iterations 2 and 3. With Yeoman installed, we'll use the `generator-webapp` generator to create our application that comes out-of-the-box with web pages, CSS stylesheets, Bootstrap 4, jQuery, Mocha, and Chai.

If you'd like to set up the Yeoman project yourself, follow the instructions in the book's GitHub repository (*https://github.com/tmarrs/json-at-work-examples/tree/master/chapter-2/Web-Project-Setup.md*). If you want to follow along with the Yeoman project provided in the code examples, `cd` to *chapter-2/speakers-web-1*. In either case, do the following to start the application from the command line:

```
gulp serve
```

This command starts a local web server and shows the main page (*index.html*) in your default browser. You should see the page in Figure 2-1 at *http://localhost:9000*.

Figure 2-1. Basic web app with Yeoman generator

Note that if you keep the application running, you can see changes take effect as you save them because this application automatically refreshes with LiveReload (*https://github.com/intesso/connect-livereload*).

The `generator-webapp` Yeoman generator creates a nice starter application, and it's time to customize it. First, let's change the title, Header, and jumbotron (i.e., remove the Splendid! button) in *index.html* as shown in Example 2-9.

Example 2-9. speakers-web-1/app/index.html

```
<!doctype html>
<html lang="">
  <head>

    ...

    <title>JSON at Work - MyConference</title>

    ...

  </head>
  <body>
    ...

    <div class="header">
      ...

      <h3 class="text-muted">JSON at Work - Speakers</h3>
    </div>

    ...

    <div class="jumbotron">
      <h1 class="display-3">Speakers</h1>
      <p class="lead">Your conference lineup.</p>
    </div>

    ...

  </body>
</html>
```

Let's add a table with some hardcoded Speaker data in the *index.html* file, as shown in Example 2-10.

Example 2-10. speakers-web-1/app/index.html

```
<!doctype html>
<html lang="">
```

```
...

<body>

  ...

  <table class="table table-striped">
    <thead>
      <tr>
        <th>Name</th>
        <th>About</th>
        <th>Topics</th>
      </tr>
    </thead>
    <tbody id="speakers-tbody">
      <tr>
        <td>Larson Richard</td>
        <td>Incididunt mollit cupidatat magna excepteur do tempor ...
        </td>
        <td>JavaScript, AngularJS, Yeoman</td>
      </tr>
      <tr>
        <td>Ester Clements</td>
        <td>Labore tempor irure adipisicing consectetur velit. ...
        </td>
        <td>REST, Ruby on Rails, APIs</td>
      </tr>
      <tr>
        <td>Christensen Fisher</td>
        <td>Proident ex Lorem et Lorem ad. Do voluptate officia ...
        </td>
        <td>Java, Spring, Maven, REST</td>
      </tr>
    </tbody>
  </table>

  ...

</body>
</html>
```

We now have a web application that displays the sample Speaker data, as shown in Figure 2-2.

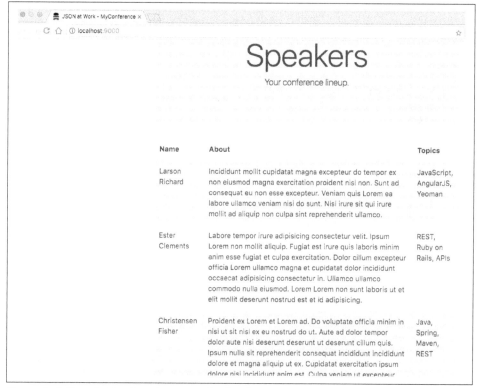

Figure 2-2. Sample Speaker data in index.html

Here are the key application files and directories generated by `generator-webapp`:

- *app/* contains the application's code (for example, HTML, JavaScript, and CSS).
  — *index.html* is the application's main page.
  — *images/* holds the application's images.
  — *scripts/* is a directory that has the application's JavaScript (and other scripting language) files.
    — *main.js* is the application's main JavaScript file. We'll work with this more in Iteration 2.
  — *styles/* is the folder that holds CSS and related styling files.
- *bower_components/* contains the project dependencies installed by Bower: Bootstrap, jQuery, Mocha, and Chai.
- *node_modules/* contains the project dependencies required by Node.js, including Gulp.

- *test/* holds test specs used by the chosen testing framework(s). In this case, we're using Mocha and Chai.
- *gulpfile.js* is the Gulp build script used to build and run the application.
- *package.json* is used by Node.js to manage dependencies that Gulp needs to execute the project scripts.
- *dist/* contains build-related artifacts created by `gulp build`.

To wrap up our discussion on `generator-webapp`, here are the other important commands you'll need to know:

Ctrl-C
Stop the application (the web server).

`gulp lint`
Use `lint` to validate the JavaScript files in the application.

`gulp +serve:test`
Test the web application. In this case, it runs PhantomJS with Mocha and Chai.

`gulp build`
Build and package the application for deployment.

`gulp clean`
Clean the artifacts generated when testing and building the application.

You can get the full list of commands by typing `gulp --tasks` at the command line.

Please shut down the web application before moving to Iteration 2.

Iteration 2—Make an HTTP Call with jQuery

In Iteration 1, we developed a web application with Speaker data hardcoded in the main page, and now it's time to add "live" content and functionality.

We'll take the following steps:

1. Factor the hardcoded Speaker data out of the main page.
2. Add a separate JSON file to hold the Speaker data.
3. Use jQuery to populate the main page with Speaker data from the JSON file.

If you'd like to set up the Yeoman project for Iteration 2 by yourself, do the following:

- Follow the instructions in the book's GitHub repository (*https://github.com/ tmarrs/json-at-work-examples/tree/master/chapter-2/Web-Project-Setup.md*).

- Don't forget to copy the *app/index.html* file from Iteration 1.

Or if you want to follow along with the Yeoman project provided in the code examples, cd to *chapter-2/speakers-web-2*. In either case, do the following to start the application from the command line:

```
gulp serve
```

This command starts the local web server as shown in Iteration 1. You should see the page in Figure 2-3 at *http://localhost:9000*.

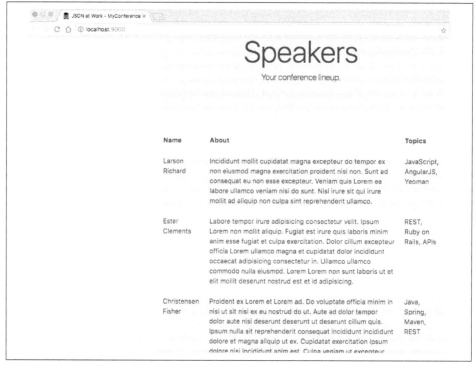

Figure 2-3. Sample Speaker data

This has the hardcoded Speaker data table in the main page (in *index.html*) that you saw earlier. Please keep the web application running so you can see changes take effect as you save them.

Now, let's remove the rows from the table body. The HTML for the speakers table now looks like Example 2-11.

Example 2-11. speakers-web-2/app/index.html

```
<!doctype html>
<html lang="">
```

```
...

<body>

  ...

  <table class="table table-striped">
    <thead>
      <tr>
        <th>Name</th>
        <th>About</th>
        <th>Topics</th>
      </tr>
    </thead>
    <tbody id="speakers-tbody">
    </tbody>
  </table>

  ...

</body>
</html>
```

In this example, we now have an empty table that has only a header row. We use
Bootstrap's `table-striped` CSS class so that we'll have zebra-striped rows. Notice the
`speakers-tbody` ID on the `<tbody>` element that holds the table's content. Later,
jQuery will use this ID to populate the table rows.

We now need a separate JSON file to hold the Speaker data. Please see the
new */speakers-web-2/app/data/speakers.json* file that has the Speaker data for the
application (this was copied from */chapter-2/data/speakers.json*).

To complete Iteration 2, the upgraded *app/scripts/main.js* file now uses jQuery to
populate the speakers table with the data from the *app/data/speakers.json* file, as
shown in Example 2-12.

Example 2-12. speakers-web-2/app/scripts/main.js

```
'use strict';

console.log('Hello JSON at Work!');

$(document).ready(function() {

  function addSpeakersjQuery(speakers) {
    $.each(speakers, function(index, speaker) {
      var tbody = $('#speakers-tbody');
      var tr = $('<tr></tr>');
      var nameCol = $('<td></td>');
```

```
        var aboutCol = $('<td></td>');
        var topicsCol = $('<td></td>');

        nameCol.text(speaker.firstName + ' ' + speaker.lastName);
        aboutCol.text(speaker.about);
        topicsCol.text(speaker.tags.join(', '));

        tr.append(nameCol);
        tr.append(aboutCol);
        tr.append(topicsCol);
        tbody.append(tr);
    });
  }

  $.getJSON('data/speakers.json',
    function(data) {
      addSpeakersjQuery(data.speakers);
    }
  );

});
```

In this example, we put the code inside jQuery's $(document).ready() so that the entire page (including the DOM) is "ready" (fully loaded). $.getJSON() is a jQuery method that makes an HTTP GET request on a URL and converts the JSON response to a JavaScript object. In this case, the *app/data/speakers.json* file is addressable as a URL through HTTP because it is deployed as a part of the web application. The $.getJSON() callback method then delegates the job of populating the speakers table to the addSpeakersjQuery() function.

The addSpeakersjQuery() method loops through the speakers array by using the jQuery .each() method. The .each() function does the following:

- Finds the <tbody> element in the speakers table by using the speakers-tbody ID we showed in the *index.html* file
- Creates a row and its columns by filling in the <tr> and <td> elements with the data from the speaker object
- Appends the new row to the <tbody> element

For more information on jQuery's getJSON() function, see the jQuery Foundation website (*http://api.jquery.com/jQuery.getJSON*).

If you kept the web application running, you should now see the screen in Figure 2-4.

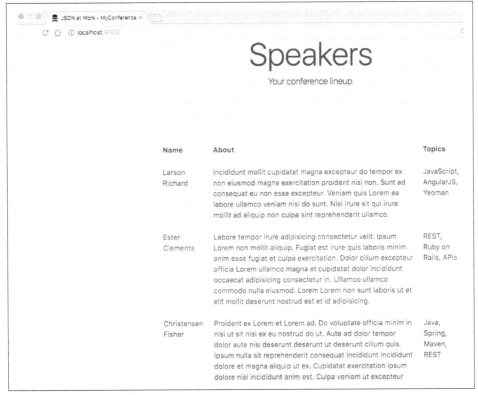

Figure 2-4. Sample Speaker data with JSON file and jQuery

The main page looks the same, but we were expecting that. We've improved the application by factoring out the hardcoded Speaker data from the main page, and we're now making an HTTP call. At this point, we have some of the elements of a real web application that populates its pages dynamically, but here are the drawbacks:

- The JSON data comes from a file within the web application, and we want it to come from a RESTful API.
- The JavaScript code knows about HTML elements on the main page. We would like to reduce the amount of HTML and DOM manipulation.

Please shut down the web application before moving to Iteration 3.

Iteration 3—Consume Speaker Data from a Stub API and Use a Template

In Iteration 2, we made an HTTP call to populate the main page with Speaker data from a JSON file, and we're now going to get the data from the Stub API provided by `json-server` that was used in Chapter 1. We're also going to factor the HTML and DOM manipulation out of the JavaScript into an external Mustache template.

We'll take the following steps:

1. Modify the HTTP call to point to the `json-server` URI.
2. Use a Mustache template to remove the HTML and DOM manipulation from JavaScript.

If you'd like to set up the Yeoman project for Iteration 2 by yourself, do the following:

- Follow the instructions in the book's GitHub Repository (*https://github.com/ tmarrs/json-at-work-examples/tree/master/chapter-2/Web-Project-Setup.md*).
- Don't forget to copy the following files from Iteration 2:
  — *app/index.html*
  — *app/scripts/main.js*

Or if you want to follow along with the Yeoman project provided in the code examples, cd to *chapter-2/speakers-web-3*.

Next, let's modify the HTTP call in *main.js* to point to the Speaker Stub API (provided by `json-server`), as shown in Example 2-13.

Example 2-13. speakers-web-3/app/scripts/main.js

```
...

  $.getJSON('http://localhost:5000/speakers',
    function(data) {
      addSpeakersjQuery(data);
    }
  );

...
```

The code now invokes the Speaker Stub API provided by `json-server`. Note that `data` is passed to `addSpeakersjQuery()` because `json-server` doesn't emit the named `speakers` Array.

First, open a new terminal session and run `json-server` on port 5000 from your command line:

```
cd chapter-2/data

json-server -p 5000 ./speakers.json
```

Start the web application (in another terminal session) from the command line:

```
gulp serve
```

This command starts the local web server as shown in Iterations 1 and 2. You should see the same Speaker data when you visit *http://localhost:9000* in your browser. But the web application is in better shape because it's using data from an API rather than a file. Please keep the web application running so you can see changes take effect as you save them.

To complete Iteration 3, let's factor out the HTML/DOM manipulation from our JavaScript code into a Mustache template. Mustache bills itself as providing *logic-less templates*, which means that there are no control statements (e.g., for or if) needed to generate HTML from JavaScript and other languages. Mustache (*http://mustache.github.io*) works with multiple languages.

Example 2-14 is our Mustache template that generates HTML content based on Speaker data.

Example 2-14. /app/templates/speakers-mustache-template.html

```
<!--
[speakers-mustache-template.html]
This is the template for items in the speakers array when the app first loads
-->
<script id="speakerTemplate" type="text/html">
  {{#.}}
    <tr>
      <td>{{firstName}} {{lastName}}</td>
      <td>{{about}}</td>
      <td>{{tags}}</td>
    </tr>
  {{/.}}
</script>
```

Note the following about this example:

- The template is an external file to keep the HTML out of our JavaScript code.
- The template code resides within a <script> element.
- The HTML is structured just as it would be in a regular web page.
- Mustache fills in the data by using variables enclosed in double parentheses.
- The context enables Mustache to loop through the Array of Speaker data. We have an anonymous (nameless) collection that we received from the HTTP call, so we enclose all our elements within a beginning {{#.}} and closing {{/.}} to set the context. Note that if we had a named Array (e.g., speakers), the context would begin with {{#speakers}} and end with {{/speakers}}.

- Each variable represents a field name within the specified context. For example, the {{firstName}} variable gets data from the firstName field for the current element in the Speaker data Array.

Please review Wern Ancheta's excellent article, "Easy Templating with Mustache.js" (*http://wernancheta.wordpress.com/2012/07/23/easy-templating-with-mustache-js*) for a deeper discussion on Mustache.

Besides Mustache, a couple of other solid templating libraries are frequently used by the JavaScript community:

Handlebars.js (http://handlebarsjs.com)
    Handlebars is very similar to Mustache.

Underscore.js (http://underscorejs.org)
    This is a general utility library, but it includes some templating functionality.

In addition, most MVC frameworks (AngularJS, Ember, and Backbone) have some form of templating. We'll cover Mustache and Handlebars more thoroughly in Chapter 7.

Example 2-15 shows our refactored *app/scripts/main.js* file that now uses Mustache.

Example 2-15. speakers-web-3/app/scripts/main.js

```
'use strict';

console.log('Hello JSON at Work!');

$(document).ready(function() {

  function addSpeakersMustache(speakers) {
    var tbody = $('#speakers-tbody');

    $.get('templates/speakers-mustache-template.html', function(templatePartial) {
      var template = $(templatePartial).filter('#speakerTemplate').html();
      tbody.append(Mustache.render(template, speakers));
    }).fail(function() {
      alert("Error loading Speakers mustache template");
    });

  }

  $.getJSON('http://localhost:5000/speakers',
    function(data) {
      addSpeakersMustache(data);
    }
  );

});
```

In this example, the addSpeakerMustache() function converts the Speaker data (that we received from json-server) into HTML by using our Mustache template. We use the jQuery's $.get() method to pull in the external Mustache template. When the $.get() call completes, we then find the main page's <tbody> element (just as before) and then use the append() method to append the HTML content that was created by Mustache.render() (based on the template and Speaker data).

But we're not quite done, because we need to add Mustache to the web application:

- Use Bower to install Mustache into the web application. From the command line in the *speakers-web-3* directory, type bower install mustache.
- Add Mustache to *app/index.html* (right after *main.js*) as shown in Example 2-16.

Example 2-16. speakers-web-3/app/index.html

```
<!doctype html>
<html lang="">

    ...

    <body>

        ...

        <script src="bower_components/mustache.js/mustache.js"></script>

        ...

    </body>
</html>
```

If you kept the web application running, you should now see the screen in Figure 2-5.

Notice that Mustache formats the Speaker data a little differently, but we improved the web application by making an API call to the Stub API (provided by json-server) and by templating the HTML with Mustache.

Of course, you can go further by using AngularJS or React, but this is left as an exercise for you.

Please don't forget to shut down both the web application and json-server with a Ctrl-C in each terminal session.

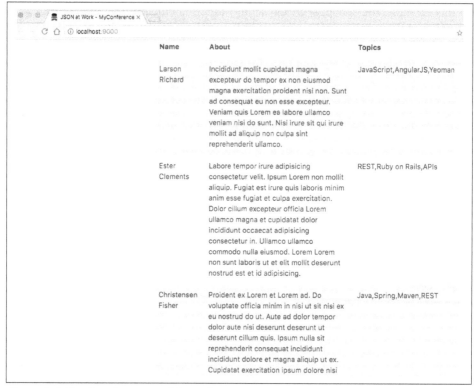

Figure 2-5. Speaker data using Mustache

How to Go Deeper with JavaScript

A deeper, more thorough knowledge of JavaScript is needed to truly understand Node.js and other JavaScript frameworks (e.g., Angular, React, Ember, Backbone, etc.), and package/build management tools such as Yeoman. If JavaScript Objects are new to you, and all the curly braces, parentheses, and semicolons are a boiling sea of syntax, then take heart because you are not alone. Every JavaScript developer encounters these issues along their path.

Here are a few websites where you can go to deepen and broaden your skills:

- JavaScriptIsSexy (*http://javascriptissexy.com*) provides excellent, freely available tutorials to help you reach an intermediate or advanced level. The main tutorials include these three:

    — How to Learn JavaScript Properly (*http://javascriptissexy.com/how-to-learn-javascript-properly*)

— Learn Intermediate and Advanced JavaScript (*http://javascriptissexy.com/learn-intermediate-and-advanced-javascript*)

— JavaScript's Apply, Call, and Bind Methods Are Essential for JavaScript Professionals (*http://javascriptissexy.com/javascript-apply-call-and-bind-methods-are-essential-for-javascript-professionals*)

As you work through these (and similar) resources, Objects and Functional Expressions will become commonplace as you reach the intermediate-to-advanced level of JavaScript. At that point, you will have a much more enjoyable and productive experience when developing with current JavaScript tools and frameworks.

What We Covered

We started with simple conversion between JavaScript and JSON and went all the way to develop a working web application and a Unit Test that makes a RESTful API call to `json-server`. For the sake of brevity and clarity, we've covered "just enough" of several technologies for you to understand core concepts and build simple applications. But we've just scratched the surface of JavaScript, Node.js, and Yeoman.

What's Next?

Now that we've developed a web application with JavaScript and JSON, we'll move on to use JSON with Ruby on Rails in Chapter 3.

JSON in Ruby on Rails

We've shown how to use JSON in JavaScript, and in this chapter we'll show how to use JSON with our second platform—Ruby on Rails (RoR).

We'll cover the following:

- Performing Ruby/JSON serialization/deserialization with `MultiJson`
- Working with Ruby Objects and JSON
- Understanding the importance of JSON camel casing
- Using JSON with Minitest
- Making RESTful API calls and testing the results with Minitest and `jq`
- Building a simple JSON-based API with Rails 5

In our examples, we'll make RESTful API calls to work with the data we deployed on `json-server` in Chapter 1. We'll then create a more realistic JSON-based Web API. But before we develop a RESTful API, let's start with the fundamentals of converting between Ruby and JSON.

Ruby on Rails Setup

Before we go any further, let's start building our development environment by installing RoR. Please go to Appendix A, and follow the instructions in "Install Ruby on Rails" on page 328.

Ruby JSON Gems

Several good JSON gems provide Ruby/JSON serialization/deserialization functionality, including these:

JSON *(https://github.com/flori/json)*
   The default JSON gem provided in Ruby.

oj *(https://github.com/ohler55/oj)*
   Optimized JSON, considered by many to be the fastest Ruby-based JSON processor available.

yajl *(https://github.com/brianmario/yajl-ruby)*
   Yet Another JSON Library.

There are many other JSON gems in addition to this list, and it's hard to choose. Rather than forcing a developer to know how to use each JSON gem, MultiJson *(https://github.com/intridea/multi_json)* encapsulates this choice by providing a wrapper that invokes the most common JSON gems on behalf of the caller by choosing the fastest JSON gem that has been loaded in an application's environment. Encapsulating JSON gems like this decouples an application from a particular JSON implementation. For further information on how MultiJson chooses a JSON implementation, see its GitHub repository *(https://github.com/intridea/multi_json)*. For detailed documentation, visit the MultiJson documentation on RubyDoc *(http://www.rubydoc.info/gems/multi_json/1.3.2/MultiJson)*.

Since MultiJson defaults to the standard JSON gem, let's install the oj gem to optimize performance.

```
gem install multi_json
gem install oj
```

Now that we've installed the oj gem, MultiJson will default to oj rather than the standard JSON gem.

JSON Serialization/Deserialization with MultiJson

Applications need to convert a Ruby Data Type to JSON (serialize) and vice versa (deserialize) to exchange JSON data with other applications.

The MultiJson Object

The MultiJson Object provides the following methods:

- MultiJson.dump() serializes Ruby to JSON.

- `MultiJson.load()` deserializes from JSON to Ruby.

Note that `MultiJson.dump()` does the following:

- Uses traditional Ruby snake case (`first_name`) rather than the recommended cross-platform camel case (`firstName`) when serializing the `speaker` Object with `oj`.
- Doesn't generate a JSON String when serializing the `speaker` Object with the JSON engine. This is because the JSON gem doesn't serialize a class unless it implements a `to_json()` method.
- Uses snake case (`first_name`) rather than camel case (`firstName`) for key names.

According to the RubyDoc `MultiJson` documentation, here is the method signature for `MultiJson.dump()`:

```
#dump(object, options = {})
```

The options provided depend on the underlying JSON implementation (in this case `oj`) because `MultiJson` is a wrapper.

JSON Serialization/Deserialization with Simple Ruby Data Types

We'll start by serializing some basic Ruby Data Types:

- Integer
- String
- Boolean
- Array
- Hash
- Object

Example 3-1 shows how to serialize/deserialize simple Ruby data types with `Multi Json` and `oj`.

Example 3-1. ruby/basic_data_types_serialize.rb

```
require 'multi_json'

puts "Current JSON Engine = #{MultiJson.current_adapter()}"
puts

age = 39 # Integer
puts "age = #{MultiJson.dump(age)}"
puts
```

```
full_name = 'Larson Richard' # String
puts "full_name = #{MultiJson.dump(full_name)}"
puts

reqistered = true # Boolean
puts "reqistered = #{MultiJson.dump(reqistered)}"
puts

tags = %w(JavaScript, AngularJS, Yeoman) # Array of Strings
puts "tags = #{MultiJson.dump(tags)}"
puts

email = { email: 'larsonrichard@ecratic.com' } # Hash
puts "email = #{MultiJson.dump(email)}"
puts

class Speaker
  def initialize(first_name, last_name, email, about,
                 company, tags, registered)
    @first_name = first_name
    @last_name = last_name
    @email = email
    @about = about
    @company = company
    @tags = tags
    @registered = registered
  end
end

speaker = Speaker.new('Larson', 'Richard', 'larsonrichard@ecratic.com',
          'Incididunt mollit cupidatat magna excepteur do tempor ex non ...',
          'Ecratic', %w(JavaScript, AngularJS, Yeoman), true)

puts "speaker (using oj gem) = #{MultiJson.dump(speaker)}"
puts
```

When you run ruby `basic_data_types_serialize.rb` from the command line, you should get the following:

`MultiJson.dump()` doesn't do much with the scalar types (Integer, String, and Boolean). Things begin to get interesting with the `speaker` Object because here `Multi Json.dump()` initially generates a valid, yet unattractive, JSON String. As you'll soon see, `MultiJson.dump()` has other parameters that enhance serialization.

To make things more readable, we'll leverage the `:pretty ⇒ true` option to pretty-print the JSON output from the `speaker` Object, as shown in Example 3-2. Although pretty-printing is more attractive to look at, it is inefficient, and should be used only for debugging purposes.

Example 3-2. ruby/obj_serialize_pretty.rb

```
require 'multi_json'

...

speaker = Speaker.new('Larson', 'Richard', 'larsonrichard@ecratic.com',
          'Incididunt mollit cupidatat magna excepteur do tempor ex non ...',
          'Ecratic', %w(JavaScript, AngularJS, Yeoman), true)

puts "speaker (using oj gem) = #{MultiJson.dump(speaker, pretty: true)}"
puts
```

Running the preceding code yields the following pretty-printed `speaker` Object:

```
json-at-work => ruby obj_serialize_pretty.rb
Current JSON Engine = MultiJson::Adapters::Oj

speaker (using oj gem) = {
  "first_name":"Larson",
  "last_name":"Richard",
  "email":"larsonrichard@ecratic.com",
  "about":"Incididunt mollit cupidatat magna excepteur do tempor ex non ...",
  "company":"Ecratic",
  "tags":[
    "JavaScript,",
    "AngularJS,",
    "Yeoman"
  ],
  "registered":true
}
```

JSON Deserialization with Objects and MultiJson

`MultiJson` can also deserialize JSON. Let's use the `MultiJson.load()` method to deserialize JSON into a Ruby `Hash`. But this causes an impedance mismatch because the `speaker` Object's `initialize()` method takes Strings (which match the `speaker` Object's attributes) as parameters. We'll need to convert `Hash` to a set of attributes to instantiate a `speaker` Object. Fortunately, it's unnecessary to write any code to convert the `Hash` because the well-known `OpenStruct` makes the `Hash` (from decoding JSON) look like an object.

Example 3-3 shows the use of `OpenStruct`.

Example 3-3. ruby/ostruct_example.rb

```ruby
require 'ostruct'

h = { first_name: 'Fred' }
m = OpenStruct.new(h)
puts m              # prints: #<OpenStruct first_name="Fred">
puts m.first_name   # prints: Fred
```

`OpenStruct` is a data structure that is similar to a `Hash`, and it allows you define key/value pairs of attributes and their values. `OpenStruct` is part of Ruby Core and provides the ability to access keys as attributes. For more information about `OpenStruct`, see the Ruby Core documentation (*http://ruby-doc.org/stdlib-2.0.0/libdoc/ostruct/rdoc/OpenStruct.html*).

When we instantiate a new `speaker` Object, it would be great to print out the new object in a readable manner for debugging purposes. With `puts`, you'd normally see something like this:

```ruby
puts speaker # #<Speaker:0x007f84412e0e38>
```

With the `awesome_print` gem, the output is much more attractive. For more information, see the `awesome_print` GitHub repository (*https://github.com/awesome-print/awesome_print*).

Before running the code in Example 3-4, install the `awesome_print` gem from the command line:

```
gem install awesome_print
```

Example 3-4. ruby/obj_deserialize.rb

```ruby
require 'multi_json'
require 'ostruct'
require 'awesome_print'

puts "Current JSON Engine = #{MultiJson.current_adapter()}"
puts

class Speaker
  def initialize(first_name, last_name, email, about,
                 company, tags, registered)
    @first_name = first_name
    @last_name = last_name
```

```
    @email = email
    @about = about
    @company = company
    @tags = tags
    @registered = registered
  end
end

speaker = Speaker.new('Larson', 'Richard', 'larsonrichard@ecratic.com',
            'Incididunt mollit cupidatat magna excepteur do tempor ex non ...',
            'Ecratic', %w(JavaScript, AngularJS, Yeoman), true)

json_speaker = MultiJson.dump(speaker, pretty: true)
puts "speaker (using oj gem) = #{MultiJson.dump(speaker)}"
puts

ostruct_spkr = OpenStruct.new(MultiJson.load(json_speaker))

speaker2 = Speaker.new(ostruct_spkr.first_name, ostruct_spkr.last_name,
                ostruct_spkr.email, ostruct_spkr.about, ostruct_spkr.company,
                ostruct_spkr.tags, ostruct_spkr.registered)

puts "speaker 2 after MultiJson.load()"
ap speaker2
puts
```

Run this example, and we'll see that the preceding code successfully deserialized the JSON String stored in json_speaker into an OpenStruct Object and finally into another speaker instance—speaker2. Note the use of awesome_print's ap method rather than the built-in puts to pretty-print the Object.

Although multi_json and oj efficiently process JSON, sometimes developers need more control over the data to be serialized.

A Word on Camel Casing and JSON

If you haven't noticed, JSON Keys/Property Names are usually in camel case form. For example, a Key that represents someone's first name would normally be expressed as firstName. But up to this point, we've seen that Ruby's JSON libraries natively express Keys in snake case (first_name). While this *may* be OK for small code examples and Unit Tests that no one else will use, snake case is incompatible with the rest of the world. Here's why:

- JSON must be interoperable. Although my stance on this will probably offend many ardent Rubyists, and others may call this *bike shedding*, the whole point of JSON and REST is interoperability across heterogeneous applications. There are other programming languages than Ruby, and the *rest* of the world is expecting camel case (`firstName`). If your API works in a way that is unexpected, people won't want to use it.
- The major players use camel-cased JSON:
  - Google has standardized on camel case in their Google JSON Style Guide (*http://bit.ly/2raShRe*).
  - The majority of JSON-based public APIs (e.g., Amazon AWS, Facebook, and LinkedIn) use camel-cased JSON.
- Avoid platform bleed-through. JSON should look the same regardless of the platform/programming language that generates or consumes it. The Ruby on Rails community prefers snake case, which is just fine within that platform, but this local programming language idiom shouldn't be reflected in an API.

JSON Serialization with Objects and ActiveSupport

The ActiveSupport gem provides functionality that has been extracted from Rails, including time zones, internationalization, and JSON encoding/decoding. ActiveSupport's JSON module provides the ability to do the following:

- Convert between camel case and snake case
- Choose which portions of an Object to serialize

You can install ActiveSupport from the command line as follows:

```
gem install activesupport
```

We'll use `ActiveSupport::JSON.encode()` to serialize a `speaker` Object into JSON, as shown in Example 3-5.

Example 3-5. ruby/obj_serialize_active_support.rb

```
require 'active_support/json'
require 'active_support/core_ext/string'

...

speaker = Speaker.new('Larson', 'Richard', 'larsonrichard@ecratic.com',
          'Incididunt mollit cupidatat magna excepteur do tempor ex non ...',
```

```
                    'Ecratic', %w(JavaScript, AngularJS, Yeoman), true)

json = ActiveSupport::JSON.encode(speaker).camelize(first_letter = :lower)
puts "Speaker as camel-cased JSON \n#{json}"
puts

json = ActiveSupport::JSON.encode(speaker,
                    only: ['first_name', 'last_name'])
                    .camelize(first_letter = :lower)

puts "Speaker as camel-cased JSON with only firstName and lastName \n#{json}"
puts
```

In the code example, you'll notice that `ActiveSupport::JSON.encode()` provides the following options:

- Camel case (`firstName`) Key names by chaining with the `camelize()` method. Note that the first letter of each Key is capitalized by default, so you'll need to use the `first_letter = :lower` parameter to get lower camel case format.
- Limit the portions of the `speaker` Object to serialize by using the `only:` parameter.

When you run the code, you should see the following:

But if you only want to convert from snake case to camel case, the `awrence` gem (*https://github.com/futurechimp/awrence*) is a simple alternative. `awrence` converts snake-cased `Hash` keys to camel case, which you can then convert to camel-cased JSON. I haven't tried this gem yet, so this is left as an exercise for you.

JSON Deserialization with Objects and ActiveSupport

ActiveSupport also has the ability to deserialize JSON. We'll now use the `decode()` method to deserialize JSON into a Ruby `Hash`. Just as before, we'll leverage `Open Struct` and `awesome_print` to help with instantiation and printing, as shown in Example 3-6.

Example 3-6. ruby/obj_deserialize_active_support.rb

```
require 'multi_json'
require 'active_support/json'
```

```
require 'active_support/core_ext/string'
require 'ostruct'
require 'awesome_print'

...

speaker = Speaker.new('Larson', 'Richard', 'larsonrichard@ecratic.com',
            'Incididunt mollit cupidatat magna excepteur do tempor ex non ...',
            'Ecratic', %w(JavaScript, AngularJS, Yeoman), true)

json_speaker = ActiveSupport::JSON.encode(speaker)
puts "speaker (using oj gem) = #{ActiveSupport::JSON.encode(speaker)}"
puts ostruct_spkr = OpenStruct.new(ActiveSupport::JSON.decode(json_speaker))

speaker2 =  Speaker.new(ostruct_spkr.first_name, ostruct_spkr.last_name,
                ostruct_spkr.email, ostruct_spkr.about, ostruct_spkr.company,
                ostruct_spkr.tags, ostruct_spkr.registered)

puts "speaker 2 after ActiveSupport::JSON.decode()"
ap speaker2
puts
```

You'll see the following result when you run the preceding code from the command line:

The plissken gem (*https://github.com/futurechimp/plissken*) is an alternative that converts from camel-cased Hash keys (that originated from JSON) to snake case. We'll use plissken in our upcoming Unit Tests.

Unit Testing with a Stub API

Now that you know how to serialize/deserialize JSON to/from a speaker Object, we're ready to run a simple server-side Unit Test against a Stub API provided by json-server (which we used in previous chapters).

Just Enough Unit Testing with Minitest

The two most common Ruby testing frameworks are Minitest, which is part of Ruby Core (*http://ruby-doc.org/stdlib-2.0.0/libdoc/minitest/rdoc/MiniTest.html*) and RSpec (*http://rspec.info*). Both Minitest and RSpec are excellent, but we can use only one of them in this chapter to keep the focus on JSON.

On one hand, Minitest

- Is part of the Ruby Standard Library, so there's nothing else to install.
- Is lightweight and simple.
- Has *most* of the functionality that RSpec provides.

On the other hand, RSpec

- Requires you to install a separate `rspec` gem, but enjoys wide acceptance in the Ruby and Rails communities.
- Is large and complex. The RSpec code base is about eight times larger than Minitest.
- Has a richer set of matchers than Minitest.

For me, it's really a matter of taste, and you'll be fine with either framework. I chose Minitest because it comes standard with Ruby.

Minitest lets you choose between BDD (`Minitest::Spec`) and TDD (`Minitest::Test`) style testing. Let's go with `Minitest::Spec` for the following reasons:

- I prefer BDD's simple English-style sentences that describe each test.
- It looks similar to RSpec, so the tests will look familiar to those developers who use RSpec.
- It's consistent with the JavaScript-base Mocha/Chai testing in the rest of this book.

This chapter covers only the basics of Minitest. To learn more, see Chris Kottom's excellent book, *The Minitest Cookbook* (*https://chriskottom.com/minitestcookbook*).

Setting Up the Unit Test

Before going further, be sure to set up your test environment. If you haven't installed Ruby on Rails yet, refer to Appendix A, and install Ruby on Rails (see "Install Ruby on Rails" on page 328 and "Install Ruby Gems" on page 329). If you want to follow along with the Ruby project provided in the code examples, `cd` to *chapter-3/speakers-test* and do the following to install all dependencies for the project:

```
bundle install
```

Bundler (*http://bundler.io*) provides dependency management for Ruby projects.

If you'd like to set up the `speakers-test` Ruby project yourself, follow the instructions in the book's GitHub repository (*https://github.com/tmarrs/json-at-work-examples/tree/master/chapter-3/Project-Setup.md*).

Test Data

We'll use the Speaker data from earlier chapters as our test data and deploy it as a RESTful API. Again, we'll leverage the json-server Node.js module to serve up the *data/speakers.json* file as a Web API. If you need to install json-server, refer to "Install npm Modules" on page 325 in Appendix A.

Here's how to run json-server on port 5000 from your local machine:

```
cd chapter-3/data

json-server -p 5000 ./speakers.json
```

You can also get a single speaker by adding the id to the URI as follows: *http://local-host:5000/speakers/1*. With the Stub API in place, it's time to write some Unit Tests.

JSON and Minitest Testing with APIs

Our Unit Test will do the following:

- Make HTTP calls to the Stub Speakers API
- Check the values from the HTTP Response Body against expected values

As in previous chapters, we'll continue to leverage the open source Unirest API wrapper (*http://unirest.io*), but this time we'll use the Ruby implementation (*http://unirest.io/ruby.html*). Please note that the Unirest gem takes the JSON in the HTTP Response Body, parses it into a Ruby Hash, and returns it to the caller (inside the HTTP Response Body). This means that the Unit Test won't be testing directly against JSON data, but rather it will test against the Hash that was populated by the JSON response from the API.

Speakers Unit Test

The Unit Test in Example 3-7 shows how to use Unirest to invoke the Speaker Stub API provided by json-server and test the response.

Example 3-7. speakers-test/test/speakers_spec.rb

```
require 'minitest_helper'

require 'unirest'
require 'awesome_print'
require 'ostruct'
require 'plissken'
require 'jq/extend'

require_relative '../models/speaker'
```

```ruby
describe 'Speakers API' do
  SPEAKERS_ALL_URI = 'http://localhost:5000/speakers'

  before do
    @res = Unirest.get SPEAKERS_ALL_URI,
                      headers:{ 'Accept' => "application/json" }

  end

  it 'should return a 200 response' do
    expect(@res.code).must_equal 200
    expect(@res.headers[:content_type]).must_equal 'application/json; charset=utf-8'
  end

  it 'should return all speakers' do
    speakers = @res.body
    expect(speakers).wont_be_nil
    expect(speakers).wont_be_empty
    expect(speakers.length).must_equal 3
  end

  it 'should validate the 3rd speaker as an Object' do
    speakers = @res.body
    ostruct_spkr3 = OpenStruct.new(speakers[2].to_snake_keys())

    expect(ostruct_spkr3.company).must_equal 'Talkola'
    expect(ostruct_spkr3.first_name).must_equal 'Christensen'
    expect(ostruct_spkr3.last_name).must_equal 'Fisher'
    expect(ostruct_spkr3.tags).must_equal ['Java', 'Spring', 'Maven', 'REST']

    speaker3 = Speaker.new(ostruct_spkr3.first_name, ostruct_spkr3.last_name,
                          ostruct_spkr3.email, ostruct_spkr3.about,
                          ostruct_spkr3.company, ostruct_spkr3.tags,
                          ostruct_spkr3.registered)

    expect(speaker3.company).must_equal 'Talkola'
    expect(speaker3.first_name).must_equal 'Christensen'
    expect(speaker3.last_name).must_equal 'Fisher'
    expect(speaker3.tags).must_equal ['Java', 'Spring', 'Maven', 'REST']
  end

  it 'should validate the 3rd speaker with jq' do
    speakers = @res.body
    speaker3 = speakers[2]

    speaker3.jq('.company') {|value| expect(value).must_equal 'Talkola'}
    speaker3.jq('.tags') {|value|
        expect(value).must_equal ['Java', 'Spring', 'Maven', 'REST']]}
    speaker3.jq('.email') {|value|
        expect(value).must_equal 'christensenfisher@talkola.com'}
```

```
    speaker3.jq('. | "\(.firstName) \(.lastName)"') {|value|
        expect(value).must_equal 'Christensen Fisher'}
  end

end
```

Note the following in this Unit Test:

- The `minitest_helper` consolidates configuration and setup and factors it out of this test. We'll cover Minitest Helpers later in this chapter.

- The test executes the Unirest `GET` request synchronously (and gets a response) with Minitest's `before` method, so that setup occurs in only one place in the code. Minitest executes `before` before running each test (i.e., `it`) within the context of the `describe`.

- The `should return all speakers` test does the following:
  — Ensures that the HTTP Response Body is not empty
  — Checks whether the Speakers API returns three `speakers`

- The `should validate the 3rd speaker as an Object` test works as follows:
  — Populate the `speakers` Hash from the HTTP Response Body (`@res.body`). At this point, the JSON from the API has already been parsed by Unirest and converted to a Ruby `Hash`.
  — Use `OpenStruct.new()` to convert the Hash for the third `speaker` into an `Open Struct`, an Object-like structure. The `to_snake_keys()` method (from the `plissken` gem) converts the camel-cased (`firstName`) Hash keys to snake case (`first_name`) for compatibility with Ruby.
  — Use Minitest BDD-style `expect` assertions to check for expected results:
    — The third `speaker`'s company, `first_name`, `last_name`, and `tags` match the values in the *speakers.json* file.

- The `should validate the 3rd speaker with jq` test works as follows:
  — Use jq (*https://stedolan.github.io/jq*) queries (e.g., `.company`) to check the same fields as in the previous test. jq simplifies Unit Testing by enabling a developer to query the JSON-based Hashes without the need to convert to an object. jq is a powerful JSON search tool, and Chapter 6 covers it in greater detail.
  — The `. | "\(.firstName) \(.lastName)"` query does a String interpolation to combine the `firsName` and `lastName` fields into the `speaker`'s full name for testing purposes.

— The `ruby-jq` gem (*https://github.com/winebarrel/ruby-jq*) provides a solid Ruby-based jq implementation.

To run this test, use `bundle exec rake` from the command line, and you should see the following:

```
json-at-work => bundle exec rake
Started with run options --seed 42108

Speakers API
  test_0001_should return a 200 response              PASS (0.01s)
  test_0004_should validate the 3rd speaker with jq   PASS (0.02s)
  test_0003_should validate the 3rd speaker as an Object  PASS (0.00s)
  test_0002_should return all speakers                PASS (0.00s)

Finished in 0.03299s
4 tests, 18 assertions, 0 failures, 0 errors, 0 skips
```

`rake` (*http://rake.rubyforge.org*) is a commonly used build utility for Ruby projects. In the `bundle exec rake` command, the following occurs:

- `rake` uses the gems that Bundler listed in this project's `Gemfile`.
- `rake` has been configured to use `test` as the default task.

The `Rakefile` defines the build tasks, and looks like Example 3-8.

Example 3-8. speakers-test/Rakefile

```
require 'rake/testtask'

Rake::TestTask.new(:test) do |t|
  t.libs = %w(lib test)
  t.pattern = 'test/**/*_spec.rb'
  t.warning = false
end

task :default => :test
```

By default, Minitest is silent and doesn't indicate that tests are passing. In the preceding Unit Test run, notice that passing tests show in the output. The `speakers-test` project leverages the `minitest-reporters` gem (*https://github.com/kern/minitest-reporters*) to make the output more readable.

The Minitest Helper in Example 3-9 configures the `minitest` and `minitest-reporters` gems for use by the `speakers_spec`.

Example 3-9. speakers-test/test/minitest_helper.rb

```
require 'minitest/spec'
require 'minitest/autorun'

require "minitest/reporters"
Minitest::Reporters.use! Minitest::Reporters::SpecReporter.new
```

For the sake of completeness, Example 3-10 shows the `Speaker` Plain Old Ruby Object (PORO) that holds the Speaker data.

Example 3-10. speakers-test/models/speaker.rb

```
class Speaker
  attr_accessor :first_name, :last_name, :email,
                :about, :company, :tags, :registered

  def initialize(first_name, last_name, email, about,
                 company, tags, registered)
    @first_name = first_name
    @last_name = last_name
    @email = email
    @about = about
    @company = company
    @tags = tags
    @registered = registered
  end
end
```

The preceding code is plain and simple:

- *speaker.rb* resides in the *models* directory to follow commonly accepted Ruby project conventions.
- `attr_accessor` defines the Speaker's data members (e.g., `first_name`) and accessor methods (getters/readers and setters/writers) for the data members.
- `initialize()` initializes the data members when `Speaker.new()` is called.

Before moving on, you can stop `json-server` by pressing Ctrl-C at the command line.

Further Reading on Ruby and Minitest

We've covered only the basics of Ruby and Minitest in this chapter. To learn more, please see the following resources:

- *Ruby in Practice*, by Jeremy McAnally and Assaf Arkin (Manning) (*https://www.manning.com/books/ruby-in-practice*)

- *The Well-Grounded Rubyist*, 2nd Ed., by David A. Black (Manning) (*https:// www.manning.com/books/the-well-grounded-rubyist-second-edition*)
- *Minitest Cookbook*, by Chris Kottam (*https://chriskottom.com/minitestcookbook*)

What Is Missing in the Unit Tests?

So far, the Unit Tests have done a decent job of testing JSON data, but something is missing. The code had to check for the existence of all the expected fields, which is clumsy and cumbersome. Imagine how arduous this would be for larger, deeper, more complex JSON documents. There's a solution for this problem: JSON Schema (this is covered in Chapter 5).

We've shown how to deploy and interact with a Stub API, and now it's time to build a small RESTful API with Ruby on Rails.

Build a Small Web API with Ruby on Rails

Now that you know how to serialize/deserialize JSON to/from a `speaker` Object and how to do a Unit Test with the Speaker Stub API (from `json-server`), we're ready to build a simple web application that leverages the API data and presents it to a user.

We'll continue to use the Speaker data to create an API with Rails 5. This version of Rails includes `rails-api`, which provides the ability to create an API-only Rails application. `rails-api` (*https://github.com/rails-api/rails-api*) began as a separate gem, but it has been merged into Rails.

We'll build two Rails-based API applications to demonstrate some of the features of AMS:

`speakers-api-1`
    Create an API with camel-cased JSON.

`speakers-api-2`
    Create an API that customizes the JSON representation.

Before we create anything, let's determine how the APIs will render JSON.

Choose a JSON Serializer

There are several options for rendering JSON in Ruby on Rails. Here's a list of the most widely used techniques:

ActiveModel::Serializers (AMS)
    AMS provides functionality to objects that need some ActiveRecord features, such as serialization and validation. AMS is part of the Rails API (*http://*

api.rubyonrails.org/classes/ActiveModel/Serializers.html), and you can find documentation on GitHub (*https://github.com/rails-api/active_model_serializers*).

Jbuilder

A Domain-Specific Language (DSL) builder that uses a separate template (i.e., outside the controller) that controls the output. For further details, please see Jbuilder on GitHub (*https://github.com/rails/jbuilder*).

RABL

Ruby API Builder Language (RABL) generates JSON, XML, PList, MessagePack, and BSON. This gem also uses a template file. The RABL GitHub repository (*https://github.com/nesquena/rabl*) has details.

Evaluation criteria

Here are a few considerations to help choose a JSON serialization approach:

- JSON generation should be done outside application objects because an object should have no knowledge of external representations. This means that you shouldn't have code in your object that renders JSON. According to Uncle Bob Martin, a class should have only one reason to change; this is known as the Single Responsibility Principle (the first of the five SOLID principles of OO Design). For further details, see his The Principles of OOD site (*http://butunclebob.com/ ArticleS.UncleBob.PrinciplesOfOod*). When you introduce JSON formatting to an Object, that Object now has a second reason to change, because it has two responsibilities (making it more difficult to change the code in the future):

  — The original functionality of the object

  — JSON encoding

- Don't clutter Controllers or Models with JSON generation. This also violates Single Responsibility and makes the Controller/Model code less flexible. Use external templates to clean up Controllers and Models and factor out messy, complex formatting logic.

- Control which attributes of an object to serialize and which ones to omit.

Although these guidelines may sound a bit strict, the whole point here is interoperability and consistency. But there are no silver bullets, and it's perfectly acceptable to have different opinions. In which case, do the following:

- Know why you believe what you believe. Back up your position with sound software engineering and architectural principles.

- Work and play well with others. Determine whether your approach fits with the overall community rather than just a single language, platform, or segment within a particular technical community.

Now that we've established some evaluation criteria, let's review the options.

AMS, RABL, or Jbuilder?

Based on the preceding considerations and a review of all the options, it's a tough decision because AMS, RABL, and Jbuilder each provide most (if not all) of what we're looking for. AMS factors out serialization into a `Serializer` Object, and RABL and Jbuilder both use external templates. Because RABL can't emit lower camel case (*https://github.com/nesquena/rabl/issues/469*), it's out of the running, which reduces our options to AMS and Jbuilder.

Choosing between AMS and Jbuilder is difficult:

- Each provides the same quality of JSON representation.
- Their performance is similar when you configure Rails to use `oj`.

It comes down to which approach you prefer:

- Programmatic JSON serialization with `Serializer` Objects (AMS) or with templates (Jbuilder)
- JSON serialization in the Controller (AMS) or in the View (Jbuilder)

There are great arguments on both sides:

Pro AMS
   Using AMS is a good approach because everything is Ruby-based. Jbuilder templates introduce the need for developers to learn a new DSL.

Pro Jbuilder
   Jbuilder forces you to think about the JSON representation first, and pushes you to decouple from the underlying database.

As many people in the Rails community would say, "it's a wash." In other words, it's a toss-up between AMS and Jbuilder; either approach produces great JSON responses for an API. I chose AMS because it's part of Rails and there's no need to learn a new DSL for templating.

speakers-api-1—Create an API with Camel-Cased JSON

We'll take the following steps to create and deploy the *speakers-api-1* API with Rails 5:

1. Set up the project.

---

2. Write source code:

- Model
- Serializer
- Controller

3. Deploy the API.
4. Test with Postman.

Set up the speakers-api-1 project

The *speakers-api-1* project already exists in the Chapter 3 code examples (*https://github.com/tmarrs/json-at-work-examples/tree/master/chapter-3*) under the *chapter-3/speakers-api-1* directory, so you don't need to create this project. But for the sake of completeness, the following sidebar explains how the project was created.

Create speakers-api-1 App with Rails

Use the following command to create the *speakers-api-1* Rails API project:

```
rails new speakers-api-1 -T --api --skip-active-record --skip-action-mailer --skip-action-cable
```

We don't need the frontend normally provided by Rails (ERB, JS, CSS, Asset Pipeline, and so forth) for our example, nor do we need a database. The preceding command creates a Rails API application without the following:

- A web-based frontend. The `--api` option leaves out these:
  — The asset pipeline
  — Views
- Tests (with the `-T` option).
- ActiveRecord (with the `--skip-active-record` option). This means that you don't need a database to run the application. While this may seem a bit strange, it's fits our purpose because it reduces application dependencies and setup.
- ActionMailer (with the `--skip-action-mailer` option). The Web API doesn't need to send emails.
- ActionCable (with the `--skip-action-cable` option). The API doesn't use Web-Socket.

The Rails generators will still create controllers, and we'll cover that in a minute.

The preceding `rails new` command created the *speakers-api-1* directory.

To install and use AMS in the project, the example code adds the following line to the Gemfile:

```
gem 'active_model_serializers'
gem 'oj'
```

As in previous examples in this chapter, we want to continue to use oj for performance reasons, but AMS doesn't require it.

Even though the project is already set up, you will need to install the gems to run the project. Do the following:

```
cd speakers-api-1
```

```
bundle exec spring binstub --all
```

In this command, Bundler installs the gems specified in the project's Gemfile.

Create the Model

The Speaker class in Example 3-11 is a PORO that represents the Speaker data that the API will render as JSON.

Example 3-11. speakers-api-1/app/models/speaker.rb

```ruby
class Speaker < ActiveModelSerializers::Model
  attr_accessor :first_name, :last_name, :email,
                :about, :company, :tags, :registered

  def initialize(first_name, last_name, email, about,
                 company, tags, registered)
    @first_name = first_name
    @last_name = last_name
    @email = email
    @about = about
    @company = company
    @tags = tags
    @registered = registered
  end
end
```

This code doesn't do much; it just provides the data members, constructors, and accessor methods (getters and setters) for a speaker. This code doesn't know anything about JSON formatting. The Speaker class inherits from ActiveModel::Serial izer so that AMS will convert it to JSON.

Create the Serializer

AMS provides Serializers (separate from Controllers and Models) that serialize Objects into JSON. The `SpeakerSerializer` already exists, but the following sidebar explains how it was created.

> ## Generate SpeakerSerializer
>
> Use the following command to generate a `SpeakerSerializer` for the existing speaker Model from the *speakers-web-1* directory:
>
> ```
> bin/rails generate serializer speaker
> ```
>
> This creates an empty shell Serializer with an `id` field:
>
> ```
> class SpeakerSerializer < ActiveModel::Serializer
>   attributes :id
> end
> ```
>
> From here, you have to add in the fields to serialize into JSON.

Example 3-12 shows the `SpeakerSerializer` that AMS uses to render `speaker` Objects as JSON.

Example 3-12. speakers-api-1/app/models/speaker_serializer.rb

```
class SpeakerSerializer < ActiveModel::Serializer
  attributes :first_name, :last_name, :email,
             :about, :company, :tags, :registered
end
```

In this code, `attributes` lists all fields to be serialized into JSON.

Create the Controller

In a Rails application, a Controller handles HTTP Requests and returns HTTP Responses. In our case, the Speaker JSON data is returned in the Response Body. The `SpeakersController` already exists, but the following sidebar explains how it was created.

> ## Generate SpeakersController
>
> Use the following command to generate a `SpeakersController` from the *speakers-web-1* directory:
>
> ```
> bin/rails generate controller speakers index show
> ```

> This creates a shell with empty index and show methods and creates the appropriate HTTP routes in *app/config/routes.rb* (more on this later).

Example 3-13 provides the full SpeakersController that implements the index and show methods.

Example 3-13. speakers-api-1/app/controllers/speakers_controller.rb

```ruby
require 'speaker'

class SpeakersController < ApplicationController
  before_action :set_speakers, only: [:index, :show]

  # GET /speakers
  def index
    render json: @speakers
  end

  # GET /speakers/:id
  def show
    id = params[:id].to_i - 1

    if id >= 0 && id < @speakers.length
      render json: @speakers[id]
    else
      render plain: '404 Not found', status: 404
    end
  end

  private

  def set_speakers
    @speakers = []

    @speakers << Speaker.new('Larson', 'Richard', 'larsonrichard@ecratic.com',
      'Incididunt mollit cupidatat magna ...', 'Ecratic',
      ['JavaScript', 'AngularJS', 'Yeoman'], true)

    @speakers << Speaker.new('Ester', 'Clements', 'esterclements@acusage.com',
      'Labore tempor irure adipisicing consectetur ...', 'Acusage',
      ['REST', 'Ruby on Rails', 'APIs'], true)

    @speakers << Speaker.new('Christensen', 'Fisher',
      'christensenfisher@talkola.com', 'Proident ex Lorem et Lorem ad ...',
      'Talkola',
      ['Java', 'Spring', 'Maven', 'REST'], true)
  end

end
```

Note the following in this code:

- The speakers Array is hardcoded, but it's for test purposes only. In a real application, a separate Data Layer would populate the speakers from a database or an external API call.

- The index method does the following:

  — Responds to HTTP GET requests on the /speakers URI.

  — Retrieves the entire speakers Array and renders it as a JSON Array in an HTTP Response Body.

- The show method does the following:

  — Responds to HTTP GET requests on the /speakers/{id} URI (where id represents a speaker ID).

  — Retrieves a speaker (based on the speaker ID) and renders it as a JSON object in an HTTP Response Body.

  — If id in the HTTP Request is out-of-bounds, the Controller renders a 404 (Not Found) HTTP Status Code with a plain-text message in the HTTP Response with render plain.

- When the Controller invokes the render method, Rails looks for a matching Serializer to serialize the speaker Object, and invokes the SpeakerSerializer by default.

The Controller and Serializer are decoupled and know nothing about each other. The serialization code exists only in the Serializer and does not reside in the Controller or the Model. The Controller, Model, and Serializer each do one thing.

In a Rails application, the *Routes* file maps URLs to Controller methods that execute when the URL is invoked. The rails generate controller command that was shown earlier created the routes shown in Example 3-14.

Example 3-14. speakers-api-1/app/config/routes.rb

```
Rails.application.routes.draw do
  get 'speakers/index'

  get 'speakers/show'

  # For details on the DSL available within this file,
  # see http://guides.rubyonrails.org/routing.html
end
```

You can shorten the *Routes* file with Resource-based routing as shown in Example 3-15.

Example 3-15. speakers-api-1/app/config/routes.rb

```
Rails.application.routes.draw do

  resources :speakers, :only => [:show, :index]

  # For details on the DSL available within this file,
  # see http://guides.rubyonrails.org/routing.html
end
```

Instead of separate routes for the `index` and `show` methods, this resourceful route
defines them with a single line of code.

Camel-casing AMS JSON output

By default, AMS renders JSON keys with snake case (`first_name` and `last_name`).
Out of the box, the serialized JSON (when the user invokes *http://localhost:3000/
speakers/1* with an HTTP GET) looks like this:

```
{
  "first_name": "Larson",
  "last_name": "Richard",
  "email": "larsonrichard@ecratic.com",
  "about": "Incididunt mollit cupidatat magna ...",
  "company": "Ecratic",
  "tags": [
    "JavaScript",
    "AngularJS",
    "Yeoman"
  ],
  "registered": true
}
```

To make our JSON output compatible with non-Ruby clients, let's add camel casing
by adding the global initializer file shown in Example 3-16.

Example 3-16. speakers-api-1/config/initializers/active_model_serializers.rb

```
ActiveModelSerializers.config.key_transform = :camel_lower
```

Deploy the API

In the *speakers-api-1* directory, run `rails s` to deploy the API at *http://localhost:
3000/speakers*, and you'll see the following:

```
json-at-work ⇒ rails s
⇒ Booting Puma
⇒ Rails 5.0.2 application starting in development on http://localhost:3000
⇒ Run `rails server -h` for more startup options
Puma starting in single mode...
* Version 3.8.2 (ruby 2.4.0-p0), codename: Sassy Salamander
* Min threads: 5, max threads: 5
* Environment: development
* Listening on tcp://localhost:3000
Use Ctrl-C to stop
```

Test the API with Postman

Now that the Speakers API is up and running, let's test with Postman (as we did in Chapter 1) to get the first `speaker`. In the Postman GUI, do the following:

- Enter the *http://localhost:3000/speakers/1* URL.
- Choose GET as the HTTP verb.
- Click the Send button.

You should see that the GET ran properly in Postman with the `speaker` JSON data in the HTTP Response Body text area and a 200 (OK) HTTP Status, as shown in Figure 3-1.

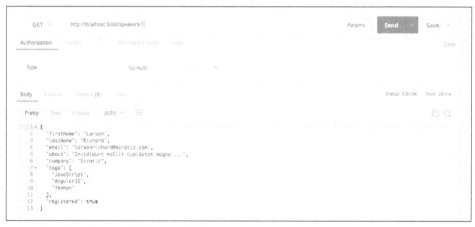

Figure 3-1. Speaker JSON data with Postman

You can stop *speakers-api-1* by pressing Ctrl-C at the command line.

speakers-api-2—Create an API that Customizes the JSON Representation

AMS's JSON customization functionality goes beyond camel-casing. The second API application will show how AMS can customize (alter) the JSON representation of each `speaker`. Except for the new `SpeakerSerializer`, *speakers-api-2* has all the same code as the original *speakers-api-1* project, so we'll just focus on serialization.

Before going further, please install the gems to run the *speakers-api-2* project. Do the following:

```
cd speakers-api-2

bundle exec spring binstub --all
```

Change the JSON representation with AMS

This new version of the `SpeakerSerializer` provides a new `name` field (which combines the `first_name` and `last_name`) without changing the original `speaker` Object, as shown in Example 3-17.

Example 3-17. speakers-api-2/app/serializers/speaker_serializer.rb

```
class SpeakerSerializer < ActiveModel::Serializer
  attributes :name, :email, :about,
             :company, :tags, :registered

  def name
    "#{object.first_name} #{object.last_name}"
  end
end
```

Note the following in this example:

- `attributes` references `name` instead of `first_name` and `last_name`.
- In the `name` method:
  - The `object` refers to the `speaker` Object being rendered.
  - Combine the `first_name` and `last_name` fields by using String interpolation to render a single `name` field. The original `Speaker` model knows nothing about the `name` attribute created by the Serializer.

The ability to customize the JSON representation with `attributes` is powerful because it decouples the Model from the JSON output.

Deploy the API

In the *speakers-api-2* directory, run `rails s` to deploy the API at *http://localhost:3000/speakers*.

Test the API with Postman

In the Postman GUI, invoke HTTP `GET` on *http://localhost:3000/speakers/1* and you should see the screen in Figure 3-2.

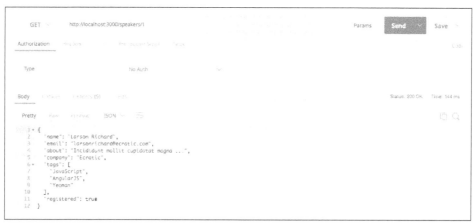

Figure 3-2. Customized Speaker JSON data with Postman

Don't forget to stop the *speakers-api-2* application by pressing Ctrl-C at the command line.

Further Reading on Rails and Rails-based APIs

We've shown just enough Rails-based APIs and AMS to get a simple API to work. To go deeper, please see the following resources:

- *Ruby on Rails Tutorial: Learn Web Development with Rails*, by Michael Hartl (*https://www.railstutorial.org/book*)

- *Learn Ruby on Rails 5*, by Daniel Kehoe (*http://learn-rails.com/learn-ruby-on-rails.html*)

- *APIs on Rails: Building REST APIs with Rails*, by Abraham Kuri (*http://apionrails.icalialabs.com/book*)

- *Get Up and Running with Rails API*, by Chris Kottam (*https://chriskottom.com/blog/2017/02/get-up-and-running-with-rails-api*)

- *Active Model Serializers, Rails, and JSON! OH MY!*, by Kendra Uzia (*https://www.sitepoint.com/active-model-serializers-rails-and-json-oh-my/*)

What We Covered

We started with simple conversions between Ruby and JSON, discussed the importance of JSON camel casing, and then demonstrated how to call a (Stub) JSON-based Web API (and tested its contents with Minitest). We then finished by creating a RESTful API with Rails 5 and tested it with Postman.

What's Next?

Now that we've developed a JSON-based application with Ruby on Rails, we'll move on to use JSON with Java (and Spring Boot) in Chapter 4.

JSON in Java

We've shown how to use JSON with JavaScript and Ruby on Rails, and we'll now move to Java, our third and final platform for this book. Here's what we'll cover:

- Performing Java/JSON serialization/deserialization with Jackson
- Working with Java Objects and JSON
- Using JSON with JUnit
- Making RESTful API calls and testing the results with JUnit and JsonUnit
- Building a small JSON-based API with Spring Boot

In our examples, we'll make RESTful API calls to work with the data we deployed on json-server in the previous chapter. We'll then move to create a more realistic JSON-based Web API. Before we develop a RESTful API, we need to start with the basics of Java serialization/deserialization with JSON, and then add more complexity.

Java and Gradle Setup

This chapter uses Gradle (*http://www.gradle.org*) for building source and test code. If you haven't installed Java and Gradle, go to Appendix A and see "Install the Java Environment" on page 331 and "Install Gradle" on page 332. After that, you will have a basic environment that enables you to run the examples.

Gradle Overview

Gradle leverages the concepts from earlier Java-based build systems—Apache Ant (*http://ant.apache.org*) and Maven (*https://maven.apache.org*). Gradle is widely used and provides the following functionality for Java projects:

- Project structure (a common/standard project directory structure)
- Dependency Management (for JAR files)
- A common build process

The `gradle init` utility initializes a project by creating a core directory structure and some initial implementations for the build script, along with simple Java source and test code. Here are the key directories and files in a Gradle project:

- *src/main/* contains source code and resources.
    - *java/* is the Java source code.
    - *resources/* contains the resources (e.g., properties, data files—JSON in our case) used by the source code.
- *test/main/* contains source code and resources.
    - *java/* is the Java source code.
    - *resources/* contains the resources (e.g., properties, data files—JSON in our case) used by the source code.
- *build/* contains the *.class* files generated by compiling the source and test code.
    - *libs/* contains the JAR or WAR files that result from building the project.
- *gradlew* is the Gradle wrapper that enables you to run a project as an executable JAR. We'll cover this in more detail in the Spring Boot section later.
- *build.gradle* is initiated for you by `gradle init`, but you need to fill it in with project-specific dependencies. Gradle uses a Groovy-based DSL for its build scripts (rather than XML).
- *build/* contains build-related artifacts created by `gradle build` or `gradle test`.

Here are the most important Gradle tasks you'll need to know in order to work with Gradle. You can see these tasks when you type `gradle tasks` on the command line:

`gradle build`
Build the project.

`gradle classes`
Compile Java source code.

`gradle clean`
Delete the *build* directory.

`gradle jar`
Compile Java source code and package it (along with Resources) into a JAR.

```
gradle javadoc
```
Generate JavaDoc documentation from the Java source code.

```
gradle test
```
Run Unit Tests (includes Java source and test code compile).

```
gradle testClasses
```
Compile Java test code.

Here's how the example projects were created:

- `gradle init --type java-application` was used to create the initial *speakers-test* and *speakers-web* applications.
- The generated *build.gradle* file and the Java application and test files are stubs. They have been replaced with actual code for the examples in this chapter.

Gradle is well-documented, and here are some tutorials and references to help you go deeper:

- Gradle User Guide (*https://docs.gradle.org/3.4.1/userguide/userguide.html*)
- Getting Started with Gradle, by Petri Kainulainen (*http://bit.ly/2tiS5kx*)
- *Gradle Beyond the Basics*, by Tim Berglund (O'Reilly)

Now that we've covered the basics of Gradle, it's time to look at Java-based JSON libraries, and then move on to coding examples.

Just Enough Unit Testing with JUnit

JUnit (*http://www.junit.org*) is a widely used Unit-Testing framework. The tests in this chapter use JUnit because of its common acceptance in the Java community. JUnit tests are procedural, so the Unit Tests are TDD-style. If you'd like to combine JUnit with BDD, Cucumber is a solid choice. To learn more about BDD and Cucumber in Java, see Micha Kops' excellent article on "BDD Testing with Cucumber, Java and JUnit" (*http://www.hascode.com/2014/12/bdd-testing-with-cucumber-java-and-junit/*).

Java-Based JSON Libraries

There are several solid JSON libraries for Java/JSON serialization/deserialization, including these:

Jackson
You can find details about Jackson in the GitHub repository (*https://github.com/FasterXML/jackson*).

Gson
> Gson is provided by Google (*https://github.com/google/gson*).

JSON-java
> This library is provided by Doug Crockford (*http://bit.ly/2sprKE6*).

Java SE (Standard Edition)
> JSON support was introduced into the Java platform in JavaEE 7 as part of the Java Specification Request (JSR) 353 (*https://jcp.org/en/jsr/detail?id=353*) initiative. JSR-353 is a standalone implementation, and you can integrate it with your Java SE applications as of Java SE 8. Java SE 9 will provide native JSON support as part of the Java Enhancement Proposal (JEP) 198 (*http://openjdk.java.net/jeps/198*) initiative.

All examples in this chapter use Jackson because it

- Is widely used (especially by the Spring community)
- Provides excellent functionality
- Has worked well for a long time
- Is well maintained with an active development community
- Has good documentation

Additionally, we'll maintain focus by sticking with one Java/JSON library. As mentioned, the other libraries work well, so feel free to try them on your own.

Let's start with the basics of Java serialization/deserialization.

JSON Serialization/Deserialization with Jackson

Java applications need to convert from Java data structures to JSON (serialize) and convert from JSON to Java (deserialize).

Serialization/Deserialization with Simple Java Data Types

As in previous chapters, we'll start by serializing some basic Java data types:

- `integer`
- `string`
- `array`
- `boolean`

Example 4-1 shows a simple Unit Test that uses Jackson and JUnit 4 to serialize/deserialize simple Java data types.

```java
package org.jsonatwork.ch4;

import static org.junit.Assert.*;

import java.io.*;
import java.util.*;

import org.junit.Test;

import com.fasterxml.jackson.core.*;
import com.fasterxml.jackson.core.type.*;
import com.fasterxml.jackson.databind.*;

public class BasicJsonTypesTest {
  private static final String TEST_SPEAKER = "age = 39\n" +
    "fullName = \"Larson Richard\"\n" +
    "tags = [\"JavaScript\",\"AngularJS\",\"Yeoman\"]\n" +
    "registered = true";

  @Test
  public void serializeBasicTypes() {
    try {
      ObjectMapper mapper = new ObjectMapper();
      Writer writer = new StringWriter();
      int age = 39;
      String fullName = new String("Larson Richard");
      List<String> tags = new ArrayList<String>(
          Arrays.asList("JavaScript", "AngularJS", "Yeoman"));

      boolean registered = true;
      String speaker = null;

      writer.write("age = ");
      mapper.writeValue(writer, age);
      writer.write("\nfullName = ");
      mapper.writeValue(writer, fullName);
      writer.write("\ntags = ");
      mapper.writeValue(writer, tags);
      writer.write("\nregistered = ");
      mapper.configure(SerializationFeature.INDENT_OUTPUT, true);
      mapper.writeValue(writer, registered);
      speaker = writer.toString();
      System.out.println(speaker);
      assertTrue(TEST_SPEAKER.equals(speaker));
      assertTrue(true);
    } catch (JsonGenerationException jge) {
      jge.printStackTrace();
      fail(jge.getMessage());
    } catch (JsonMappingException jme) {
      jme.printStackTrace();
```

```
        fail(jme.getMessage());
    } catch (IOException ioe) {
      ioe.printStackTrace();
      fail(ioe.getMessage());
    }
  }

  @Test
  public void deSerializeBasicTypes() {
    try {
      String ageJson = "{ \"age\": 39 }";
      ObjectMapper mapper = new ObjectMapper();
      Map<String, Integer> ageMap = mapper.readValue(ageJson,
          new TypeReference<HashMap<String,Integer>>() {});

      Integer age = ageMap.get("age");

      System.out.println("age = " + age + "\n\n\n");
      assertEquals(39, age.intValue());
      assertTrue(true);
    } catch (JsonMappingException jme) {
      jme.printStackTrace();
      fail(jme.getMessage());
    } catch (IOException ioe) {
      ioe.printStackTrace();
      fail(ioe.getMessage());
    }
  }

}
```

In this example, the @Test annotation tells JUnit to run the serializeBasicTypes()
and deSerializeBasicTypes() methods as part of the test. These Unit Tests don't do
many assertions on the JSON data itself. We'll cover assertions in more detail later
when we test against a Web API.

Here are the most important Jackson classes and methods that serialize/deserialize to/
from JSON:

- ObjectMapper converts between Java and JSON constructs.

- ObjectMapper.writeValue() converts a Java data type to JSON (and in this case,
  outputs to a Writer).

- ObjectMapper.readValue() converts JSON to a Java data type.

Run a single Unit Test from the command line as follows:

```
cd chapter-4/speakers-test

+gradle test --tests org.jsonatwork.ch4.BasicJsonTypesTest+
```

You should see these results:

```
json-at-work => gradle test --tests org.jsonatwork.ch4.BasicJsonTypesTest
:compileJava
:processResources NO-SOURCE
:classes
:compileTestJava
:processTestResources
:testClasses
:test

org.jsonatwork.ch4.BasicJsonTypesTest > deSerializeBasicTypes STANDARD_OUT
    age = 39



org.jsonatwork.ch4.BasicJsonTypesTest > serializeBasicTypes STANDARD_OUT
    age = 39
    fullName = "Larson Richard"
    tags = ["JavaScript","AngularJS","Yeoman"]
    registered = true

BUILD SUCCESSFUL
```

This example isn't too exciting right now because it serializes/deserializes only simple data types to/from JSON. Serialization/deserialization gets more interesting when Objects are involved.

Serialization/Deserialization with Java Objects

Now that we have a decent grasp of Jackson and how to work with simple Java data types, let's wade in deeper with Objects. Example 4-2 shows how to use Jackson to serialize/deserialize a single `speaker` Object, and then how to deserialize a JSON file into multiple `speaker` Objects.

Example 4-2. speakers-test/src/test/java/org/jsonatwork/ch4/
SpeakerJsonFlatFileTest.java

```java
package org.jsonatwork.ch4;

import static org.junit.Assert.*;

import java.io.*;
import java.net.*;
import java.util.*;

import org.junit.Test;

import com.fasterxml.jackson.core.*;
import com.fasterxml.jackson.databind.*;
```

```java
import com.fasterxml.jackson.databind.type.*;

public class SpeakerJsonFlatFileTest {

private static final String SPEAKER_JSON_FILE_NAME = "speaker.json";
private static final String SPEAKERS_JSON_FILE_NAME = "speakers.json";
private static final String TEST_SPEAKER_JSON = "{\n" +
    "  \"id\" : 1,\n" +
    "  \"age\" : 39,\n" +
    "  \"fullName\" : \"Larson Richard\",\n" +
    "  \"tags\" : [ \"JavaScript\", \"AngularJS\", \"Yeoman\" ],\n" +
    "  \"registered\" : true\n" +
  "}";

@Test
public void serializeObject() {
    try {
      ObjectMapper mapper = new ObjectMapper();
      Writer writer = new StringWriter();
      String[] tags = {"JavaScript", "AngularJS", "Yeoman"};
      Speaker speaker = new Speaker(1, 39, "Larson Richard", tags, true);
      String speakerStr = null;

      mapper.configure(SerializationFeature.INDENT_OUTPUT, true);
      speakerStr = mapper.writeValueAsString(speaker);
      System.out.println(speakerStr);
      assertTrue(TEST_SPEAKER_JSON.equals(speakerStr));
      assertTrue(true);
    } catch (JsonGenerationException jge) {
      jge.printStackTrace();
      fail(jge.getMessage());
    } catch (JsonMappingException jme) {
      jme.printStackTrace();
      fail(jme.getMessage());
    } catch (IOException ioe) {
      ioe.printStackTrace();
      fail(ioe.getMessage());
    }
  }

  private File getSpeakerFile(String speakerFileName) throws URISyntaxException {
    ClassLoader classLoader = Thread.currentThread().getContextClassLoader();
    URL fileUrl = classLoader.getResource(speakerFileName);
    URI fileUri = new URI(fileUrl.toString());
    File speakerFile = new File(fileUri);

    return speakerFile;
  }

  @Test
  public void deSerializeObject() {
    try {
```

```java
    ObjectMapper mapper = new ObjectMapper();
    File speakerFile = getSpeakerFile(
        SpeakerJsonFlatFileTest.SPEAKER_JSON_FILE_NAME);

    Speaker speaker = mapper.readValue(speakerFile, Speaker.class);

    System.out.println("\n" + speaker + "\n");
    assertEquals("Larson Richard", speaker.getFullName());
    assertEquals(39, speaker.getAge());
    assertTrue(true);
  } catch (URISyntaxException use) {
    use.printStackTrace();
    fail(use.getMessage());
  } catch (JsonParseException jpe) {
    jpe.printStackTrace();
    fail(jpe.getMessage());
  } catch (JsonMappingException jme) {
    jme.printStackTrace();
    fail(jme.getMessage());
  } catch (IOException ioe) {
    ioe.printStackTrace();
    fail(ioe.getMessage());
  }
}

@Test
public void deSerializeMultipleObjects() {
  try {
    ObjectMapper mapper = new ObjectMapper();
    File speakersFile = getSpeakerFile(
        SpeakerJsonFlatFileTest.SPEAKERS_JSON_FILE_NAME);

    JsonNode arrNode = mapper.readTree(speakersFile).get("speakers");
    List<Speaker> speakers = new ArrayList<Speaker>();
      if (arrNode.isArray()) {
        for (JsonNode objNode : arrNode) {
        System.out.println(objNode);
        speakers.add(mapper.convertValue(objNode, Speaker.class));
      }
    }

    assertEquals(3, speakers.size());
    System.out.println("\n\n\nAll Speakers\n");
    for (Speaker speaker: speakers) {
      System.out.println(speaker);
    }

    System.out.println("\n");
    Speaker speaker3 = speakers.get(2);
    assertEquals("Christensen Fisher", speaker3.getFullName());
    assertEquals(45, speaker3.getAge());
    assertTrue(true);
```

```
    } catch (URISyntaxException use) {
      use.printStackTrace();
      fail(use.getMessage());
    } catch (JsonParseException jpe) {
      jpe.printStackTrace();
      fail(jpe.getMessage());
    } catch (JsonMappingException jme) {
      jme.printStackTrace();
      fail(jme.getMessage());
    } catch (IOException ioe) {
      ioe.printStackTrace();
      fail(ioe.getMessage());
    }
  }

}
```

Note the following in this JUnit test:

- `serializeObject()` creates a `Speaker` Object and serializes it to Standard Output by using the `ObjectMapper.writeValueAsString()` method and `System.out.println()`. The test sets the `SerializationFeature.INDENT_OUT PUT` to `true` to indent/pretty-print the JSON output.

- `deSerializeObject()` calls `getSpeakerFile()` to read a JSON input file (which contains a single `speaker` JSON Object), and uses the `ObjectMapper.read Value()` method to deserialize it into a `Speaker` Java Object.

- `deSerializeMultipleObjects()` does the following:

  — Calls `getSpeakerFile()` to read a JSON input file, which contains an array of JSON `speaker` Objects.

  — Invokes the `ObjectMapper.readTree()` method to get a `JsonNode` Object, which is a pointer to the root node of the JSON document that was in the file.

  — Visits each node in the JSON tree and uses the `ObjectMapper.convert Value()` method to deserialize each `speaker` JSON object into a `Speaker` Java Object.

  — Prints out each `Speaker` Object in the list.

- `getSpeakerFile()` finds a file on the classpath and does the following:

  — Gets the `ContextClassLoader` from the current `Thread` of execution.

  — Uses the `ClassLoader.getResource()` method to find the filename as a resource within the current classpath.

  — Constructs a `File` Object based on the URI of the filename.

Each of the preceding tests uses JUnit's assertion methods (*http://junit.sourceforge.net/javadoc/org/junit/Assert.html*) to test the results of JSON serialization/deserialization.

You'll see the following when you run the test from the command line using `gradle test --tests org.jsonatwork.ch4.SpeakerJsonFlatFileTest`:

```
json-at-work => gradle test --tests org.jsonatwork.ch4.SpeakerJsonFlatFileTest
:compileJava UP-TO-DATE
:processResources NO-SOURCE
:classes UP-TO-DATE
:compileTestJava UP-TO-DATE
:processTestResources UP-TO-DATE
:testClasses UP-TO-DATE
:test

org.jsonatwork.ch4.SpeakerJsonFlatFileTest > serializeObject STANDARD_OUT
    {
      "id" : 1,
      "age" : 39,
      "fullName" : "Larson Richard",
      "tags" : [ "JavaScript", "AngularJS", "Yeoman" ],
      "registered" : true
    }

org.jsonatwork.ch4.SpeakerJsonFlatFileTest > deSerializeObject STANDARD_OUT

    Speaker [id=1, age=39, fullName=Larson Richard, tags=[JavaScript, AngularJS, Yeoman], registered=true]

org.jsonatwork.ch4.SpeakerJsonFlatFileTest > deSerializeMultipleObjects STANDARD_OUT
    {"id":1,"fullName":"Larson Richard","tags":["JavaScript","AngularJS","Yeoman"],"age":39,"registered":true}
    {"id":2,"fullName":"Ester Clements","tags":["REST","Ruby on Rails","APIs"],"age":29,"registered":true}
    {"id":3,"fullName":"Christensen Fisher","tags":["Java","Spring","Maven","REST"],"age":45,"registered":false}


    All Speakers

    Speaker [id=1, age=39, fullName=Larson Richard, tags=[JavaScript, AngularJS, Yeoman], registered=true]
    Speaker [id=2, age=29, fullName=Ester Clements, tags=[REST, Ruby on Rails, APIs], registered=true]
    Speaker [id=3, age=45, fullName=Christensen Fisher, tags=[Java, Spring, Maven, REST], registered=false]

BUILD SUCCESSFUL
```

Jackson offers much more functionality than can be shown in this chapter. Refer to the following resources for some great tutorials:

- Java Jackson Tutorial (*http://www.baeldung.com/jackson*), by Eugen Paraschiv

- Jackson Tutorial (*http://www.tutorialspoint.com/jackson*), Tutorials Point

- Jackson JSON Java Parser API Example Tutorial (*http://www.journaldev.com/2324/jackson-json-processing-api-in-java-example-tutorial*), by Pankaj (Journal-Dev)

- Java JSON Jackson Introduction (*http://www.studytrails.com/java/json/java-jackson-introduction.jsp*), by Mithil Shah

Unit Testing with a Stub API

Until now, we've been using JUnit to test against the data from JSON flat files. We'll now do a more realistic test against an API. But we need an API to test against without writing a lot of code or creating lots of infrastructure. We'll show how to create a simple Stub API (which produces a JSON response) without writing a single line of code.

Test Data

To create the Stub, we'll use the Speaker data from earlier chapters as our test data, which is available at GitHub (*https://github.com/tmarrs/json-at-work-examples/tree/master/chapter-4/speakers-test/src/test/resources*) and deploy it as a RESTful API. We'll leverage the `json-server` Node.js module to serve up the *speakers.json* file as a Web API. If you need to install `json-server`, refer to "Install npm Modules" on page 325 in Appendix A. Here's how to run `json-server` on port 5000 from your local machine (using a second terminal session):

```
cd chapter-4/speakers-test/src/test/resources

json-server -p 5000 ./speakers.json
```

You can also get a single speaker by adding the `id` to the URI as follows: *http://localhost:5000/speakers/1*. With the Stub API in place, it's time to write some Unit Tests.

JSON and JUnit Testing with APIs

Our Unit Test will do the following:

- Make HTTP calls to the Stub Speakers API
- Check the JSON (from the HTTP Response) against expected values

As in earlier chapters, we'll continue to leverage the open source Unirest API wrapper, but this time we'll use the Java version (*http://unirest.io/java.html*).

In the previous JUnit tests in the chapter, we ensured that only bare minimum functionality was working (no exceptions were thrown), and it's now time to make our tests a bit more sophisticated. The remaining Unit Tests will look at the JSON content returned from an HTTP Response, and verify that it matches the expected output. We could search through the data and do a comparison with custom code, or we could use a library to reduce the amount of work. JsonUnit (*https://github.com/lukas-krecan/JsonUnit*) has many helpful matchers to simplify JSON comparison in JUnit tests. We'll cover the basics of JsonUnit in these Unit Tests, but it provides much deeper functionality than we can cover here, including the following:

- Regular Expressions
- More matchers
- The ability to ignore specific fields and values

The Unit Test in Example 4-3 pulls everything together by invoking the Stub API and comparing the JSON response with expected values.

Example 4-3. speakers-test/src/test/java/org/jsonatwork/ch4/SpeakersJsonApiTest.java

```java
package org.jsonatwork.ch4;

import static org.junit.Assert.*;

import java.io.*;
import java.net.*;
import java.util.*;

import org.apache.http.*;
import org.junit.Test;

import com.fasterxml.jackson.core.*;
import com.fasterxml.jackson.databind.*;
import com.mashape.unirest.http.HttpResponse;
import com.mashape.unirest.http.Unirest;
import com.mashape.unirest.http.exceptions.*;
import com.mashape.unirest.request.*;

import static net.javacrumbs.jsonunit.fluent.JsonFluentAssert.assertThatJson;

public class SpeakersApiJsonTest {
  private static final String SPEAKERS_ALL_URI = "http://localhost:5000/speakers";
  private static final String SPEAKER_3_URI = SPEAKERS_ALL_URI + "/3";

  @Test
  public void testApiAllSpeakersJson() {
    try {
      String json = null;
      HttpResponse <String> resp = Unirest.get(
        SpeakersApiJsonTest.SPEAKERS_ALL_URI).asString();

      assertEquals(HttpStatus.SC_OK, resp.getStatus());
      json = resp.getBody();
      System.out.println(json);
      assertThatJson(json).node("").isArray();
      assertThatJson(json).node("").isArray().ofLength(3);
      assertThatJson(json).node("[0]").isObject();
      assertThatJson(json).node("[0].fullName")
              .isStringEqualTo("Larson Richard");
      assertThatJson(json).node("[0].tags").isArray();
```

```
          assertThatJson(json).node("[0].tags").isArray().ofLength(3);
          assertThatJson(json).node("[0].tags[1]").isStringEqualTo("AngularJS");
          assertThatJson(json).node("[0].registered").isEqualTo(true);
          assertTrue(true);
        } catch (UnirestException ue) {
          ue.printStackTrace();
        }
      }

    @Test
    public void testApiSpeaker3Json() {
      try {
        String json = null;
        HttpResponse <String> resp = Unirest.get(
          SpeakersApiJsonTest.SPEAKER_3_URI).asString();

        assertEquals(HttpStatus.SC_OK, resp.getStatus());
        json = resp.getBody();
        System.out.println(json);
        assertThatJson(json).node("").isObject();
        assertThatJson(json).node("fullName")
              .isStringEqualTo("Christensen Fisher");
        assertThatJson(json).node("tags").isArray();
        assertThatJson(json).node("tags").isArray().ofLength(4);
        assertThatJson(json).node("tags[2]").isStringEqualTo("Maven");
        assertTrue(true);
      } catch (UnirestException ue) {
        ue.printStackTrace();
      }
    }

}
```

Note the following in this JUnit test:

- testApiAllSpeakersJson():

  — Gets a list of all speakers from the Speakers API by calling Unirest.get() with *http://localhost:5000/speakers*

  — Verifies that the HTTP Status Code is OK (200).

  — Gets the JSON document (which contains an array of speaker Objects) from the HTTP Response Body.

  — Makes a series of assertions on the JSON document with JSONUnit's assert ThatJson() to verify that

    — We have an array of three speaker objects.

    — Each field (for example, fullName, tags, and registered) in each speaker object matches the expected values.

— When you run `gradle test`, you should see the following as part of the output:

```
org.jsonatwork.ch4.SpeakersApiJsonTest > testApiAllSpeakersJson STANDARD_OUT
[
  {
    "id": 1,
    "fullName": "Larson Richard",
    "tags": [
      "JavaScript",
      "AngularJS",
      "Yeoman"
    ],
    "age": 39,
    "registered": true
  },
  {
    "id": 2,
    "fullName": "Ester Clements",
    "tags": [
      "REST",
      "Ruby on Rails",
      "APIs"
    ],
    "age": 29,
    "registered": true
  },
  {
    "id": 3,
    "fullName": "Christensen Fisher",
    "tags": [
      "Java",
      "Spring",
      "Maven",
      "REST"
    ],
    "age": 45,
    "registered": false
  }
]
BUILD SUCCESSFUL
```

- `testApiSpeaker3Json()`:

  — Gets speaker 3 from the Speakers API by calling `Unirest.get()` with *http://localhost:5000/speakers/3*

  — Verifies that the HTTP Response Code is `OK` (200)

  — Gets the JSON document (which contains a single `speaker` Object) from the HTTP Response Body.

— Makes a series of assertions on the JSON document with JSONUnit's `assert`
`ThatJson()` to verify that

   — We have a single `speaker` Object.

   — Each field in the `speaker` Object has the expected values.

— When you run `gradle test`, you should see the following as part of the
output:

```
org.jsonatwork.ch4.SpeakersApiJsonTest > testApiSpeaker3Json STANDARD_OUT
    {
        "id": 3,
        "fullName": "Christensen Fisher",
        "tags": [
            "Java",
            "Spring",
            "Maven",
            "REST"
        ],
        "age": 45,
        "registered": false
    }
```

This Unit Test only touches upon the basics of the Unirest Java library, which also
provides the following:

- Full HTTP verb coverage (GET, POST, PUT, DELETE, PATCH)
- The ability to do custom mappings from an HTTP Response Body to a Java
  Object
- Asynchronous (i.e., nonblocking) requests
- Timeouts
- File uploads
- And much more

Visit the Unirest website (*http://unirest.io/java.html*) for further information on the
Unirest Java library.

Before moving on, you can stop `json-server` by pressing Ctrl-C at the command
line.

We've shown how to deploy and interact with a Stub API, and now it's time to build a
small RESTful API.

Build a Small Web API with Spring Boot

We'll continue to use the Speaker data to create an API (*chapter-4/speakers-api* in the examples) with Spring Boot. The Spring Framework (*https://spring.io*) makes it easier to develop and deploy Java-based Web applications and RESTful APIs. Spring Boot (*https://projects.spring.io/spring-boot*) makes it easier to create Spring-based applications by providing defaults. With Spring Boot:

- There are no tedious, error-prone XML-based configuration files.
- Tomcat and/or Jetty can be embedded, so there is no need to deploy a WAR (Web application ARchive) separately. You still *could* use Spring Boot and Gradle to build and deploy a WAR file to Tomcat. But as you'll see, an executable JAR simplifies a developer's environment because it reduces the amount of setup and installations, which enables iterative application development.

We'll take the following steps to create and deploy the Speakers API with Spring Boot:

1. Write source code:
   - Model
   - Controller
   - Application

2. Create a build script (*build.gradle*).
3. Deploy an embedded JAR with `gradlew`.
4. Test with Postman.

Create the Model

The `Speaker` class in Example 4-4 is a Plain Old Java Object (POJO) that represents the Speaker data that the API will render as JSON.

Example 4-4. speakers-api/src/main/java/org/jsonatwork/ch4/Speaker.java

```
package org.jsonatwork.ch4;

import java.util.ArrayList;
import java.util.Arrays;
import java.util.List;

public class Speaker {
  private int id;
  private int age;
```

```java
private String fullName;
private List<String> tags = new ArrayList<String>();
private boolean registered;

public Speaker() {
  super();
}

public Speaker(int id, int age, String fullName, List<String> tags,
               boolean registered) {
  super();
  this.id = id;
  this.age = age;
  this.fullName = fullName;
  this.tags = tags;
  this.registered = registered;
}

public Speaker(int id, int age, String fullName, String[] tags,
               boolean registered) {
  this(id, age, fullName, Arrays.asList(tags), registered);
}

public int getId() {
  return id;
}

public void setId(int id) {
  this.id = id;
}

public int getAge() {
  return age;
}

public void setAge(int age) {
  this.age = age;
}

public String getFullName() {
  return fullName;
}

public void setFullName(String fullName) {
  this.fullName = fullName;
}

public List<String> getTags() {
  return tags;
}

public void setTags(List<String> tags) {
```

```
    this.tags = tags;
  }

  public boolean isRegistered() {
    return registered;
  }

  public void setRegistered(boolean registered) {
    this.registered = registered;
  }

  @Override
  public String toString() {
    return String.format(
      "Speaker [id=%s, age=%s, fullName=%s, tags=%s, registered=%s]",
      id, age, fullName, tags, registered);
  }

}
```

There's nothing exciting in this code. It just provides the data members, constructors, and accessor methods (getters and setters) for a speaker. This code doesn't know anything about JSON because (as you'll soon see) Spring automatically converts this object to JSON.

Create the Controller

In a Spring application, the Controller handles the HTTP Requests and returns HTTP Responses. In our case, the speaker JSON data is returned in the response body. Example 4-5 shows the SpeakerController.

Example 4-5. speakers-api/src/main/java/org/jsonatwork/ch4/SpeakerController.java

```
package org.jsonatwork.ch4;

import java.util.*;
import org.springframework.web.bind.annotation.*;
import org.springframework.http.*;

@RestController
public class SpeakerController {

  private static Speaker speakers[] = {
    new Speaker(1, 39, "Larson Richard",
              new String[] {"JavaScript", "AngularJS", "Yeoman"}, true),
    new Speaker(2, 29, "Ester Clements",
              new String[] {"REST", "Ruby on Rails", "APIs"}, true),
    new Speaker(3, 45, "Christensen Fisher",
              new String[] {"Java", "Spring", "Maven", "REST"}, false)
  };
```

```
@RequestMapping(value = "/speakers", method = RequestMethod.GET)
public List<Speaker> getAllSpeakers() {
  return Arrays.asList(speakers);
}

@RequestMapping(value = "/speakers/{id}", method = RequestMethod.GET)
public ResponseEntity<?>  getSpeakerById(@PathVariable long id) {
  int tempId = ((new Long(id)).intValue() - 1);

  if (tempId >= 0 && tempId < speakers.length) {
    return new ResponseEntity<Speaker>(speakers[tempId], HttpStatus.OK);
  } else {
    return new ResponseEntity(HttpStatus.NOT_FOUND);
  }
}
}
```

Note the following in this code:

- The `@RestController` annotation identifies the `SpeakerController` class as a Spring MVC Controller that processes HTTP Requests.

- The `speakers` array is hardcoded, but it's for test purposes only. In a real application, a separate Data Layer would populate the `speakers` from a database or an external API call.

- The `getAllSpeakers()` method does the following:
  - Responds to HTTP `GET` requests on the */speakers* URI.
  - Retrieves the entire `speakers` Array as an `ArrayList` and returns it as a JSON Array in an HTTP Response Body.
  - The `@RequestMapping` annotation binds the */speakers* URI to the `getAllSpeak ers()` method for an HTTP `GET` Request.

- The `getSpeakerById()` method does the following:
  - Responds to HTTP `GET` requests on the */speakers/{id}* URI (where `id` represents a speaker ID).
  - Retrieves a `speaker` (based on the speaker ID) and returns it as a JSON Object in an HTTP Response Body.
  - The `@PathVariable` annotation binds the speaker ID from the HTTP Request path to the `id` parameter for lookup.
  - The `ResponseEntity` return value type enables you to set the HTTP Status Code and/or the `speakers` in the HTTP Response.

In both of the preceding methods, the `Speaker` Object is automatically converted to JSON without any extra work. By default, Spring is configured to use Jackson behind the scenes to do the Java-to-JSON conversion.

Register the Application

As mentioned earlier, we could package the Speakers API as a WAR file and deploy it on an application server such as Tomcat. But it's easier to run our API as a standalone application from the command line. To do this we need to do the following:

- Add a Java `main()` method
- Package the application as an executable JAR

The `Application` class in Example 4-6 provides the `main()` method that we need.

Example 4-6. speakers-api/src/main/java/org/jsonatwork/ch4/Application.java

```
package org.jsonatwork.ch4;

import org.springframework.boot.SpringApplication;
import org.springframework.boot.autoconfigure.SpringBootApplication;

@SpringBootApplication
public class Application {

  public static void main(String[] args) {
    SpringApplication.run(Application.class, args);
  }
}
```

In this example, the `@SpringBootApplication` annotation registers our application with Spring and wires up the `SpeakerController` and `Speaker`.

That's all the code that we need. Now, let's look at the *build.gradle* script to build the application.

Write the Build Script

Gradle uses a script called *build.gradle* to build an application. Example 4-7 shows the build script for the *speakers-api* project.

Example 4-7. speakers-api/build.gradle

```
buildscript {
  repositories {
    mavenCentral()
  }
```

```
dependencies {
    classpath("org.springframework.boot:spring-boot-gradle-plugin:1.5.2.RELEASE")
  }
}

apply plugin: 'java'
apply plugin: 'org.springframework.boot'

ext {
  jdkVersion = "1.8"
}

sourceCompatibility = jdkVersion
targetCompatibility = jdkVersion

tasks.withType(JavaCompile) {
  options.encoding = 'UTF-8'
}

jar {
  baseName = 'speakers-api'
  version =  '0.0.1'
}

repositories {
  mavenCentral()
}

test {
  testLogging {
    showStandardStreams = true // Show standard output & standard error.
  }
  ignoreFailures = false
}

dependencies {
  compile (
    [group: 'org.springframework.boot', name: 'spring-boot-starter-web']
  )
}
```

Note the following in this *build.gradle* script:

- The Spring Boot Gradle plug-in does the following:
  — Packages all build artifacts into a single, executable JAR
  — Searches for a class in *src/main/java* that has a main() method (in this case, Application.java) to deploy our API within the executable JAR
- The jar block defines the name of the application's JAR file

- `repositories` tells Gradle to pull application dependencies from the Maven Central Repository (*https://search.maven.org*).

- `testLogging` tells Gradle to show Standard Output and Standard Error when running tests.

- `dependencies` defines the JARs that the *speakers-api* depends on.

This is a simple build, but Gradle has far more powerful build functionality. Visit the "Wiring Gradle Build Scripts" section of the Gradle User Guide (*http://bit.ly/2tiWYKa*) to learn more.

We've covered the build script, and now it's time to deploy the Speakers API.

Deploy the API

The *gradlew* script was generated by the `gradle init` command that was used to create the *speakers-api* project. To learn more about how to create a Gradle project, see "Creating New Gradle Builds" from the Gradle User Guide (*https://guides.gradle.org/creating-new-gradle-builds*).

gradlew pulls everything together and simplifies deployment by taking the following steps:

- Invokes the *build.gradle* script to build the application and uses the Spring Boot plug-in to build the executable JAR

- Deploys the Speakers API (as an executable JAR) to *http://localhost:8080/speakers* on an embedded (bundled) Tomcat server

In the *speakers-api* directory, run `./gradlew bootRun` to deploy the application, and you'll see the following (at the end of all the log messages):

```
2017-03-31 16:06:08.975  INFO 23433 --- [      main] org.apache.catalina.core.StandardEngine  : Starting Servlet Engine: Apache Tomcat
/8.5.11
2017-03-31 16:06:09.084  INFO 23433 --- [ost-startStop-1] o.a.c.c.C.[Tomcat].[localhost].[/]      : Initializing Spring embedded WebAppli
ationContext
2017-03-31 16:06:09.084  INFO 23433 --- [ost-startStop-1] o.s.web.context.ContextLoader          : Root WebApplicationContext: initialize
tion completed in 1288 ms
2017-03-31 16:06:09.215  INFO 23433 --- [ost-startStop-1] o.s.b.w.servlet.ServletRegistrationBean  : Mapping servlet: 'dispatcherServlet'
o [/]
2017-03-31 16:06:09.220  INFO 23433 --- [ost-startStop-1] o.s.b.w.servlet.FilterRegistrationBean   : Mapping filter: 'characterEncodingFil
er' to: [/*]
2017-03-31 16:06:09.221  INFO 23433 --- [ost-startStop-1] o.s.b.w.servlet.FilterRegistrationBean   : Mapping filter: 'hiddenHttpMethodFilt
r' to: [/*]
2017-03-31 16:06:09.221  INFO 23433 --- [ost-startStop-1] o.s.b.w.servlet.FilterRegistrationBean   : Mapping filter: 'httpPutFormContentFi
ter' to: [/*]
2017-03-31 16:06:09.221  INFO 23433 --- [ost-startStop-1] o.s.b.w.servlet.FilterRegistrationBean   : Mapping filter: 'requestContextFilter
 to: [/*]
2017-03-31 16:06:09.517  INFO 23433 --- [      main] s.w.s.m.m.a.RequestMappingHandlerAdapter : Looking for @ControllerAdvice: org.sp
ingframework.boot.context.embedded.AnnotationConfigEmbeddedWebApplicationContext@3d0f8e03: startup date [Fri Mar 31 16:06:07 MDT 2017]; ro
t of context hierarchy
2017-03-31 16:06:09.599  INFO 23433 --- [      main] s.w.s.m.m.a.RequestMappingHandlerMapping : Mapped "{[/speakers],methods=[GET]}"
nto public java.util.List<org.jsonatwork.ch4.Speaker> org.jsonatwork.ch4.SpeakerController.getAllSpeakers()
2017-03-31 16:06:09.600  INFO 23433 --- [      main] s.w.s.m.m.a.RequestMappingHandlerMapping : Mapped "{[/speakers/{id}],methods=[GE
]}" onto public org.springframework.http.ResponseEntity<?> org.jsonatwork.ch4.SpeakerController.getSpeakerById(long)
2017-03-31 16:06:09.604  INFO 23433 --- [      main] s.w.s.m.m.a.RequestMappingHandlerMapping : Mapped "{[/error]}" onto public org.s
ringframework.http.ResponseEntity<java.util.Map<java.lang.String, java.lang.Object>> org.springframework.boot.autoconfigure.web.BasicError
ontroller.error(javax.servlet.http.HttpServletRequest)
2017-03-31 16:06:09.605  INFO 23433 --- [      main] s.w.s.m.m.a.RequestMappingHandlerMapping : Mapped "{[/error],produces=[text/html
}" onto public org.springframework.web.servlet.ModelAndView org.springframework.boot.autoconfigure.web.BasicErrorController.errorHtml(java
.servlet.http.HttpServletRequest,javax.servlet.http.HttpServletResponse)
2017-03-31 16:06:09.643  INFO 23433 --- [      main] o.s.w.s.handler.SimpleUrlHandlerMapping   : Mapped URL path [/webjars/**] onto ha
dler of type [class org.springframework.web.servlet.resource.ResourceHttpRequestHandler]
2017-03-31 16:06:09.644  INFO 23433 --- [      main] o.s.w.s.handler.SimpleUrlHandlerMapping   : Mapped URL path [/**] onto handler of
type [class org.springframework.web.servlet.resource.ResourceHttpRequestHandler]
2017-03-31 16:06:09.690  INFO 23433 --- [      main] o.s.w.s.handler.SimpleUrlHandlerMapping   : Mapped URL path [/**/favicon.ico] ont
handler of type [class org.springframework.web.servlet.resource.ResourceHttpRequestHandler]
2017-03-31 16:06:09.863  INFO 23433 --- [      main] o.s.j.e.a.AnnotationMBeanExporter         : Registering beans for JMX exposure on
startup
2017-03-31 16:06:09.934  INFO 23433 --- [      main] s.b.c.e.t.TomcatEmbeddedServletContainer : Tomcat started on port(s): 8080 (http)
2017-03-31 16:06:09.940  INFO 23433 --- [      main] org.jsonatwork.ch4.Application           : Started Application in 2.536 seconds
JVM running for 2.922)
> Building 80% > :bootRun
```

Test the API with Postman

Now that the Speakers API is up and running, let's test with Postman (as we did in Chapter 1) to get the first speaker. In the Postman GUI, do the following:

1. Enter the *http://localhost:8080/speakers/1* URL.

2. Choose GET as the HTTP verb.

3. Click the Send button.

You should see that the GET ran properly in Postman with the speaker JSON data in the HTTP Response Body text area and a 200 (OK) HTTP Status, as shown in Figure 4-1.

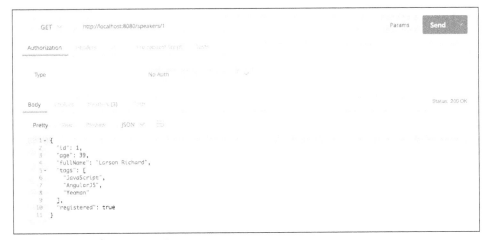

Figure 4-1. Speakers API on Postman

You can stop *gradlew* by pressing Ctrl-C at the command line.

As promised, development and deployment is simpler because we didn't do any of the following:

- Create or modify XML-based configuration metadata for Spring or Java EE (i.e., *web.xml*)
- Deploy a WAR file
- Install Tomcat

Note that we took these deployment steps to show how to set up a simple development environment for a Web API. You still need to deploy a WAR file to an application server when you move into shared (e.g., Staging, User Acceptance Testing, Production) environments so that you have the ability to tune and load-test the application.

What We Covered

We started with simple conversion between Java and JSON constructs, and then demonstrated how to call a (Stub) JSON-based Web API and test its contents with JUnit. We then finished by creating a RESTful API with Spring Boot and tested it with Postman.

What's Next?

With the basics of JSON usage on several core platforms (JavaScript, Ruby on Rails, and Java) behind us, we'll move deeper into the JSON ecosystem in the next three chapters:

- JSON Schema
- JSON Search
- JSON Transform

In Chapter 5, we'll show how to structure and validate JSON documents with JSON Schema.

PART II

The JSON Ecosystem

CHAPTER 5

JSON Schema

We've covered the basics of JSON using our core platforms (JavaScript, Ruby on Rails, and Java), and now it's time to wade in deeper. In this chapter, we'll show how to leverage JSON Schema to define the structure and format of JSON documents exchanged between applications:

- JSON Schema overview
- Core JSON Schema—basics and tooling
- How to design and test an API with JSON Schema

In our examples, we'll design an API with JSON Schema after we progressively walk through the concepts of JSON Schema. As noted in the preface, from now on we will write all our examples in Node.js to keep the size of the chapters to a minimum. But know that the other platforms work well with JSON Schema. If you haven't installed Node.js already, now would be a great time. Follow the instructions in Appendix A.

JSON Schema Overview

Many architects and developers are unfamiliar with JSON Schemas. Before going into details, it's important to know what a JSON Schema is, how it helps, and why/when to use it. Along the way, we'll look at the JSON Schema Specification and show a simple example.

What Is JSON Schema?

A JSON Schema specifies a JSON document (or message)'s content, structure, and format. A JSON Schema validates a JSON document, so you may be wondering why plain JSON validation isn't enough. Unfortunately, *validation* is an overloaded term.

Syntactic Versus Semantic Validation

The difference is in the *type* of validation. When you validate a JSON document without a Schema, you're validating only the syntax of the document. This type of validation guarantees only that the document is well-formed (i.e., matching braces, double quotes for keys, and so forth). This type of validation is known as *syntactic validation*, and we've done this before with tools such as JSONLint, and the JSON parsers for each platform.

How does a JSON Schema help?

Syntactic validation is a good start, but at times you need to validate at a deeper level by using semantic validation. What if you have the following situations:

- You (as an API Consumer) need to ensure that a JSON response from an API contains a valid `Speaker`, or a list of `Orders`?

- You (as an API Producer) need to check incoming JSON to make sure that the Consumer can send you only the fields you're expecting?

- You need to check the format of a phone number, a date/time, a postal code, an email address, or a credit card number?

This is where JSON Schema shines, and this type of validation is known as *semantic validation*. In this case, you're validating the *meaning* of the data, not just the syntax. JSON Schema is also great for API Design because it helps define the interface, and we'll cover that later in this chapter.

A Simple Example

Before talking too much more about JSON Schema, let's look at Example 5-1 to get a feel for the syntax.

Example 5-1. ex-1-basic-schema.json

```
{
  "$schema": "http://json-schema.org/draft-04/schema#",
  "type": "object",
  "properties": {
    "email": {
      "type": "string"
    },
    "firstName": {
      "type": "string"
    },
    "lastName": {
      "type": "string"
    }
```

```
    }
}
```

This Schema specifies that a document can have three fields (email, firstName, and lastName), where each one is a string. We'll gloss over Schema syntax for now, but don't worry—we'll cover it soon. Example 5-2 shows a sample JSON instance document that corresponds to the preceding Schema.

Example 5-2. ex-1-basic.json

```
{
  "email": "larsonrichard@ecratic.com",
  "firstName": "Larson",
  "lastName": "Richard"
}
```

JSON Schema on the Web

The *json-schema.org* site, shown in Figure 5-1, is the starting place to go for all things related to JSON Schema, including copious documentation and examples.

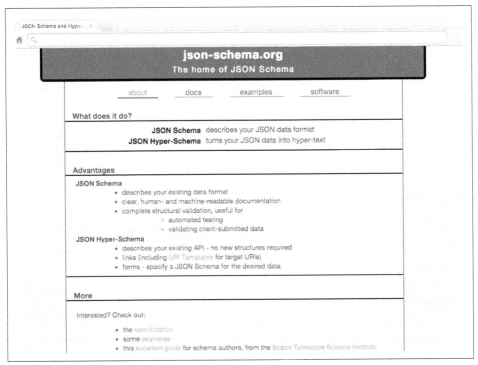

Figure 5-1. json-schema.org site

From here, you can find example Schemas, great validation libraries for most major platforms, along with the JSON Schema Standard GitHub repository (*https://github.com/json-schema-org/json-schema-spec*) (where the standard is maintained). The GitHub repository is shown in Figure 5-2.

Figure 5-2. json-schema GitHub repository

Here you can track updates, issues, and progress with the JSON Schema standard (more on that later in "The Current State of the JSON Schema Standard" on page 119).

Why JSON Schema?

JSON Schema provides the ability to validate the content and semantics of a document, and here are some real-world use cases:

Security

The Open Web Application Project (OWASP) Web Service Security Cheat Sheet (*http://bit.ly/2rXAfpa*) recommends that Web Services should validate their payloads by using a Schema. Granted, they still talk about XML Schema, but their concern is still applicable to JSON. OWASP calls for validation of field lengths (min/max) and fixed format fields (e.g., phone number or postal code) to help secure a service.

Message Design

JSON isn't just for APIs anymore. Many enterprises use JSON as the preferred format to send payloads over messaging systems such as Apache Kafka (we'll cover this in more detail in Chapter 10). The message Producer and Consumer are completely decoupled in this style of architecture, and JSON Schema can help ensure that the reader receives messages in a format that it's expecting.

API Design

JSON is a first-class citizen in API Design. JSON Schema helps define an API's contract by specifying the format, content, and structure of a document.

Prototyping

With the structure and rigor of JSON Schema, this may seem counterintuitive. We'll show a streamlined prototyping workflow with JSON Schema and related tooling when we design an API later in this chapter.

My Journey with JSON Schema

As mentioned in the Preface, as of 2009 I wasn't sure that JSON was ready for the enterprise. I loved its speed and simplicity, but I didn't see a way to guarantee the structure and content of JSON documents between applications. But when I learned about JSON Schema in 2010, I changed my position and came to accept JSON as a viable enterprise-class data format.

The Current State of the JSON Schema Standard

The JSON Schema Specification is at implementation draft 4 (v0.4), and the next implementation draft 6 (v0.6) is on the way. Draft 5 (v0.5) was published late last year as a working draft to capture work in progress and was not an implementation draft. But don't let the 0.*x* version number concern you. As you'll see in our examples, JSON Schema is robust, provides solid validation capabilities today, and there is a wide variety of working JSON Schema libraries for every major programming platform. You can find more details in the JSON Schema draft 4 spec (*https:// tools.ietf.org/html/draft-zyp-json-schema-04*).

JSON Schema and XML Schema

JSON Schema fills the same role with JSON as XML Schema did with XML documents, but with the following differences:

- A JSON document does not reference a JSON Schema. It's up to an application to validate a JSON document against a Schema.
- JSON Schemas have no namespace.

• JSON Schema files have a *.json* extension.

Core JSON Schema—Basics and Tooling

Now that you have an overview of JSON Schema, it's time to go deeper. JSON Schema is powerful, but it can be tedious, and we'll show some tools to make it easier. We'll then cover basic data types and core keywords that provide a foundation for working with JSON Schema on real-world projects.

JSON Schema Workflow and Tooling

JSON Schema syntax can be a bit daunting, but developers don't have to code everything by hand. Several excellent tools can make life much easier.

JSON Editor Online

We've already covered JSON Editor Online in Chapter 1, but it's worth another brief mention. Start modeling a JSON document with this tool to get a feel for the data. Use this tool to generate the JSON document and avoid all the typing. When you're finished, save the JSON document to the clipboard.

JSONSchema.net

Once you have your core concept, the JSONSchema.net application generates a JSON Schema based on the JSON document that was created earlier with JSON Editor Online (see Figure 5-3). The JSONSchema.net application alone will save you 80 percent of the typing required to create a Schema. I always start my Schema work with this application and then make incremental upgrades.

Here are the steps to generate the initial Schema with JSONSchema.net:

1. Paste in a JSON document on the left side.
2. Start with the default settings, and make the following changes:

   • Turn off "Use absolute IDs."
   • Turn off "Allow additional properties."
   • Turn off "Allow additional items."

3. Click the Generate Schema button.
4. Copy the generated Schema to your clipboard.

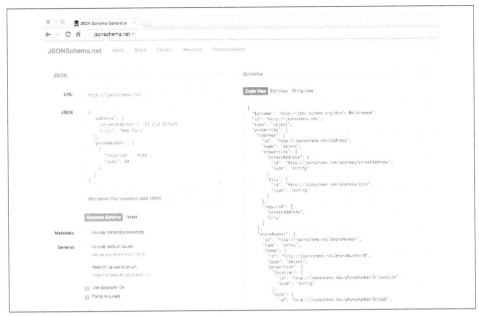

Figure 5-3. Speakers Schema on JSONSchema.net

JSON Validate

After you've created a JSON Schema, the JSON Validate (*http://jsonvalidate.com*) application validates a JSON document against that Schema, as shown in Figure 5-4.

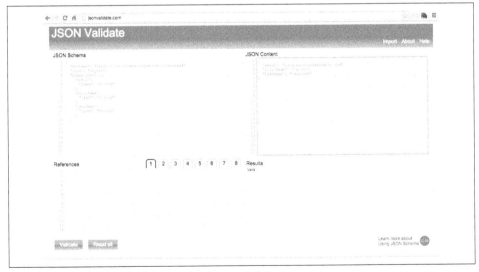

Figure 5-4. Valid Speakers Schema on jsonvalidate.com

To validate the JSON document against the Schema, do the following:

1. Paste the JSON document and Schema into the JSON Validate application.
2. Remove all id fields from the Schema because they're not needed.
3. Click the Validate button to validate the document.

NPM modules on the CLI: validate and jsonlint

But sometimes you don't have good internet connectivity, so it's great to have tools that run locally. Plus, if you have sensitive data, it's safer to run examples on your machine from the command-line interface (CLI). The `validate` module is the Node.js equivalent of the *jsonvalidate.com* site. To install and run it, follow the instructions in Appendix A (see "Install npm Modules" on page 325).

Both *jsonvalidate.com* and `validate` are part of the Using JSON Schema site (a great Schema resource), which can be found on GitHub (*http://usingjsonschema.github.io/*). You've already seen the JSONLint site in Chapter 1, but you can also use JSONLint from the command line by using the `jsonlint` Node.js module. To install and run it, follow the instructions in Appendix A (see "Install npm Modules" on page 325).

I've used `jsonlint` only for syntactic validation, but if you run `jsonlint --help` from the command line, you'll notice that it can also do semantic validation with a Schema. For more information, see the `jsonlint` documentation on GitHub (*https://github.com/zaach/jsonlint*).

We'll leverage `validate` from the command line to work through the examples.

Core Keywords

Here are the core keywords in any JSON Schema:

`$schema`
> Specifies the JSON Schema (spec) version. For example, "`$schema`": "`http://json-schema.org/draft-04/schema#`" specifies that the schema conforms to version 0.4, while `http://json-schema.org/schema#` tells a JSON Validator to use the current/latest version of the specification (which is 0.4 as of this writing). Using the latter of these two options is risky because some JSON Validators default to a previous version, so an earlier version (and not the current/latest) version will be used. To play it safe, *always* specify the version so that you (and the JSON Validator) are sure about the version you're using.

`type`
> Specifies the data type for a field. For example: "`type`": "`string`".

`properties`
   Specifies the fields for an object. It contains `type` information.

Basic Types

The document in Example 5-3 contains the basic JSON types (for example, `string`, `number`, `boolean`) that you've seen before.

Example 5-3. ex-2-basic-types.json

```
{
  "email": "larsonrichard@ecratic.com",
  "firstName": "Larson",
  "lastName": "Richard",
  "age": 39,
  "postedSlides": true,
  "rating": 4.1
}
```

JSON Schema uses the same basic data types as the Core JSON data types from Chapter 1 (`string`, `number`, `array`, `object`, `boolean`, `null`), but adds an `integer` type that specifies whole numbers. The `number` type still allows both whole and floating-point numbers.

The JSON Schema in Example 5-4 describes the structure of the preceding document.

Example 5-4. ex-2-basic-types-schema.json

```
{
  "$schema": "http://json-schema.org/draft-04/schema#",
  "type": "object",
  "properties": {
    "email": {
      "type": "string"
    },
    "firstName": {
      "type": "string"
    },
    "lastName": {
      "type": "string"
    },
    "age": {
      "type": "integer"
    },
    "postedSlides": {
      "type": "boolean"
    },
    "rating": {
      "type": "number"
```

```
        }
      }
    }
```

In this example, note the following:

- The $schema field indicates that JSON Schema v0.4 rules will be used for validating the document.

- The first type field mentioned indicates that there is an Object at the root level of the JSON document that contains all the fields in the document.

- email, firstName, lastName are of type string

- age is an integer. Although JSON itself has only a number type, JSON Schema provides the finer-grained integer type. postedSlides is a boolean. rating is a number, which allows for floating-point values.

Run the preceding example using validate, and you'll see that the document is valid for this Schema.

```
json-at-work => validate ex-2-basic-types.json ex-2-basic-types-schema.json
JSON content in file ex-2-basic-types.json is valid
json-at-work => 
```

Although the preceding Schema is a decent start, it doesn't go far enough. Let's try the following changes to the JSON document that we want to validate:

- Add an extra field (e.g., company).

- Remove one of the expected fields (e.g., postedSlides).

Example 5-5 shows our modified JSON document.

Example 5-5. ex-2-basic-types-invalid.json

```
{
  "email": "larsonrichard@ecratic.com",
  "firstName": "Larson",
  "lastName": "Richard",
  "age": 39,
  "rating": 4.1,
  "company": "None"
}
```

Right now there's nothing to prevent you from invalidating the document, as you'll see in the following run:

```
json-at-work => validate ex-2-basic-types-invalid.json ex-2-basic-types-schema.json
JSON content in file ex-2-basic-types-invalid.json is valid
json-at-work =>
```

Basic types validation

At this point, you might be thinking that JSON Schema isn't useful because it's not validating as expected. But we can make the validation process function as expected by adding simple constraints. First, to prevent extra fields, use the code in Example 5-6.

Example 5-6. ex-3-basic-types-no-addl-props-schema.json

```
{
  "$schema": "http://json-schema.org/draft-04/schema#",
  "type": "object",
  "properties": {
    "email": {
      "type": "string"
    },
    "firstName": {
      "type": "string"
    },
    "lastName": {
      "type": "string"
    },
    "postedSlides": {
      "type": "boolean"
    },
    "rating": {
      "type": "number"
    }
  },
  "additionalProperties": false
}
```

In this example, setting `additionalProperties` to `false` disallows any extra fields in the document root `Object`. Copy the previous JSON document (*ex-2-basic-types-invalid.json*) to a new version (*ex-3-basic-types-no-addl-props-invalid.json*) and try validating against the preceding Schema. You should now see the following:

```
json-at-work => validate ex-3-basic-types-no-addl-props-invalid.json ex-3-basic-types-no-addl-props-schema.json
Invalid: Additional properties not allowed
JSON Schema element: /additionalProperties
JSON Content path: /age
```

This is getting better, but it still isn't what we want because there's no guarantee that all the expected fields will be in the document. To reach a core level of semantic validation, we need to ensure that all required fields are present, as shown in Example 5-7.

Example 5-7. ex-4-basic-types-validation-req-schema.json

```
{
  "$schema": "http://json-schema.org/draft-04/schema#",
  "type": "object",
  "properties": {
    "email": {
      "type": "string"
    },
    "firstName": {
      "type": "string"
    },
    "lastName": {
      "type": "string"
    },
    "postedSlides": {
      "type": "boolean"
    },
    "rating": {
      "type": "number"
    }
  },
  "additionalProperties": false,
  "required": ["email", "firstName", "lastName", "postedSlides", "rating"]
}
```

In this example, the required Array specifies the fields that are required, so these fields *must* be present for a document to be considered valid. Note that a field is considered optional if not mentioned in the required Array.

Example 5-8 shows the modified JSON document (without the required rating field, plus an unexpected age field) to validate.

Example 5-8. ex-4-basic-types-validation-req-invalid.json

```
{
  "email": "larsonrichard@ecratic.com",
  "firstName": "Larson",
  "lastName": "Richard",
  "postedSlides": true,
  "age": 39
}
```

When running this example from the command line, the document is now considered invalid:

```
json-at-work => validate ex-4-basic-types-validation-req-invalid.json ex-4-basic-types-validation-req-schema.json
Invalid: Missing required property: rating
JSON Schema element: /required/4
JSON Content path:
```

We finally have what we want:

- No extra fields are allowed.
- All fields are required.

Now that we have basic semantic validation in place, let's move on to validating number fields in JSON documents.

Numbers

As you'll recall, a JSON Schema number type can be a floating-point or whole number. The Schema in Example 5-9 validates the average rating for a speaker's conference presentation, where the range varies from 1.0 (poor) to 5.0 (excellent).

Example 5-9. ex-5-number-min-max-schema.json

```
{
  "$schema": "http://json-schema.org/draft-04/schema#",
  "type": "object",
  "properties": {
    "rating": {
      "type": "number",
      "minimum": 1.0,
      "maximum": 5.0
    }
  },
  "additionalProperties": false,
  "required": ["rating"]
}
```

Example 5-10 is a valid JSON document because the rating is within the 1.0–5.0 range.

Example 5-10. ex-5-number-min-max.json

```
{
  "rating": 4.99
}
```

Example 5-11 is an invalid document, where the rating is greater than 5.0.

Example 5-11. ex-5-number-min-max-invalid.json

```
{
  "rating": 6.2
}
```

Run this from the command line, and you'll see that the preceding document is invalid:

```
json-at-work => validate ex-5-number-min-max-invalid.json ex-5-number-min-max-schema.json
Invalid: Value 6.2 is greater than maximum 5
JSON Schema element: /properties/rating/maximum
JSON Content path: /rating
```

Arrays

JSON Schema provides the ability to validate Arrays. Arrays can hold any of the JSON Schema basic types (`string`, `number`, `array`, `object`, `boolean`, `null`). The Schema in Example 5-12 validates the `tags` field, which is an Array of type `string`.

Example 5-12. ex-6-array-simple-schema.json

```
{
  "$schema": "http://json-schema.org/draft-04/schema#",
  "type": "object",
  "properties": {
    "tags": {
      "type": "array",
        "items": {
        "type": "string"
      }
    }
  },
  "additionalProperties": false,
  "required": ["tags"]
}
```

Example 5-13 is a valid JSON document for the preceding Schema.

Example 5-13. ex-6-array-simple.json

```
{
  "tags": ["fred"]
}
```

The document in Example 5-14 is not valid because we've added an integer to the `tags` Array.

Example 5-14. ex-6-array-simple-invalid.json

```
{
  "tags": ["fred", 1]
}
```

Run the preceding example to verify that the document is invalid:

```
json-at-work => validate ex-6-array-simple-invalid.json ex-6-array-simple-schema.json
Invalid: invalid type: number (expected string)
JSON Schema element: /properties/tags/items/type
JSON Content path: /tags/1
```

JSON Schema provides the ability to specify the minimum (`minItems`) and maximum (`maxItems`) number of items in an Array. The Schema in Example 5-15 allows for two to four items in the `tags` Array.

Example 5-15. ex-7-array-min-max-schema.json

```
{
  "$schema": "http://json-schema.org/draft-04/schema#",
  "type": "object",
  "properties": {
    "tags": {
      "type": "array",
      "minItems": 2,
      "maxItems": 4,
      "items": {
        "type": "string"
      }
    }
  },
  "additionalProperties": false,
  "required": ["tags"]
}
```

The JSON document conforms in Example 5-16 to the preceding Schema.

Example 5-16. ex-7-array-min-max.json

```
{
  "tags": ["fred", "a"]
}
```

The document in Example 5-17 is invalid because the `tags` Array has five items.

Example 5-17. ex-7-array-min-max-invalid.json

```
{
  "tags": ["fred", "a", "x", "betty", "alpha"]
}
```

Run the preceding example to verify:

```
json-at-work => validate ex-7-array-min-max-invalid.json ex-7-array-min-max-schema.json
Invalid: Array is too long (5), maximum 4
JSON Schema element: /properties/tags/maxItems
JSON Content path: /tags
```

Enumerated Values

The enum keyword constrains a field's value to a fixed set of unique values, specified in an Array. The Schema in Example 5-18 limits the set of allowable values in the tags Array to one of "Open Source", "Java", "JavaScript", "JSON", or "REST".

Example 5-18. ex-8-array-enum-schema.json

```
{
  "$schema": "http://json-schema.org/draft-04/schema#",
  "type": "object",
  "properties": {
    "tags": {
      "type": "array",
      "minItems": 2,
      "maxItems": 4,
      "items": {
        "enum": [
          "Open Source", "Java", "JavaScript", "JSON", "REST"
        ]
      }
    }
  },
  "additionalProperties": false,
  "required": ["tags"]
}
```

The document in Example 5-19 is valid based on the preceding Schema.

Example 5-19. ex-8-array-enum.json

```
{
  "tags": ["Java", "REST"]
}
```

This document in Example 5-20 is not valid because the value "JS" is not one of the values in the Schema's enum.

Example 5-20. ex-8-array-enum-invalid.json

```
{
  "tags": ["Java", "REST", "JS"]
}
```

Run this example to show that the document is invalid:

```
json-at-work => validate ex-8-array-enum-invalid.json ex-8-array-enum-schema.json
Invalid: No enum match for: "JS"
JSON Schema element: /properties/tags/items/type
JSON Content path: /tags/2
```

Objects

JSON Schema enables you to specify an object. This is the heart of semantic validation because it enables you to validate Objects exchanged between applications. With this capability, both an API's Consumer and Producer can agree on the structure and content of important business concepts such as a person or order. The Schema in Example 5-21 specifies the content of a speaker Object.

Example 5-21. ex-9-named-object-schema.json

```
{
  "$schema": "http://json-schema.org/draft-04/schema#",
  "type": "object",
  "properties": {
    "speaker": {
      "type": "object",
      "properties": {
        "firstName": {
          "type": "string"
        },
        "lastName": {
          "type": "string"
        },
        "email": {
          "type": "string"
        },
        "postedSlides": {
          "type": "boolean"
        },
        "rating": {
          "type": "number"
        },
        "tags": {
```

```
      "type": "array",
      "items": {
        "type": "string"
      }
    }
  }
},
"additionalProperties": false,
"required": ["firstName", "lastName", "email",
  "postedSlides", "rating", "tags"
]
}
},
"additionalProperties": false,
"required": ["speaker"]
}
```

This Schema is similar to previous examples, with the addition of a top-level `speaker` object nested inside the root `object`.

The JSON document in Example 5-22 is valid against the preceding Schema.

Example 5-22. ex-9-named-object.json

```
{
  "speaker": {
    "firstName": "Larson",
    "lastName": "Richard",
    "email": "larsonrichard@ecratic.com",
    "postedSlides": true,
    "rating": 4.1,
    "tags": [
      "JavaScript", "AngularJS", "Yeoman"
    ]
  }
}
```

The document in Example 5-23 is invalid because the `speaker` Object is missing the required `rating` field.

Example 5-23. ex-9-named-object-invalid.json

```
{
  "speaker": {
    "firstName": "Larson",
    "lastName": "Richard",
    "email": "larsonrichard@ecratic.com",
    "postedSlides": true,
    "tags": [
      "JavaScript", "AngularJS", "Yeoman"
    ]
```

```
    }
}
```

Run the example on the command line to ensure that the preceding document is invalid:

```
json-at-work => validate ex-9-named-object-invalid.json ex-9-named-object-schema.json
Invalid: Missing required property: rating
JSON Schema element: /properties/speaker/required/4
JSON Content path: /speaker
```

We've now covered the most important basic types, and we'll move on to more-complex schemas.

Pattern Properties

JSON Schema provides the ability to specify repeating fields (with similar names) through pattern properties (with the `patternProperties` keyword) based on Regular Expressions. Example 5-24 defines the fields in an address.

Example 5-24. ex-10-pattern-properties-schema.json

```
{
  "$schema": "http://json-schema.org/draft-04/schema#",
  "type": "object",
  "properties": {
    "city": {
      "type": "string"
    },
    "state": {
      "type": "string"
    },
    "zip": {
      "type": "string"
    },
    "country": {
      "type": "string"
    }
  },
  "patternProperties": {
    "^line[1-3]$": {
      "type": "string"
    }
  },
  "additionalProperties": false,
  "required": ["city", "state", "zip", "country", "line1"]
}
```

In this example, the ^line[1-3]$ Regular Expression allows for the following address fields in a corresponding JSON document: line1, line2, and line3. Here's how to interpret this Regular Expression:

- ^ represents the beginning of the string.
- line translates to the literal string "line".
- [1-3] allows for a single integer between 1 and 3.
- $ indicates the end of the string.

Note that only line1 is required, and the others are optional.

The document in Example 5-25 will validate against the preceding Schema.

Example 5-25. ex-10-pattern-properties.json

```
{
  "line1": "555 Main Street",
  "line2": "#2",
  "city": "Denver",
  "state": "CO",
  "zip": "80231",
  "country": "USA"
}
```

Example 5-26 is invalid because it has a line4 field, which is out of range.

Example 5-26. ex-10-pattern-properties-invalid.json

```
{
  "line1": "555 Main Street",
  "line4": "#2",
  "city": "Denver",
  "state": "CO",
  "zip": "80231",
  "country": "USA"
}
```

Run this example to see that the preceding document is invalid:

```
json-at-work => validate ex-10-property-patterns-invalid.json ex-10-property-patterns-schema.json
Invalid: Additional properties not allowed
JSON Schema element: /additionalProperties
JSON Content path: /line4
```

Regular Expressions

JSON Schema also uses Regular Expressions to constrain field values. The Schema in Example 5-27 limits the value of the email field to a standard email address format as specified in IETF RFC 2822 (*http://www.faqs.org/rfcs/rfc2822.html*).

Example 5-27. ex-11-regex-schema.json

```
{
  "$schema": "http://json-schema.org/draft-04/schema#",
  "type": "object",
  "properties": {
    "email": {
      "type": "string",
      "pattern": "^[\\w|-|.]+@[\\w]+\\.[A-Za-z]{2,4}$"
    },
    "firstName": {
      "type": "string"
    },
    "lastName": {
      "type": "string"
    }
  },
  "additionalProperties": false,
  "required": ["email", "firstName", "lastName"]
}
```

In this example, the Regular Expression specifies a valid email address. Here's how to interpret this Regular Expression:

- ^ represents the beginning of the string.
- [\\w|-|.]+ matches one-to-many instances of the following pattern:
  — [\\w|-|.] matches a word character (a-zA-Z0-9_), a dash (-), or a dot(.).
- @ indicates the literal "@".
- [\\w]+ matches one-to-many instances of the following pattern:
  — [\\w] matches a word character (a-zA-Z0-9_).
- \\. indicates the literal "."
- [A-Za-z]{2,4} matches two to four occurrences of the following pattern:
  — [A-Za-z] matches an alphabetic character.
- $ indicates the end of the string.

The double backslash (\\) is used by JSON Schema to denote special characters within regular expressions because the single backslash (\) normally used in standard

Regular Expressions won't work in this context. This is due to that fact the a single backslash is already used in core JSON document syntax to escape special characters (e.g., \b for a backspace).

The following document in Example 5-28 is valid because the email address follows the pattern specified in the Schema.

Example 5-28. ex-11-regex.json

```
{
  "email": "larsonrichard@ecratic.com",
  "firstName": "Larson",
  "lastName": "Richard"
}
```

The document in Example 5-29 is invalid because the email address field is missing the trailing .com.

Example 5-29. ex-11-regex-invalid.json

```
{
  "email": "larsonrichard@ecratic",
  "firstName": "Larson",
  "lastName": "Richard"
}
```

Run the preceding example to prove that it's invalid:

```
json-at-work => validate ex-11-regex-invalid.json ex-11-regex-schema.json
Invalid: String does not match pattern: ^[\w|-]+@[\w|-]+\.[A-Za-z]{2,4}$
JSON Schema element: /properties/email/pattern
JSON Content path: /email
```

Going deeper with Regular Expressions

Regular Expressions can be daunting and complex at times. Although a full tutorial on Regular Expressions is far beyond the scope of this book, here are some resources to help you master Regular Expressions:

- *Introducing Regular Expressions* by Michael Fitzgerald (O'Reilly).
- *Regular Expressions Cookbook, Second Edition* by Jan Goyvaerts and Steven Levithan (O'Reilly).
- *Mastering Regular Expressions, Third Edition* by Jeffrey E. F. Friedl (O'Reilly).
- Regular Expressions 101 (*https://regex101.com*)—this is my favorite Regex site.

- RegExr (*http://regexr.com*)
- Regular-Expressions.info (*http://www.regular-expressions.info*)

Dependent Properties

Dependent Properties introduce dependencies between fields in a Schema: one field depends on the presence of the other. The `dependencies` keyword is an object that specifies the dependent relationship(s), where field x maps to an array of fields that must be present if y is populated. In Example 5-30 `tags` must be present if `favorite Topics` is provided in the corresponding JSON document (that is, `favoriteTopic` depends on `tags`).

Example 5-30. ex-12-dependent-properties-schema.json

```
{
  "$schema": "http://json-schema.org/draft-04/schema#",
  "type": "object",
  "properties": {
    "email": {
      "type": "string",
      "pattern": "^[\\w|-|.]+@[\\w]+\\.[A-Za-z]{2,4}$"
    },
    "firstName": {
      "type": "string"
    },
    "lastName": {
      "type": "string"
      },
    "tags": {
      "type": "array",
        "items": {
          "type": "string"
        }
    },
    "favoriteTopic": {
      "type": "string"
    }
  },
  "additionalProperties": false,
  "required": ["email", "firstName", "lastName"],
  "dependencies": {
    "favoriteTopic": ["tags"]
  }
}
```

The JSON document in Example 5-31 is valid because the `favoriteTopic` is present, and the `tags` Array is populated.

Example 5-31. ex-12-dependent-properties.json

```
{
  "email": "larsonrichard@ecratic.com",
  "firstName": "Larson",
  "lastName": "Richard",
  "tags": [
    "JavaScript", "AngularJS", "Yeoman"
  ],
  "favoriteTopic": "JavaScript"
}
```

The JSON document in Example 5-32 is invalid because the `favoriteTopic` is present, but the `tags` Array is missing.

Example 5-32. ex-12-dependent-properties-invalid.json

```
{
  "email": "larsonrichard@ecratic.com",
  "firstName": "Larson",
  "lastName": "Richard",
  "favoriteTopic": "JavaScript"
}
```

Run the preceding example, and you'll see that the document is invalid:

```
json-at-work => validate ex-12-dependent-properties-invalid.json ex-12-dependent-properties-schema.json
Invalid: Dependency failed - key must exist: tags (due to key: favoriteTopic)
JSON Schema element: /dependencies/favoriteTopic/0
JSON Content path:
```

Internal References

References provide the ability to reuse definitions/validation rules. Think of references as *DRY* (Do Not Repeat Yourself) for Schema. References can be either Internal (inside the same Schema) or External (in a separate/external Schema). We'll start with Internal References.

In Example 5-33, you'll notice that the Regular Expression for the `email` field has been replaced by a `$ref`, a Uniform Resource Identifier (URI) to the actual definition/validation rule for the `email` field:

- `#` indicates that the definition exists locally within the Schema.

- `/definitions/` is the path to the `definitions` object in this Schema. Note that the `definitions` keyword indicates the use of a reference.

- `emailPattern` is the path to the `emailPattern` specification within the `definitions` object.

- JSON Schema leverages JSON Pointer (covered in Chapter 7) to specify URIs (e.g., `#/definitions/emailPattern`).

Example 5-33. ex-13-internal-ref-schema.json

```
{
  "$schema": "http://json-schema.org/draft-04/schema#",
  "type": "object",
  "properties": {
    "email": {
      "$ref": "#/definitions/emailPattern"
    },
    "firstName": {
      "type": "string"
    },
    "lastName": {
      "type": "string"
    }
  },
  "additionalProperties": false,
  "required": ["email", "firstName", "lastName"],
  "definitions": {
    "emailPattern": {
      "type": "string",
      "pattern": "^[\\w|-|.]+@[\\w]+\\.[A-Za-z]{2,4}$"
    }
  }
}
```

Other than the new `definitions` object, there's nothing really that new here. We've just moved the definition for email addresses to a common location that can be used throughout the Schema by multiple fields.

Example 5-34 shows a JSON document that conforms to the preceding Schema.

Example 5-34. ex-13-internal-ref.json

```
{
  "email": "larsonrichard@ecratic.com",
  "firstName": "Larson",
  "lastName": "Richard"
}
```

Example 5-35 is invalid because `email` is missing the trailing `.com`.

Example 5-35. ex-13-internal-ref-invalid.json

```
{
  "email": "larsonrichard@ecratic",
  "firstName": "Larson",
  "lastName": "Richard"
}
```

Validate this document from the command line, and you'll see that it's invalid:

```
json-at-work => validate ex-13-internal-ref-invalid.json ex-13-internal-ref-schema.json
Invalid: String does not match pattern: ^[\w|-]+@[\w|-]+\.[A-Za-z]{2,4}$
JSON Schema element: /properties/email/pattern
JSON Content path: /email
```

External References

External References provide a way to specify validation rules in an external Schema file. In this case, Schema A references Schema B for a particular set of validation rules. External References enable a development team (or several teams) to reuse common Schemas and definitions across the enterprise.

Example 5-36 shows our speaker Schema that now references an external (second) Schema.

Example 5-36. ex-14-exernal-ref-schema.json

```
{
  "$schema": "http://json-schema.org/draft-04/schema#",
  "type": "object",
  "properties": {
    "email": {
      "$ref":
        "http://localhost:8081/ex-14-my-common-schema.json#/definitions/emailPattern"
    },
    "firstName": {
      "type": "string"
    },
    "lastName": {
      "type": "string"
    }
  },
  "additionalProperties": false,
  "required": ["email", "firstName", "lastName"]
}
```

Notice the two key differences:

- The definitions Object has been factored out of this schema. Don't worry; it comes back really soon.

- The `email` field's `$ref` now points to an external Schema (*ex-14-my-common-schema.json*) to find the definition/validation rule for this field. We'll cover the HTTP address to the external Schema later in this chapter.

Example 5-37 shows the External Schema.

Example 5-37. ex-14-my-common-schema.json

```
{
  "$schema": "http://json-schema.org/draft-04/schema#",
  "id": "http://localhost:8081/ex-14-my-common-schema.json",

  "definitions": {
    "emailPattern": {
      "type": "string",
      "pattern": "^[\\w|-|.]+@[\\w]+\\.[A-Za-z]{2,4}$"
    }
  }
}
```

The `definitions` object that contains the `emailPattern` validation rule now resides in the external Schema. But at this point, you may be asking the follow questions:

- How does the reference actually work?
- How does a JSON Schema Validator locate the external Schema?

Here's how it all connects:

- In *ex-14-exernal-ref-schema.json*, the URI prefix (`http://localhost:8081/ex-14-my-common-schema.json`) before the # in the `$ref` tells the JSON Schema processor to look for the `emailPattern` definition in an external Schema.
- In *ex-14-my-common-schema.json* (the external Schema), the `id` field (a JSON Schema keyword) at the root of the Schema makes the content of the Schema available to external access.
- The URI in `$ref` and `id` should be an exact match to make the reference work properly.
- The `definitions` object works the same as it did for internal references.

Example 5-38 shows a JSON document that conforms to the Schema. Notice that this document has neither changed nor is it aware of the external Schema.

Example 5-38. ex-14-external-ref.json

```
{
  "email": "larsonrichard@ecratic.com",
```

```
  "firstName": "Larson",
  "lastName": "Richard"
}
```

Example 5-39 shows a document that won't validate against the Schema because the email is missing the trailing .com.

Example 5-39. ex-14-external-ref-invalid.json

```
{
  "email": "larsonrichard@ecratic",
  "firstName": "Larson",
  "lastName": "Richard"
}
```

There are two ways to validate the preceding document against the Schema:

- The filesystem
- The web

Let's start by validating on the filesystem by using the validate tool that we've been using all along:

```
json-at-work => validate ex-14-external-ref-invalid.json ex-14-external-ref-schema.json
Invalid: String does not match pattern: ^[\w|-]+@[\w|-]+\.[A-Za-z]{2,4}$
JSON Schema element: /properties/email/pattern
JSON Content path: /email
```

The JSON document (*ex-14-external-ref-invalid.json*) is invalid as in previous runs, but notice the inclusion of both the main (*ex-14-external-ref-schema.json*) and external (*ex-14-my-common-schema.json*) Schemas on the command line.

Now let's use the web to validate against the external Schema. In this case, we'll deploy this file as static content on a web server so that the URI in the $ref and id (http://localhost:8081/ex-14-my-common-schema.json#/definitions/emailPat tern) will work properly. If you haven't done so before, now would be a great time to install the http-server Node.js module. To install and run it, follow the instructions in Appendix A (see "Install npm Modules" on page 325).

Run http-server (on port 8081) in the same directory where the external Schema resides, and your command line should look like this:

```
json-at-work => http-server -p 8081
Starting up http-server, serving ./ on: http://0.0.0.0:8081
Hit CTRL-C to stop the server
[Wed, 02 Sep 2015 03:44:00 GMT] "GET /ex-14-my-common-schema.json" "undefined"
[Wed, 02 Sep 2015 03:44:16 GMT] "GET /ex-14-my-common-schema.json" "undefined"
```

When you visit *http://localhost:8081/ex-14-my-common-schema.json* in your browser, you should see the screen in Figure 5-5.

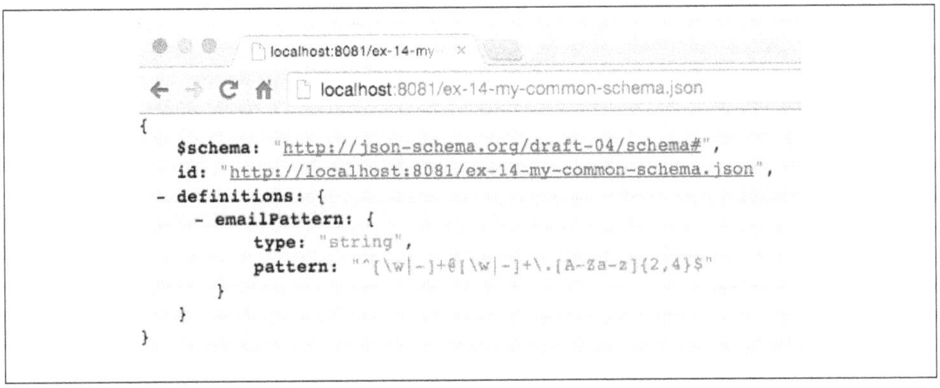

```
                 localhost:8081/ex-14-my      ×

         C                 localhost:8081/ex-14-my-common-schema.json
{
    $schema: "http://json-schema.org/draft-04/schema#",
    id: "http://localhost:8081/ex-14-my-common-schema.json",
  - definitions: {
    - emailPattern: {
          type: "string",
          pattern: "^[\w|-]+@[\w|-]+\.[A-Za-z]{2,4}$"
      }
    }
}
```

Figure 5-5. Web-addressable external Schema

Now that the external Schema is web addressable, we can do the validation, and you'll see that the document is invalid:

```
json-at-work => validate ex-14-external-ref-invalid.json ex-14-external-ref-schema.json
Invalid: String does not match pattern: ^[\w|-]+@[\w|-]+\.[A-Za-z]{2,4}$
JSON Schema element: /properties/email/pattern
JSON Content path: /email
```

Choosing Validation Rules

In addition to the `requires` and `dependencies` keywords, JSON Schema provides finer-grained mechanisms to tell the Schema processor which validation rules to use. These additional keywords are as follows:

`oneOf`
> One, and only one, rule must match successfully.

`anyOf`
> One or more rules must match successfully.

`allOf`
> All rules must match successfully.

oneOf

The `oneOf` keyword enforces an exclusive choice between validation rules. In the Schema in Example 5-40, the value of the `rating` field can either be less than 2.0 or less than 5.0, but not both.

Example 5-40. ex-15-one-of-schema.json

```json
{
  "$schema": "http://json-schema.org/draft-04/schema#",
  "type": "object",
  "properties": {
    "email": {
      "type": "string",
      "pattern": "^[\\w|-|.]+@[\\w]+\\.[A-Za-z]{2,4}$"
    },
    "firstName": {
      "type": "string"
    },
      "type": "string"
    },
    "postedSlides": {
      "type": "boolean"
    },
    "rating": {
      "type": "number",
      "oneOf": [
        {
          "maximum": 2.0
        },
        {
          "maximum": 5.0
        }
      ]
    }
  },
  "additionalProperties": false,
  "required": [ "email", "firstName", "lastName", "postedSlides", "rating" ]
}
```

Example 5-41 is valid because the value of the `rating` field is 4.1, which matches only one of the validation rules (< 5.0), but not both.

Example 5-41. ex-15-one-of.json

```json
{
  "email": "larsonrichard@ecratic.com",
  "firstName": "Larson",
  "lastName": "Richard",
  "postedSlides": true,
  "rating": 4.1
}
```

The JSON document in Example 5-42 is invalid because the value of the `rating` field is 1.9, which matches both validation rules (< 2.0 and < 5.0).

Example 5-42. ex-15-one-of-invalid.json

```
{
  "email": "larsonrichard@ecratic.com",
  "firstName": "Larson",
  "lastName": "Richard",
  "postedSlides": true,
  "rating": 1.9
}
```

Validate the preceding document from the command line, and you'll see that it's invalid:

```
json-at-work => validate ex-15-one-of-invalid.json ex-15-one-of-schema.json
Invalid: Data is valid against more than one schema from "oneOf": indices 0 and 1
JSON Schema element: /properties/rating/oneOf
JSON Content path: /rating
```

anyOf

The `anyOf` keyword allows for a match against any (one or more) of the validation rules. In Example 5-43, we've expanded the potential values of `postedSlides` to allow for `[Y|y]es` and `[N|n]o` in addition to a `boolean`.

Example 5-43. ex-16-any-of-schema.json

```
{
  "$schema": "http://json-schema.org/draft-04/schema#",
  "type": "object",
  "properties": {
    "email": {
      "type": "string",
      "pattern": "^[\\w|-|.]+@[\\w]+\\.[A-Za-z]{2,4}$"
    },
    "firstName": {
      "type": "string"
    },
    "lastName": {
      "type": "string"
    },
    "postedSlides": {
      "anyOf": [
        {
          "type": "boolean"
        },
        {
          "type": "string",
          "enum": [ "yes", "Yes", "no", "No" ]
        }
      ]
    }
}
```

```
    },
    "rating": {
      "type": "number"
    }
  },
  "additionalProperties": false,
  "required": [ "email", "firstName", "lastName", "postedSlides", "rating" ]
}
```

Example 5-44 is valid because the value of postedSlides is "yes".

Example 5-44. ex-16-any-of.json

```
{
  "email": "larsonrichard@ecratic.com",
  "firstName": "Larson",
  "lastName": "Richard",
  "postedSlides": "yes",
  "rating": 4.1
}
```

Example 5-45 is invalid because the value of the postedSlides field is "maybe", which is not in the set of allowed values.

Example 5-45. ex-16-any-of-invalid.json

```
{
  "email": "larsonrichard@ecratic.com",
  "firstName": "Larson",
  "lastName": "Richard",
  "postedSlides": "maybe",
  "rating": 4.1
}
```

Validate this document from the command line, and you'll see that it's invalid:

```
json-at-work => validate ex-16-any-of-invalid.json ex-16-any-of-schema.json
Invalid: Data does not match any schemas from "anyOf"
JSON Schema element: /properties/postedSlides/anyOf
JSON Content path: /postedSlides
```

allOf

With the allOf keyword, the data must match all of the validation rules. In the Schema in Example 5-46, the lastName *must* be a string with a length < 20.

Example 5-46. ex-17-all-of-schema.json

```json
{
  "$schema": "http://json-schema.org/draft-04/schema#",
  "type": "object",
  "properties": {
    "email": {
      "type": "string",
      "pattern": "^[\\w|-|.]+@[\\w]+\\.[A-Za-z]{2,4}$"
    },
    "firstName": {
      "type": "string"
    },
    "lastName": {
      "allOf": [
        { "type": "string" },
        { "maxLength": 20 }
      ]
    },
    "postedSlides": {
      "type": "boolean"
    },
    "rating": {
      "type": "number",
      "maximum": 5.0
    }
  },
  "additionalProperties": false,
  "required": [
    "email",
    "firstName",
    "lastName",
    "postedSlides",
    "rating"
  ]
}
```

Example 5-47 is valid because the length of the lastName is ≤ 20.

Example 5-47. ex-17-all-of.json

```json
{
  "email": "larsonrichard@ecratic.com",
  "firstName": "Larson",
  "lastName": "Richard",
  "postedSlides": true,
  "rating": 4.1
}
```

Example 5-48 is invalid because the length of the lastName exceeds 20 characters.

Example 5-48. ex-17-all-of-invalid.json

```
{
  "email": "larsonrichard@ecratic.com",
  "firstName": "Larson",
  "lastName": "ThisLastNameIsWayTooLong",
  "postedSlides": true,
  "rating": 4.1
}
```

Validate the preceding document, and you'll see that it's invalid:

```
json-at-work => validate ex-17-all-of-invalid.json ex-17-all-of-schema.json
Invalid: String is too long (24 chars), maximum 20
JSON Schema element: /properties/lastName/allOf/1/maxLength
JSON Content path: /lastName
```

We've covered the basics of JSON Schema and syntax, and now it's time to design an API with JSON Schema.

How to Design and Test an API with JSON Schema

JSON Schema is all about the semantics (the meaning) and structure of the data exchanged by applications and APIs. In the context of API Design, think of a JSON Schema as part of the contract (interface). In this last portion of the chapter, we'll go from concept to a running Stub API that other applications and APIs can start testing and using.

Our Scenario

We'll use the same `speaker` model that we've been using all along, and iteratively add constraints and capabilities. Here are the steps we need in order to go from a concept to a running Stub API:

1. Model a JSON document.
2. Generate a JSON Schema.
3. Generate sample data.
4. Deploy a Stub API with `json-server`.

Model a JSON Document

Before creating a Schema, we need to know the data that we're exchanging. Besides the fields and their formats, it's important to get a good look-and-feel for the data itself. To do this, we need to overcome one of the major issues with JSON itself: creating documents by hand is tedious and error-prone. Use a modeling tool rather than doing a lot of typing. There are several good tools to support this, and my favorite is JSON Editor Online. Refer to "Model JSON Data with JSON Editor Online" on page 18 in Chapter 1 for further details on the features of JSON Editor Online.

Figure 5-6 shows our speaker model.

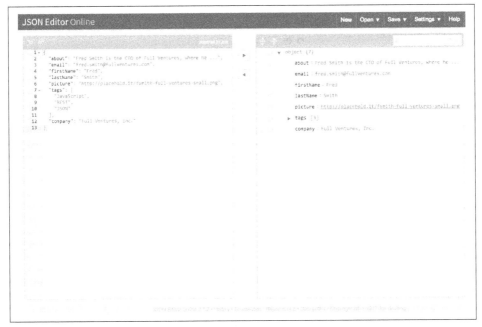

Figure 5-6. Speaker model on jsoneditoronline.com

Rather than typing the JSON document, use JSON Editor Online to model the data, and generate a JSON document. In the JSON model on the righthand portion of the screen, click the icon next to an element (i.e., Object, key/value pair, Array) and you'll see a menu. Select Append or Insert to add elements:

- Objects
- Name/value pairs
- Arrays

After entering a few fields, press the left-arrow button (in the middle of the page) to create the JSON document. You can then iteratively add, test, and review the content of your document until it looks good. Then, save the JSON document, shown in Example 5-49, into a file (with the Save to Disk option under the Save menu).

Example 5-49. ex-18-speaker.json

```
{
  "about": "Fred Smith is the CTO of Full Ventures, where he ...",
  "email": "fred.smith@fullventures.com",
  "firstName": "Fred",
  "lastName": "Smith",
  "picture": "http://placehold.it/fsmith-full-ventures-small.png",
  "tags": [
    "JavaScript",
    "REST",
    "JSON"
  ],
  "company": "Full Ventures, Inc."
}
```

Before going any further, it would be a good idea to validate the JSON document by using JSONLint (either with the CLI or web app). This should validate because JSON Editor Online produces valid JSON, but it's always good to double-check.

Generate a JSON Schema

With a valid JSON document in hand, we can now use JSONSchema.net to generate a corresponding JSON Schema based on the document structure and content. Again, save yourself a lot of typing by letting a tool do most of the work for you.

Visit *http://jsonschema.net* and paste in the JSON document on the left side, as shown in Figure 5-7.

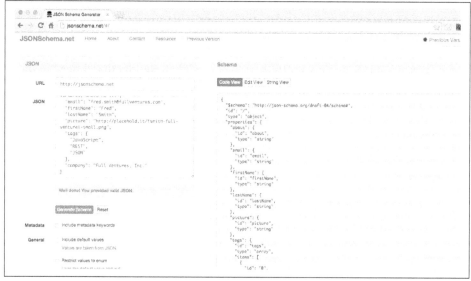

Figure 5-7. Generate Speakers Schema on JSONSchema.net

To generate a Schema, start with the default settings, and make the following changes:

- Turn off "Use absolute IDs."
- Turn off "Allow additional properties."
- Click the Generate Schema button.
- Copy the generated Schema (on the righthand side) to your clipboard.

After saving your clipboard to a file, we now have the Schema in Example 5-50.

Example 5-50. ex-18-speaker-schema-generated.json

```json
{
  "$schema": "http://json-schema.org/draft-04/schema#",
  "id": "/",
  "type": "object",
  "properties": {
    "about": {
      "id": "about",
      "type": "string"
    },
    "email": {
      "id": "email",
      "type": "string"
    },
    "firstName": {
      "id": "firstName",
      "type": "string"
    },
    "lastName": {
      "id": "lastName",
      "type": "string"
    },
    "picture": {
      "id": "picture",
      "type": "string"
    },
    "tags": {
      "id": "tags",
      "type": "array",
      "items": [{
        "id": "0",
        "type": "string"
      }, {
        "id": "1",
        "type": "string"
      }, {
        "id": "2",
        "type": "string"
      }]
```

```
    },
    "company": {
      "id": "company",
      "type": "string"
    }
  },
  "additionalProperties": false,
  "required": [
    "about",
    "email",
    "firstName",
    "lastName",
    "picture",
    "tags",
    "company"
  ]
}
```

JSONSchema.net is great at generating a base Schema, but it adds fields that we don't use, plus it doesn't do enum, pattern, and so forth. The main takeaway is that JSON-Schema.net does about 80 percent of the work for you, and then you need to fill in a few pieces yourself. We don't need the id fields at this time, but we do need to add a Regular Expression to validate the email field (just use the Regex from previous examples). After making these changes, the Schema should look like Example 5-51.

Example 5-51. ex-18-speaker-schema-generated-modified.json

```
{
  "$schema": "http://json-schema.org/draft-04/schema#",
  "type": "object",
  "properties": {
    "about": {
      "type": "string"
    },
    "email": {
      "type": "string",
      "pattern": "^[\\w|-|.]+@[\\w]+\\.[A-Za-z]{2,4}$"
    },
    "firstName": {
      "type": "string"
    },
    "lastName": {
      "type": "string"
    },
    "picture": {
      "type": "string"
    },
    "tags": {
      "type": "array",
      "items": [
```

```
      {
        "type": "string"
      }
    ]
  },
  "company": {
    "type": "string"
  }
},
"additionalProperties": false,
"required": [ "about", "email", "firstName",
              "lastName", "picture", "tags", "company"
]
}
```

Validate the JSON Document

Now that we have a JSON Schema, let's validate the document against the Schema by using the JSON Validate web app. Visit *http://jsonvalidate.com/* and paste in the JSON document and Schema, as shown in Figure 5-8.

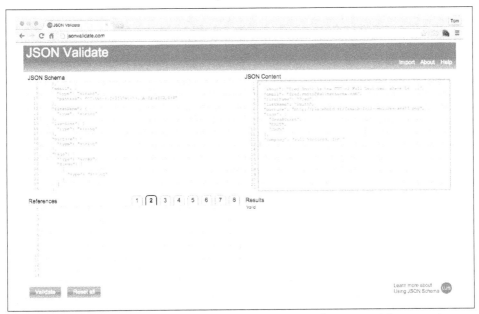

Figure 5-8. Validate Speakers JSON document against Speakers JSON Schema on json-validate.com

Click the Validate button, and the document should validate against the Schema. You could have used the `validate` CLI tool we've been using throughout this chapter, but the web app is a great visual.

Generate Sample Data

At this point, we have a JSON document with its corresponding Schema, but we need more data to create an API for testing. We could use JSON Editor Online to generate test data, but there are a couple of issues with this approach because a human would have to randomize and generate massive amounts of data. Even with a GUI, it's a big manual effort.

JSON Editor Online is great for creating a small JSON document to get the design process going, but we need another approach to generate randomized bulk JSON data for API testing. We'll use JSON Generator to create our data; visit *http://www.json-generator.com/* and you should see the screen in Figure 5-9.

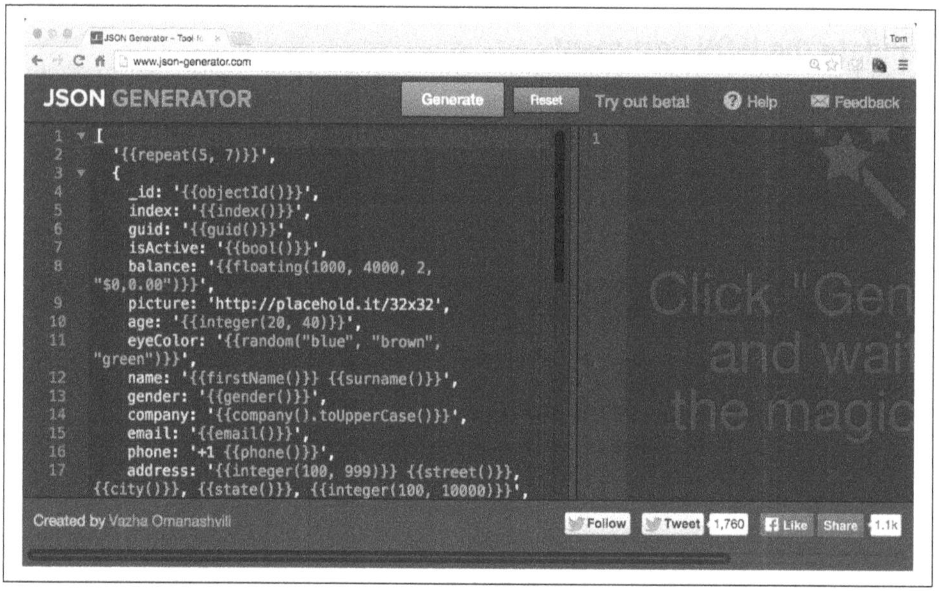

Figure 5-9. json-generator site

The code on the left side is a template (in the form of a JavaScript Object Literal) that JSON Generator uses to generate sample JSON data. Notice that this tool has the ability to generate sample/random data for paragraphs, numbers, names, globally unique identifiers (GUIDs), names, gender, email addresses, etc. Plus, it has the ability to do this in bulk with the `{{repeat}}` tag at the top of the template. Click the Help button for detailed documentation on the tags.

But these default settings are way more than we need. Let's pare this template down to the fields we need to generate three `speaker` objects with random data (see Example 5-52).

Example 5-52. ex-18-speaker-template.js

```
// Template for http://www.json-generator.com/

[
  '{{repeat(3)}}', {
    id: '{{integer()}}',
    picture: 'http://placehold.it/32x32',
    name: '{{firstName()}}',
    lastName: '{{surname()}}',
    company: '{{company()}}',
    email: '{{email()}}',
    about: '{{lorem(1, "paragraphs")}}'
  }
]
```

After clicking the Generate button, you should see the following JSON document in the web app shown in Figure 5-10 (if you want more than the three speaker objects, just change the 3 in the repeat tag to a higher number).

Figure 5-10. Create a Speaker JSON document with json-generator

Now, click the Copy to Clipboard button on the righthand side, and paste into a file, as shown in Example 5-53.

Example 5-53. ex-18-speakers-generated.json

```
[
  {
    "id": 5,
    "picture": "http://placehold.it/32x32",
    "name": "Allen",
```

```
    "lastName": "Strickland",
    "company": "Coriander",
    "email": "allenstrickland@coriander.com",
    "about": "Quis enim labore ..."
  },
  {
    "id": 9,
    "picture": "http://placehold.it/32x32",
    "name": "Merle",
    "lastName": "Prince",
    "company": "Xylar",
    "email": "merleprince@xylar.com",
    "about": "Id voluptate duis ..."
  },
  {
    "id": 8,
    "picture": "http://placehold.it/32x32",
    "name": "Salazar",
    "lastName": "Ewing",
    "company": "Zentime",
    "email": "salazarewing@zentime.com",
    "about": "Officia qui id ..."
  }
]
```

We're almost there, but we need to tweak the data just a bit so that we can deploy the file as an API:

- We already have an Array. Let's name it `speakers`, and then wrap it with the { and }. We now have a JSON document with the `speakers` Array as the root element.

- Let's redo the `id` fields so that they start at 0.

Our file now looks like Example 5-54.

Example 5-54. ex-18-speakers-generated-modified.json

```
{
  "speakers": [
    {
      "id": 0,
      "picture": "http://placehold.it/32x32",
      "name": "Allen",
      "lastName": "Strickland",
      "company": "Coriander",
      "email": "allenstrickland@coriander.com",
      "about": "Quis enim labore ..."
    },
    {
      "id": 1,
```

```
      "picture": "http://placehold.it/32x32",
      "name": "Merle",
      "lastName": "Prince",
      "company": "Xylar",
      "email": "merleprince@xylar.com",
      "about": "Id voluptate duis ..."
    },
    {
      "id": 2,
      "picture": "http://placehold.it/32x32",
      "name": "Salazar",
      "lastName": "Ewing",
      "company": "Zentime",
      "email": "salazarewing@zentime.com",
      "about": "Officia qui id ..."
    }
  ]
}
```

At this point, you're probably wondering why we needed to make those modifications. The changes were needed so that json-server has the proper URIs (routes) for the Speaker data:

- We get the *http://localhost:5000/speakers* route by encapsulating with the speakers array, with all the data addressable from there.

- We can access the first element with this route: *http://localhost:5000/speakers/0*.

But we're getting ahead of ourselves. Let's get json-server up and running, and then start browsing the API.

Deploy a Stub API with json-server

Now that we have a Schema and some test data, it's time to deploy the sample data as an API so consumers can start testing it and provide feedback. If you haven't done so before, now would be a great time to install the json-server Node.js module. To install and run it, follow the instructions in Appendix A (see "Install npm Modules" on page 325).

Run json-server (on port 5000) in the same directory where the *ex-18-speakers-generated-modified.json* file resides, and your command line should look like this:

```
json-at-work => json-server -p 5000 ./ex-18-speakers-generated-modified.json
{^_^} Hi!

Loading database from ./ex-18-speakers-generated-modified.json
  http://localhost:5000/speakers

You can now go to http://localhost:5000/

Enter `s` at any time to create a snapshot of the db

GET /speakers 200 11.750 ms - 1667
GET /speakers 304 4.027 ms - -
GET /speakers/0 200 3.170 ms - 574
GET /speakers/0 304 2.556 ms - -
GET /speakers/0 304 1.350 ms - -
GET /speakers 304 1.437 ms - -
```

When you visit *http://localhost:5000/speakers* in your browser, you should see the screen in Figure 5-11.

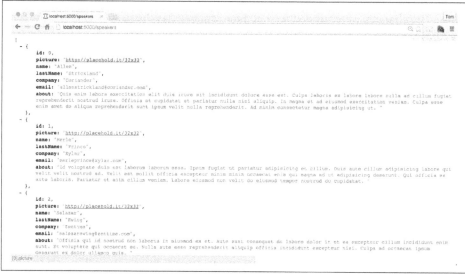

Figure 5-11. Speakers Stub API on json-server

You now have a testable API without writing a single line of code; we just deployed a static JSON file. The beauty of this approach is that this looks, acts, and feels like an API. From here, you can interact with it just as you would with other APIs. You could use your browser, cURL, or make HTTP calls from your favorite language to begin interacting with it.

Now there are limits. With json-server, you can do an HTTP GET only on the data—it's read only.

Final Thoughts on API Design and Testing with JSON Schema

After going through this exercise, you should have an appreciation for the powerful JSON-based open source tools that can shorten your API development life cycle. Here's the bottom line:

- Use JSON modeling tools before committing to the final data structure. Iterate with stakeholders early and often.
- Writing a JSON document or Schema by hand is tedious and error-prone. Let the tools do most of the work for you and avoid as much typing as possible.
- Validate early and often.
- Generate bulk randomized JSON data rather than creating it yourself.
- Spinning up a Stub API is simple. Don't write your own testing infrastructure, because someone else has already done it for you. Just use what's out there. You have better things to do with your time.

Validation Using a JSON Schema Library

We've shown how to use the `validate` command-line tool and the JSON Validate web app to validate a JSON document against a Schema, but the ultimate goal is to validate from an application.

But JSON Schema isn't only just for JavaScript and Node.js. Most major platforms have excellent support for JSON Schema v4:

Ruby on Rails
> `json-schema` gem (*https://rubygems.org/gems/json-schema/versions/2.5.1*).

Java
> `json-schema-validator` (*https://github.com/fge/json-schema-validator*).

PHP
> `jsv4-php` (*https://github.com/geraintluff/jsv4-php*).

Python
> `jsonschema` (*https://github.com/Julian/jsonschema*).

Clojure
> Just use the Java-based `json-schema-validator`.

Node.js
> Node.js has several good JSON Schema processors. I've had success with the following:

- `ajv` is my favorite library to use from a Node.js-based application because it's clean and simple. `ajv` is compatible with popular Node.js-based testing suites (e.g., Mocha/Chai, Jasmine, and Karma). You can find more information on `ajv` on the npm site (*https://www.npmjs.com/package/ajv*) and on GitHub (*https://github.com/epoberezkin/ajv*). We'll show how to use `ajv` in Chapter 10.

- `ujs-jsonvalidate` is a processor we've been using all through this chapter to validate against a Schema from the command line. You can find further usage information on GitHub (*http://bit.ly/2reROyx*). You can find the `ujs-jsonvalidate` npm module at *http://bit.ly/2tj4ODI*.

Where to Go Deeper with JSON Schema

We've covered the basics of JSON Schema, but a definitive guide is far beyond the scope of this chapter. In addition to the *json-schema.org* site mentioned previously, here are a few more resources:

- Using JSON Schema by Joe McIntyre (*http://usingjsonschema.com/*) provides a wealth of JSON Schema-related reference information and tools, including these:
  - The *Using JSON Schema* ebook (*http://usingjsonschema.com/downloads/*)
  - The `jsonvalidate` application (*http://jsonvalidate.com/*)
  - The `ujs-validate` npm module (*https://github.com/usingjsonschema/ujs-jsonvalidate-nodejs*)

- Understanding JSON Schema by Michael Droettboom et al. (*http://spacetele scope.github.io/understanding-json-schema/UnderstandingJSONSchema.pdf*)

- A Short Guide to JSON Schema (*https://bugventure.github.io/jsen/json-schema*)

What We Covered

We introduced JSON Schema and how it helps in application architecture. We then designed and tested an API with JSON Schema, and leveraged JSON Schema-related tooling along the way.

What's Next?

Now that we've shown how to structure and validate JSON instance documents with JSON Schema, we'll show to how search JSON documents in Chapter 6.

JSON Search

JSON Search libraries and tools make it easier to search JSON documents and quickly access the fields that you're looking for. JSON Search shines when you need to search through a large JSON document returned from a Web API.

In this chapter, we'll cover the following:

- Making your job easier with JSON Search
- Using the major JSON Search libraries and tools
- Writing Unit Tests that search the content of JSON documents returned by a Web API

In our examples, we'll use several JSON Search technologies to search JSON data from a Web API deployed on your local machine. We'll create Unit Tests to execute the searches and check results.

Why JSON Search?

Imagine that the result set from an API call has several hundred (or more) JSON Objects, and you want to use only a subset of the data (key/value pairs) or apply a search filter (based on your criteria). Without JSON Search, you would have to parse the JSON document and sift through a large data structure by writing custom code. This low-level approach is a tedious, code-intensive chore. You have better things to do with your time. The JSON Search libraries and tools shown in this chapter will reduce your work and make your job easier.

JSON Search Libraries and Tools

Many libraries (callable from an application) and command-line tools can search JSON documents. Here are the most common, widely used libraries, which we'll explore later in this chapter:

- JSONPath
- JSON Pointer
- jq

Honorable Mention

Many high-quality JSON Search libraries and command-line tools are available to search and filter JSON content, but we can't cover all of them. Here are some others that are worth a look, but we can not discuss them further in this chapter for the sake of brevity:

SpahQL

  SpahQL is like jQuery for JSON Objects. The SpahQL library is available in a GitHub repository (*https://github.com/danski/spahql*).

json

  A command-line tool available on GitHub (*https://github.com/zpoley/json-command*), and on the npm repository (*https://www.npmjs.com/package/json*). Even though we won't use json's search capabilities in this chapter, we'll still use it to pretty-print JSON documents.

jsawk

  jsawk (*https://github.com/micha/jsawk*) is a command-line tool that transforms a JSON document in addition to searching.

Even though we're not covering these tools, one or more could also be right for your project. Compare them with JSONPath, JSON Pointer, and jq to see which one works best for you.

What to Look For

Many libraries and tools are available, and it's hard to choose which one(s) to use. Here are my criteria:

Mindshare

  Does it appear to be widely used? How many hits do you see when you do an internet search?

Developer community

Is the code on GitHub? Is it well maintained?

Platforms

Does it run on multiple platforms? Do multiple providers support the specification or library interfaces?

Intuitive

Is it well-documented? How easy is it to install? How intuitive is the interface? How easy is it to use?

Standards

Is the library associated with a standard (e.g., IETF, WC3, or Ecma)?

We'll use these guidelines to evaluate each JSON Search product.

Test Data

We need more realistic test data and a larger, richer JSON document to search against, and the web has an abundant supply. For this chapter and the next, we'll use an open data set available from a public API rather than the Speaker data from previous chapters. We'll leverage the cities/weather data from the OpenWeatherMap API (*http://openweathermap.org*). See the full API documentation (*http://openweather map.org/current*).

The *chapter-6/data/cities-weather-orig.json* file contains weather data from the Open-WeatherMap API for cities within a rectangle by latitude/longitude (in this case, Southern California, United States). Note that the weather data from OpenWeather-Map changes frequently, so the data I've captured for the book example will not match the current data from the API. Let's modify the weather data before we use it with json-server. First, look at the *data/cities-weather-orig.json* file, and notice that the weather data is stored in an Array called list. I've renamed it to cities for the sake of clarity and testability and saved the changes in the *data/cities-weather.json* file. Additionally, I moved the cod, calctime, and cnt fields (at the beginning of the document) into an Object. This second change was needed for compatibility with json-server, which accepts only Objects or an Array of Objects. We'll continue to leverage the json-server Node.js module from earlier chapters to deploy the city weather data as a Web API. Example 6-1 shows the modified weather data.

Example 6-1. data/cities-weather.json

```
{
  "other": {
    "cod": 200,
    "calctime": 0.006,
    "cnt": 110
```

```
  },
  "cities": [
  ...
  ]
}
```

Now, run `json-server` as follows:

```
json-server -p 5000 ./cities-weather.json
```

Visit *http://localhost:5000/cities* in your browser, and you should see the screen in Figure 6-1.

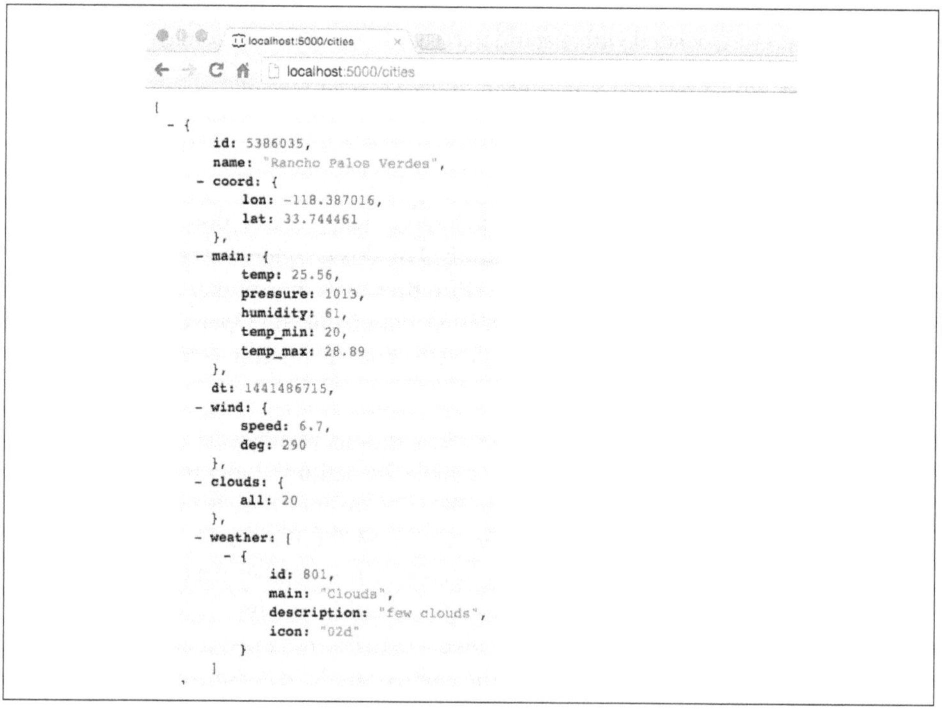

Figure 6-1. OpenWeather API data on json-server viewed from the browser

We now have test JSON data deployed as a Stub API, and we'll use it for Unit Testing throughout this chapter.

Setting Up Unit Tests

All tests in this chapter will continue to leverage Mocha/Chai within a Node.js environment, just as you saw in previous chapters. Before going further, be sure to set up your test environment. If you haven't installed Node.js yet, refer to Appendix A, and install Node.js (see "Install Node.js" on page 320 and "Install npm Modules" on page

325). If you want to follow along with the Node.js project provided in the code examples, cd to *chapter-6/cities-weather-test* and do the following to install all dependencies for the project:

```
npm install
```

If you'd like to set up the Node.js project yourself, follow the instructions in the book's GitHub repository (*https://github.com/tmarrs/json-at-work-examples/tree/master/chapter-6/Project-Setup.md*).

Now that we've set up a testing environment, it's time to start working with JSONPath and the other JSON Search libraries.

Comparing JSON Search Libraries and Tools

Now that we've covered the basics of JSON Search, we will compare the following libraries and tools:

- JSONPath
- JSON Pointer
- jq

JSONPath

JSONPath (*http://goessner.net/articles/JsonPath*) was developed by Stefan Goessner in 2007 to search for and extract data from JSON documents. The original library was developed in JavaScript, but because of its popularity, most modern languages and platforms now support JSONPath.

JSONPath query syntax

JSONPath query syntax is based on XPath (which is used to search XML documents). Table 6-1 lists some JSONPath queries based on our cities example.

Table 6-1. JSONPath queries

JSONPath query	Description
`$.cities`	Get all elements in the cities Array.
`$.cities.length`	Get the number of elements in the cities Array.
`$.cities[0::2]`	Get every other element in the cities array. See the description of `slice()` in the following list.
`$.cities[(@.length-1)]` or `$.cities[-1:]`	Get the last element in the cities Array.
`$..weather`	Get all weather subelements.

JSONPath query	Description
`$.cities[:3]`	Get the first three elements in cities Array.
`$.cities[:3].name`	Get the city name for first three elements in the cities Array.
`$.cities[?(@.main.temp > 84)]`	Get the cities where the temp > 84.
`$.cities[?(@.main.temp >= 84 && @.main.temp <= 85.5)]`	Get the cities where the temp is between 84 and 85.5.
`$.cities[?(@.weather[0].main == 'Clouds')]`	Get the cities with cloudy weather.
`$.cities[?(@.weather[0].main.match(/ Clo/))]`	Get the cities with cloudy weather by using regex.

These example queries use JSONPath keywords and symbols:

- `$` represents the document root-level object.
- `..` returns all elements and subelements that have a particular name.
- `[]` with an index is an Array query, and the index is based on the JavaScript `slice()` function. The Mozilla Developer Network (MDN) provides a full description (*https://mzl.la/2rRu4BH*). Here's a brief overview of JSONPath `slice()`:
  — It provides the ability to select a portion of an Array.
  — The `begin` parameter (as with JS `slice()`) is the beginning index, is zero-based, and defaults to zero if omitted.
  — The `end` parameter (as with JS `slice()`) is the end index (noninclusive), and defaults to the end of the Array if omitted.
  — The `step` parameter (added by JSONPath `slice()`) represents the step, and defaults to 1. A `step` value of 1 returns all Array elements specified by the `begin` and `end` parameters; a value of 2 returns every other (or second) element, and so on.
- `@` represents the current element.
- `[?(...)]` enables a conditional search. The code inside the parentheses can be any valid JS expression, including conditionals (e.g., `==` or `>`) and Regular Expressions.

JSONPath online tester

A couple of online JSONPath testers enable you to practice JSONPath queries before writing a single line of code. I like the tester provided by Kazuki Hamasaki (*http://ashphy.com/JSONPathOnlineEvaluator*). Just paste in the *data/cities-weather.json* document (from the Chapter 6 code examples (*https://github.com/tmarrs/json-at-*

work-examples/tree/master/chapter-6)) in the left text box, and enter a JSONPath query. The results appear in the text box on the righthand side of the page as shown in Figure 6-2.

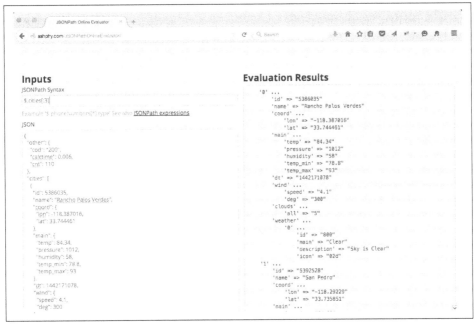

Figure 6-2. JSONPath Online Evaluator with OpenWeather API data

You'll notice that only the data values are returned in the JSONPath results text box, and that the keys are not returned.

JSONPath Unit Test

The Unit Test in Example 6-2 exercises several of the example JSONPath queries that were shown earlier. This code leverages the `jsonpath` Node.js module to search against the JSON data returned by the Cities API that runs on your local machine. See *https://github.com/dchester/jsonpath* for a detailed description of the `jsonpath` module.

Example 6-2. cities-weather-test/test/jsonpath-spec.js

```
'use strict';

/* Attribution: Cities Weather data provided by OpenWeatherMap API
   ([http://openweathermap.org]) under Creative Commons Share A Like
   License (https://creativecommons.org/licenses/by-sa/4.0).
   Changes were made to the data to work with json-server.
   This does not imply an endorsement by the licensor.
```

```
    This code is distributed under Creative Commons Share A Like License.
*/

var expect = require('chai').expect;
var jp = require('jsonpath');
var unirest = require('unirest');

describe('cities-jsonpath', function() {
  var req;

  beforeEach(function() {
    req = unirest.get('http://localhost:5000/cities')
      .header('Accept', 'application/json');
  });

  it('should return a 200 response', function(done) {
    req.end(function(res) {
      expect(res.statusCode).to.eql(200);
      expect(res.headers['content-type']).to.eql(
        'application/json; charset=utf-8');
      done();
    });
  });

  it('should return all cities', function(done) {
    req.end(function(res) {
      var cities = res.body;

      expect(cities.length).to.eql(110);
      done();
    });
  });

  it('should return every other city', function(done) {
    req.end(function(res) {
      var cities = res.body;
      var citiesEveryOther = jp.query(cities, '$[0::2]');

      expect(citiesEveryOther[1].name).to.eql('Rosarito');
      expect(citiesEveryOther.length).to.eql(55);
      done();
    });
  });

  it('should return the last city', function(done) {
    req.end(function(res) {
      var cities = res.body;
      var lastCity = jp.query(cities, '$[(@.length-1)]');

      expect(lastCity[0].name).to.eql('Moreno Valley');
      done();
```

```
    });
  });

  it('should return the 1st 3 cities', function(done) {
    req.end(function(res) {
      var cities = res.body;
      var citiesFirstThree = jp.query(cities, '$[:3]');
      var citiesFirstThreeNames = jp.query(cities, '$[:3].name');

      expect(citiesFirstThree.length).to.eql(3);
      expect(citiesFirstThreeNames.length).to.eql(3);
      expect(citiesFirstThreeNames).to.eql(['Rancho Palos Verdes',
        'San Pedro', 'Rosarito'
      ]);

      done();
    });
  });

  it('should return cities within a temperature range', function(done) {
    req.end(function(res) {
      var cities = res.body;
      var citiesTempRange = jp.query(cities,
        '$[?(@.main.temp >= 84 && @.main.temp <= 85.5)]'
      );

      for (var i = 0; i < citiesTempRange.length; i++) {
        expect(citiesTempRange[i].main.temp).to.be.at.least(84);
        expect(citiesTempRange[i].main.temp).to.be.at.most(85.5);
      }

      done();
    });
  });

  it('should return cities with cloudy weather', function(done) {
    req.end(function(res) {
      var cities = res.body;
      var citiesWeatherCloudy = jp.query(cities,
        '$[?(@.weather[0].main == "Clouds")]'
      );

      checkCitiesWeather(citiesWeatherCloudy);
      done();
    });
  });

  it('should return cities with cloudy weather using regex', function(done) {
    req.end(function(res) {
      var cities = res.body;
      var citiesWeatherCloudyRegex = jp.query(cities,
        '$[?(@.weather[0].main.match(/Clo/))]'
```

```
      );

    checkCitiesWeather(citiesWeatherCloudyRegex);
    done();
  });
});

function checkCitiesWeather(cities) {
  for (var i = 0; i < cities.length; i++) {
    expect(cities[i].weather[0].main).to.eql('Clouds');
  }
}
});
```

Note the following in this example:

- The test sets up the URI and `Accept` for `unirest` using Mocha's `beforeEach()` method, so that setup occurs in only one place in the code. Mocha executes `beforeEach()` before running each test (i.e., `it`) within the context of the `describe`.

- Each test exercises one or more example JSONPath queries and uses `expect`-style assertions.

- The calls to the `jsonpath` module work as follows:
  - `jp.query()` takes a JavaScript Object and a String-based JSONPath query as parameters, and synchronously returns the result set as a JavaScript Object.

- Each JSONPath query omits the leading `.cities` because `json-server` takes the name of the `cities` Array (from the *cities-weather.json* file) and adds `cities` to the URI:
  - The URI address is *http://localhost:5000/cities.*
  - Use `$[:3]` to get the first three cities, rather than `$.cities[:3]`.

To run this test from the command line (in a second terminal session), do the following:

```
cd cities-weather-test
```

```
npm test
```

You should see the following results:

```
json-at-work => npm test

...

> mocha test

...
```

```
cities-jsonpath
  ✓ should return a 200 response
  ✓ should return all cities
  ✓ should return every other city
  ✓ should return the last city
  ✓ should return 1st 3 cities
  ✓ should return cities within a temperature range
  ✓ should return cities with cloudy weather
  ✓ should return cities with cloudy weather using regex


  ...
```

If you call `console.log()` with the `cities` variable in any of the preceding tests, you'll see that the `jsonpath` module returns a valid JSON document with key/value pairs.

JSONPath on other platforms

JSONPath is not limited to JavaScript and Node.js. Most major platforms have excellent support for JSONPath, including these:

- Ruby on Rails (*https://github.com/joshbuddy/jsonpath*)
- Python (*https://pypi.python.org/pypi/jsonpath/*)
- Java (*https://github.com/jayway/JsonPath*)

There are other good JSONPath libraries are available, but please verify that they follow the syntax mentioned in Stefan Goessner's article (*http://goessner.net/articles/Json Path*). Otherwise, it's not really JSONPath. To borrow a phrase from *The Princess Bride*, "You keep using that word, but I do not think it means what you think it means."

JSONPath scorecard

Table 6-2 provides a scorecard for JSONPath based on the evaluation criteria from the beginning of this chapter.

Table 6-2. JSONPath scorecard

Mindshare	Y
Dev community	Y
Platforms	JavaScript, Node.js, Java, Ruby on Rails
Intuitive	Y
Standard	N

JSONPath provides a rich set of set of search features and works across most major platforms. The only downsides are that JSONPath is not a standard and lacks a CLI implementation, but don't let that stop you from using it. JSONPath enjoys wide community usage and acceptance, and has an excellent online tester. JSONPath reduces the amount of code needed to search and access a JSON document, and gets the subset of data that you need.

JSON Pointer

JSON Pointer is a standard for accessing a single value within a JSON document. The JSON Pointer specification provides further details (*http://tools.ietf.org/html/rfc6901*). JSON Pointer's main purpose is to support the JSON Schema specification's `$ref` functionality in locating validation rules within a Schema (see Chapter 5).

JSON Pointer query syntax

For example, consider the following document:

```
{
  "cities": [
    {
      "id": 5386035,
      "name": "Rancho Palos Verdes"
    },
    {
      "id": 5392528,
      "name": "San Pedro"
    },
    {
      "id": 5358705,
      "name": "Huntington Beach"
    }
  ]
}
```

Table 6-3 describes the preceding document's common JSON Pointer query syntax:

Table 6-3. JSON Pointer queries

JSON Pointer query	Description
/cities	Get all cities in the Array.
/cities/0	Get the first city.
/cities/1/name	Get the name of the second city.

JSON Pointer query syntax is quite simple, and works as follows:

- / is a path separator.

- Array indexing is zero-based.

You'll notice that in the JSON Pointer specification, only the data values are returned when making a query, and that the keys are not returned.

JSON Pointer Unit Test

The Unit Test in Example 6-3 exercises some of the example JSON Pointer queries that were shown earlier. This code leverages the `json-pointer` Node.js module to search against the `cities` API. See *https://github.com/manuelstofer/json-pointer* for a detailed description of the `json-pointer` module.

Example 6-3. cities-weather-test/test/json-pointer-spec.js

```
'use strict';

/* Attribution: Cities Weather data provided by OpenWeatherMap API
   ([http://openweathermap.org]) under Creative Commons Share A Like
   License (https://creativecommons.org/licenses/by-sa/4.0).
   Changes were made to the data to work with json-server.
   This does not imply an endorsement by the licensor.

   This code is distributed under Creative Commons Share A Like License.
*/

var expect = require('chai').expect;
var pointer = require('json-pointer');
var unirest = require('unirest');

describe('cities-json-pointer', function() {
  var req;

  beforeEach(function() {
    req = unirest.get('http://localhost:5000/cities')
                 .header('Accept', 'application/json');
  });

  it('should return a 200 response', function(done) {
    req.end(function(res) {
      expect(res.statusCode).to.eql(200);
      expect(res.headers['content-type']).to.eql(
                 'application/json; charset=utf-8');
      done();
    });
  });

  it('should return the 1st city', function(done) {
    req.end(function(res) {
      var cities = res.body;
      var firstCity = null;
```

```
      firstCity = pointer.get(cities, '/0');
      expect(firstCity.name).to.eql('Rancho Palos Verdes');
      expect(firstCity.weather[0].main).to.eql('Clear');
      done();
    });
  });

  it('should return the name of the 2nd city', function(done) {
    req.end(function(res) {
      var cities = res.body;
      var secondCityName = null;

      secondCityName = pointer.get(cities, '/1/name');
      expect(secondCityName).to.eql("San Pedro");
      done();
    });
  });
});
```

Note the following in this example:

- Each test runs an example JSON Pointer query and leverages expect-style asser-tions.
- The calls to the json-pointer module work as follows:
  - pointer.get() takes a JavaScript Object and a String-based JSON Pointer query as parameters, and synchronously returns the result set as a JavaScript Object.
- Each JSON Pointer query omits the leading .cities because json-server takes the name of the cities Array (from the *cities-weather.json* file) and adds cities to the URI:
  - The URI address is *http://localhost:5000/cities*.
  - Use /0 to get the first city, rather than /cities/0.

To run this test from the command line, do the following:

```
cd cities-weather-test

npm test
```

You should see the following results:

```
json-at-work => npm test

...

> mocha test
```

```
...
cities-json-pointer
  ✓ should return a 200 response
  ✓ should return the 1st city
  ✓ should return the name of the 2nd city

...
```

If you invoke `console.log()` on the `firstCity` variable in the `should return the 1st city` test above, you'll see that the `json-pointer` module returns a valid JSON document with key/value pairs.

JSON Pointer on other platforms

In addition to Node.js, most major platforms have a JSON Pointer library:

- Ruby on Rails (*https://github.com/tent/json-pointer-ruby*)
- Python (*https://github.com/stefankoegl/python-json-pointer*)
- Java—Jackson currently supports JSON Pointer (*https://github.com/fge/jackson-coreutils*), but JavaEE 8 will provide JSON Pointer support as part of JSR 374, Java API for JSON Processing 1.1 (*http://bit.ly/2reREao*).

Several tools claim to implement JSON Pointer, but they really don't follow the JSON Pointer specification. When evaluating a JSON Pointer library or tool, be sure it follows RFC 6901 (*http://tools.ietf.org/html/rfc6901*). Again, if it doesn't expressly mention RFC 6901, it's not JSON Pointer.

JSON Pointer scorecard

Table 6-4 shows a scorecard for JSON Pointer based on our criteria.

Table 6-4. JSON Pointer scorecard

Mindshare	Y
Dev community	Y
Platforms	JavaScript, Node.js, Java, Ruby on Rails
Intuitive	Y
Standard	Y—RFC 6901

JSON Pointer provides a limited set of search capabilities. Each query returns only a single field from a JSON document. JSON Pointer's main purpose is to support JSON Schema's `$ref` syntax.

jq

jq is a JSON Search tool that provides JSON command-line processing, including filtering and array slicing. Per the jq GitHub repository (*https://stedolan.github.io/jq*), jq is like sed for JSON. But jq is not limited to the command line; several good libraries enable you to use jq from your favorite Unit-Testing framework ("jq Unit Test" on page 180 covers this).

Integration with cURL

Many people in the UNIX community use cURL (*http://curl.haxx.se*) to make HTTP calls to Web APIs from the command line. cURL provides the ability to communicate over multiple protocols in addition to HTTP. To install cURL, please see "Install cURL" on page 333 in Appendix A.

We'll start by using cURL to make a GET request from the command against the Cities API as follows:

```
curl  -X GET 'http://localhost:5000/cities'
```

Now that we're able to get a JSON response from the Cities API, let's pipe the content to jq to filter the Cities API data from the command line. Here's a simple example:

```
curl  -X GET 'http://localhost:5000/cities' | jq .[0]
```

Run this command, and you should see the following:

```
json-at-work => curl -X GET 'http://localhost:5000/cities' | jq .[0]
  % Total    % Received % Xferd  Average Speed   Time    Time     Time  Current
                                 Dload  Upload   Total   Spent    Left  Speed
100 57510  100 57510     0     0   806k      0 --:--:-- --:--:-- --:--:--  802k
{
  "id": 5386035,
  "name": "Rancho Palos Verdes",
  "coord": {
    "lon": -118.387016,
    "lat": 33.744461
  },
  "main": {
    "temp": 84.34,
    "pressure": 1012,
    "humidity": 58,
    "temp_min": 78.8,
    "temp_max": 93
  },
  "dt": 1442171078,
  "wind": {
    "speed": 4.1,
    "deg": 300
  },
  "clouds": {
    "all": 5
  },
  "weather": [
    {
      "id": 800,
      "main": "Clear",
      "description": "Sky is Clear",
      "icon": "02d"
    }
  ]
}
```

Note the following in this example:

- cURL makes an HTTP GET call to the OpenWeatherMap API and pipes the JSON response to Standard Output.

- jq reads the JSON from Standard Input, selects the first city from the API, and outputs the JSON to Standard Output.

cURL is a valuable and powerful part of an API developer's toolkit. cURL also provides the ability to test an API with all the main HTTP verbs (GET, POST, PUT, and DELETE). We've just scratched the surface with cURL; visit the main site (*http://curl.haxx.se*) to learn more.

jq query syntax

Table 6-5 shows some basic jq queries.

Table 6-5. jq queries

jq query	Description
`.cities[0]`	Get the first city. jq Array filtering starts at 0.
`.cities[-1]`	Get the last city. An index of -1 indicates the last element of an Array.
`.cities[0:3]`	Get the first three cities, where 0 is the start index (inclusive), and 3 is the end index (exclusive).
`.cities[:3]`	Get the first three cities. This is shorthand, and it omits the start index.
`.cities[] | select (.main.temp >= 80 and (.main.temp_min >= 79 and .main.temp_max <= 92))`	Get all cities whose current temperature is >= 80 degrees Fahrenheit and whose min and max temperature ranges between 79 and 92 degrees Fahrenheit (inclusive).

Here's how to execute a jq query to get the last city at the command line:

```
cd chapter-6/data

jq '.cities[-1]' cities-weather.json
```

You should see the following:

```
json-at-work => jq '.cities[-1]' cities-weather.json
{
  "id": 5374732,
  "name": "Moreno Valley",
  "coord": {
    "lon": -117.230591,
    "lat": 33.937519
  },
  "main": {
    "temp": 87.84,
    "pressure": 1013,
    "humidity": 42,
    "temp_min": 82.4,
    "temp_max": 98.6
  },
  "dt": 1442171075,
  "wind": {
    "speed": 1,
    "deg": 0
  },
  "clouds": {
    "all": 1
  },
  "weather": [
    {
      "id": 800,
      "main": "Clear",
      "description": "Sky is Clear",
      "icon": "01d"
    }
  ]
}
```

Let's go deeper with a more concrete example.

jq online tester—jqPlay

jqPlay (*https://jqplay.org*) is a web-based tester for jq, and provides the ability to iteratively test jq queries against JSON data. To test jqPlay, do the following to get a new Array of Objects that contain the id and name of the first three cities:

1. Visit *https://jqplay.org* and paste the contents of the *chapter-6/data/cities-weather.json* file into the JSON text area on the left.

2. Paste the following jq query into the Filter text box: [[].cities[0:3] | .[] | { id, name }]

You should see the screen in Figure 6-3.

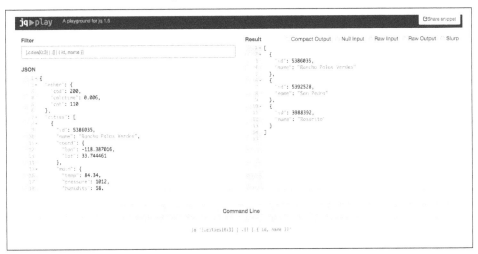

Figure 6-3. Search OpenWeather API data with jqPlay

Here's a breakdown of the [.cities[0:3] | .[] | { id, name }] query:

- The | enables you to chain your filters.
- .cities[0:3] selects the first three elements from the cities Array as a subarray.
- .[] returns all elements from the subarray.
- { id, name } selects only the id and name fields:
    — The curly braces ({ and }) tell jq to create a new Object.
    — The id and name tell jq to include only these fields in the new Object.
- The surrounding Array braces ([and]) convert the result set to an Array.

Scroll to the bottom of the `jqplay` page, and you'll see that it has a cheat sheet with links to more examples and documentation, as shown in Figure 6-4.

Figure 6-4. jq cheat sheet on jqPlay

jq-tutorial

In addition to an online tester, the Node.js community has contributed a nice `jq` tutorial, which is available on the npm repository (*https://www.npmjs.com/package/jq-tutorial*). Install this tutorial as follows:

```
npm install -g jq-tutorial
```

Run `jq-tutorial` from the command line, and you should see this:

```
json-at-work => jq-tutorial
Run jq-tutorial with one of the following:
    * pick
    * objects
    * mapping
    * filtering
    * output
    * reduce
```

This shows all the available `jq` tutorials. Then, choose one of the tutorials like this:

```
jq-tutorial objects
```

This tutorial will show how to use objects with `jq`. Follow each learning path, and increase your overall `jq` skill level.

jq Unit Test

The Unit Test in Example 6-4 exercises several of the example `jq` queries that were shown earlier. This code leverages the `node-jq` Node.js module (*https://www.npmjs.com/package/*) to search against the JSON data returned by the `Cities`

API that runs on your local machine. See the `node-jq` documentation on GitHub (*https://github.com/sanack/node-jq*) for a detailed description.

Example 6-4. cities-weather-test/test/jq-spec.js

```
'use strict';

/* Attribution: Cities Weather data provided by OpenWeatherMap API
   ([http://openweathermap.org]) under Creative Commons Share A Like
   License (https://creativecommons.org/licenses/by-sa/4.0).
   Changes were made to the data to work with json-server.
   This does not imply an endorsement by the licensor.

   This code is distributed under Creative Commons Share A Like License.
*/

var expect = require('chai').expect;
var jq = require('node-jq');
var unirest = require('unirest');
var _ = require('underscore');


describe('cities-jq', function() {
  var req;

  beforeEach(function() {
    req = unirest.get('http://localhost:5000/cities')
      .header('Accept', 'application/json');
  });

  it('should return a 200 response', function(done) {
    req.end(function(res) {
      expect(res.statusCode).to.eql(200);
      expect(res.headers['content-type']).to.eql(
        'application/json; charset=utf-8');
      done();
    });
  });

  it('should return all cities', function(done) {
    req.end(function(res) {
      var cities = res.body;

      expect(cities.length).to.eql(110);
      done();
    });
  });

  it('should return the last city', function(done) {
    req.end(function(res) {
      var cities = res.body;
```

```
    jq.run('.[-1]', cities, {
        input: 'json'
      })
      .then(function(lastCityJson) { // Returns JSON String.
        var lastCity = JSON.parse(lastCityJson);
        expect(lastCity.name).to.eql('Moreno Valley');
        done();
      })
      .catch(function(error) {
        console.error(error);
        done(error);
      });
  });
});

it('should return the 1st 3 cities', function(done) {
  req.end(function(res) {
    var cities = res.body;

    jq.run('.[:3]', cities, {
        input: 'json'
      })
      .then(function(citiesFirstThreeJson) { // Returns JSON String.
        var citiesFirstThree = JSON.parse(citiesFirstThreeJson);
        var citiesFirstThreeNames = getCityNamesOnly(
          citiesFirstThree);

        expect(citiesFirstThree.length).to.eql(3);
        expect(citiesFirstThreeNames.length).to.eql(3);
        expect(citiesFirstThreeNames).to.eql([
          'Rancho Palos Verdes',
          'San Pedro', 'Rosarito'
        ]);

        done();
      })
      .catch(function(error) {
        console.error(error);
        done(error);
      });
  });
});

function getCityNamesOnly(cities) {
  return _.map(cities,
    function(city) {
      return city.name;
    });
}

it('should return cities within a temperature range', function(done) {
```

```javascript
      req.end(function(res) {
        var cities = res.body;

        jq.run(
            '[.[] | select (.main.temp >= 84 and .main.temp <= 85.5)]',
            cities, {
              input: 'json'
            })
          .then(function(citiesTempRangeJson) { // Returns JSON String.
            var citiesTempRange = JSON.parse(citiesTempRangeJson);

            for (var i = 0; i < citiesTempRange.length; i++) {
              expect(citiesTempRange[i].main.temp).to.be.at.least(
                84);
              expect(citiesTempRange[i].main.temp).to.be.at.most(
                85.5);
            }

            done();
          })
          .catch(function(error) {
            console.error(error);
            done(error);
          });
      });
    });

    it('should return cities with cloudy weather', function(done) {
      req.end(function(res) {
        var cities = res.body;

        jq.run(
            '[.[] | select(.weather[0].main == "Clouds")]',
            cities, {
              input: 'json'
            })
          .then(function(citiesWeatherCloudyJson) { // Returns JSON String.
            var citiesWeatherCloudy = JSON.parse(
              citiesWeatherCloudyJson);

            checkCitiesWeather(citiesWeatherCloudy);

            done();
          })
          .catch(function(error) {
            console.error(error);
            done(error);
          });
      });
    });

    it('should return cities with cloudy weather using regex', function(done) {
```

```
req.end(function(res) {
  var cities = res.body;

  jq.run(
      '[.[] | select(.weather[0].main | test("^Clo"; "i"))]',
      cities, {
        input: 'json'
      })
    .then(function(citiesWeatherCloudyJson) { // Returns JSON String.
      var citiesWeatherCloudy = JSON.parse(
        citiesWeatherCloudyJson);

      checkCitiesWeather(citiesWeatherCloudy);

      done();
    })
    .catch(function(error) {
      console.error(error);
      done(error);
    });
  });
});

function checkCitiesWeather(cities) {
  for (var i = 0; i < cities.length; i++) {
    expect(cities[i].weather[0].main).to.eql('Clouds');
  }
}

});
```

Note the following in this example:

- The test sets up the URI and Accept for unirest using Mocha's beforeEach() method, so that setup occurs in only one place in the code. Mocha executes beforeEach() before running each test (i.e., it) within the context of the describe.

- Each test exercises one or more example jq queries and uses expect-style assertions.

- The calls to the node-jq module work as follows. jq.run() does the following:

  — Takes a String-based jq query as the first parameter.

  — Uses an optional second parameter (an Object) that specifies the type of input:

    — { input: 'json' } is a JavaScript Object. The Unit Tests use this option because unirest returns Objects from the HTTP call to the Stub API provided by json-server.

— { input: 'file' } is a JSON file. This is the default if the caller doesn't specify an input option.

— { input: 'string' } is a JSON String.

— Uses an ES6 JavaScript Promise to asynchronously return the result set as a JSON String. In this case, the Unit Tests all need to do the following:

— Wrap their code within the then and catch constructs of the Promise.

— Use JSON.parse() to parse the result into a corresponding JavaScript object structure.

— Visit the MDN site (*https://mzl.la/2r0Q4sy*) to learn more about the new Promise syntax.

- Each jq query omits the leading .cities because json-server takes the name of the cities Array (from the *cities-weather.json* file) and adds cities to the URI:

— The URI address is *http://localhost:5000/cities*.

— Use $[:3] to get the first three cities, rather than $.cities[:3].

To run this test from the command line (in a second terminal session), do the following:

```
cd cities-weather-test

npm test
```

You should see the following results:

```
json-at-work => npm test

...

> mocha test

...

  cities-jq
    ✓ should return a 200 response
    ✓ should return all cities
    ✓ should return the last city
    ✓ should return the 1st 3 cities
    ✓ should return cities within a temperature range
    ✓ should return cities with cloudy weather
    ✓ should return cities with cloudy weather using regex

...
```

If you call console.log() with the cities variable in any of these tests, you'll see that the node-jq module returns a valid JSON document with key/value pairs.

jq on other platforms

In addition to Node.js, other major platforms have a jq library:

Ruby

    The ruby-jq gem is available at RubyGems.org (*https://rubygems.org/gems/ruby-jq*), and you can also find it on GitHub (*https://github.com/winebarrel/ruby-jq*).

Java

    jackson-jq (*https://github.com/eiiches/jackson-jq*) plugs into the Java Jackson library (from Chapter 4).

jq scorecard

Table 6-6 shows how jq stacks up against our evaluation criteria.

Table 6-6. jq scorecard

Mindshare	Y
Dev community	Y
Platforms	CLI—Linux/macOS/Windows, Node.js, Java, Ruby on Rails
Intuitive	Y
Standard	N

jq is excellent because it

- Enjoys solid support in most languages.
- Has excellent documentation.
- Provides a rich set of search and filtering capabilities.
- Can pipe query results to standard UNIX CLI tools (for example, sort, grep, and uniq).
- Works great on the command line with the widely used cURL HTTP client.
- Has a fantastic online tester. jqPlay enables you to test jq queries from a simple web interface. This rapid feedback enables you to iterate to a solution before writing any code.
- Has a useful interactive tutorial (see the "jq-tutorial" section).

The only downside to jq is the initial learning curve. The sheer number of options along with the query syntax can seem overwhelming at first, but the time you spend to learn jq is well worth it.

We've covered the basics of jq in this chapter. jq has excellent documentation, and you can find more detailed information at the following websites:

- jq Manual (*https://stedolan.github.io/jq/manual*)

- jq Tutorial (*https://stedolan.github.io/jq/tutorial*)

- jq Cookbook (*https://github.com/stedolan/jq/wiki/Cookbook*)

- HyperPolyGlot JSON Tools: Jq (*http://hyperpolyglot.org/json*)

- Ubuntu jq man pages (*http://bit.ly/2rt8qBH*)

JSON Search Library and Tool Evaluations—The Bottom Line

Based on the evaluation criteria and overall usability, I rank the JSON Search libraries in the following order:

1. jq
2. JSONPath
3. JSON Pointer

Although JSON Pointer is a standard and it *can* search a JSON document, I rank JSONPath in second place over JSON Pointer for the following reasons:

- JSONPath has a richer query syntax.

- A JSONPath query returns multiple elements in a document.

But jq is my overwhelming favorite JSON Search tool because it

- Works from the command line (JSONPath and JSON Pointer don't provide this capability). If you work with JSON in automated DevOps environments, you need a tool that works from the command line.

- Has an online tester, which makes development faster.

- Has an interactive tutorial.

- Provides a rich query language.

- Has solid library support in most programming languages.

- Enjoys a large mindshare in the JSON community.

I've successfully used jq to search through JSON responses from other Web APIs (not from OpenWeatherMap) that contained over 2 million lines of data, and jq performed flawlessly in a production environment. jq enjoys great mindshare in the JSON community—just do a web search on "jq tutorial" and you'll see several excellent tutorials that will help you go deeper.

What We Covered

We've shown some of the more widely used JSON Search libraries and tools, and how to test search results. Hopefully, you're now convinced to use one or more of these JSON Search technologies to reduce your work rather than writing your own custom utilities.

What's Next?

Now that we've shown how to efficiently search JSON documents, we'll move on to transforming JSON in Chapter 7.

CHAPTER 7

JSON Transform

Your application(s) may take in data from multiple APIs, and you'll often need to convert their JSON response data to a format that integrates with your application architecture.

Many JSON Transform technologies enable you to convert between a JSON document and other data formats (e.g., HTML or XML) or a different JSON structure. Many developers will be familiar with some of these libraries (e.g., Mustache and Handlebars), but we'll show how to use them in nontraditional ways (more on that later). We'll also cover libraries (e.g., JSON-T) that are not well-known to the community at large, but are commonly used by members of the JSON community.

Types of JSON Transformation

Typical types of transformations include the following:

JSON-to-HTML
> Many web and mobile applications have to handle JSON data from APIs, and this is the most common type of JSON transformation.

JSON-to-JSON
> Sometimes the JSON response from a Web API isn't quite what you're looking for, and you'd like to change the format of the data to make it easier to work with. In this case, you can alter the structure by modifying values and/or removing, adding, and deleting fields. Some of the libraries are analogous to eXtensible Stylesheet Language Transformations (XSLT) for XML (which is used to transform XML documents) in that they use a separate template to describe the transformation.

JSON-XML

SOAP/XML-based Web Services still exist, and sometimes you need to consume XML and convert it to JSON for compatibility with newer applications in the enterprise that are based on REST and JSON. Conversely, your applications may need to send XML payloads to SOAP/XML-based Web Services. In this case, you'll need to convert from JSON to XML.

In this chapter, we'll show how to do the following:

- Convert JSON to HTML
- Convert a JSON document to a new (JSON) structure
- Convert between XML and JSON
- Use JSON Transform libraries
- Write Unit Tests that transform the content of JSON documents returned by a Web API

What to Look For in a JSON Transform Library

Just as you saw with JSON Search, several libraries are available for each type of transformation, and it's hard to choose which one(s) to use. We'll use the same criteria we did in Chapter 6:

Mindshare
Does it appear to be widely used? How many hits do you see when you do an internet search?

Developer community
Is the code on GitHub? Is it well maintained?

Platforms
Does it run on multiple platforms? Do multiple providers support the specification or library interfaces?

Intuitive
Is it well-documented? How easy is it to install? How intuitive is the interface? How easy is it to use? How much code do I need to write?

Standards
Is the library associated with an official standard (e.g., IETF, WC3, or Ecma)?

Test Input Data

We'll use the same OpenWeatherMap API data that we used in previous chapters for our examples. The original OpenWeatherMap API data was captured in *chapter-7/ data/cities-weather.json*. For the sake of brevity, Example 7-1 provides a shortened version of the data.

Example 7-1. data/cities-weather-short.json

```json
{
  "cities": [
    {
      "id": 5386035,
      "name": "Rancho Palos Verdes",
      "coord": {
        "lon": -118.387016,
        "lat": 33.744461
      },
      "main": {
        "temp": 84.34,
        "pressure": 1012,
        "humidity": 58,
        "temp_min": 78.8,
        "temp_max": 93
      },
      "dt": 1442171078,
      "wind": {
        "speed": 4.1,
        "deg": 300
      },
      "clouds": {
        "all": 5
      },
      "weather": [
        {
          "id": 800,
          "main": "Clear",
          "description": "Sky is Clear",
          "icon": "02d"
        }
      ]
    },
    {
      "id": 5392528,
      "name": "San Pedro",
      "coord": {
      "lon": -118.29229,
      "lat": 33.735851
      },
      "main": {
```

```
      "temp": 84.02,
      "pressure": 1012,
      "humidity": 58,
      "temp_min": 78.8,
      "temp_max": 91
    },
    "dt": 1442171080,
    "wind": {
      "speed": 4.1,
      "deg": 300
    },
    "clouds": {
      "all": 5
    },
    "weather": [
      {
        "id": 800,
        "main": "Clear",
        "description": "Sky is Clear",
        "icon": "02d"
      }
    ]
  },
  {
    "id": 3988392,
    "name": "Rosarito",
    "coord": {
      "lon": -117.033333,
      "lat": 32.333328
    },
    "main": {
      "temp": 82.47,
      "pressure": 1012,
      "humidity": 61,
      "temp_min": 78.8,
      "temp_max": 86
    },
    "dt": 1442170905,
    "wind": {
      "speed": 4.6,
      "deg": 240
    },
    "clouds": {
      "all": 32
    },
    "weather": [
      {
        "id": 802,
        "main": "Clouds",
        "description": "scattered clouds",
        "icon": "03d"
      }
```

```
          ]
        }
      ]
  }
}
```

Let's start with a JSON-to-HTML transformation.

JSON-to-HTML Transformation

Most developers should be familiar with converting JSON from an API response to HTML. For this type of conversion, we'll look at the following libraries:

- Mustache
- Handlebars

Target HTML Document

Refer to "Test Input Data" on page 191. We want to simplify the Cities data and display it in an HTML table as shown in Example 7-2.

Example 7-2. data/weather.html

```
<!DOCTYPE html>
<html>

  <head>
    <meta charset="UTF-8" />
    <title>OpenWeather - California Cities</title>
    <link rel="stylesheet" href="weather.css">
  </head>

  <body>
    <h1>OpenWeather - California Cities</h1>
    <table class="weatherTable">
      <thead>
        <tr>
          <th>City</th>
          <th>ID</th>
          <th>Current Temp</th>
        </tr>
      </thead>
      <tr>
        <td>Santa Rosa</td>
        <td>5201</td>
        <td>75</td>
      </tr>
    </table>
  </body>
```

```
</html>
```

We'll compare how each library converts the sample JSON input data to the target HTML document.

Mustache

Mustache uses templates that provide a declarative (codeless) way to convert data into other formats. In this case, we'll use it to convert JSON data to an HTML document. The Mustache team uses the term *logicless* to describe their library because templates contain only simple tags without if/then/else clauses or looping constructs. Based on the specification, Mustache expands the tags in a template file with values from a hash or an object that is populated by an application. The beauty of templates (regardless of whether you use Mustache or Handlebars, which reintroduces some conditional logic) is that this approach provides a separation of concerns by factoring out the transformation from application code to external files. External templates enable you to easily add/remove data formats or change how you do the data formatting without modifying application code.

For more information, see the following sites:

- Mustache main site (*http://mustache.github.io/*)
- Mustache GitHub repository (*https://github.com/janl/mustache.js*)
- Mustache 5 Specification (*http://mustache.github.io/mustache.5.html*)

Mustache template syntax

The Mustache template in Example 7-3 converts the OpenWeatherMap JSON data to HTML.

Example 7-3. templates/transform-html.mustache

```
<!DOCTYPE html>
<html>

  <head>
    <meta charset="UTF-8" />
    <title>OpenWeather - California Cities</title>
    <link rel="stylesheet" href="weather.css">
  </head>
  <body>
    <h1>OpenWeather - California Cities</h1>
    <table class="weatherTable">
      <thead>
        <tr>
```

```
      <th>City</th>
      <th>ID</th>
      <th>Current Temp</th>
      <th>Low Temp</th>
      <th>High Temp</th>
      <th>Humidity</th>
      <th>Wind Speed</th>
      <th>Summary</th>
      <th>Description</th>
    </tr>
  </thead>
  {{#cities}}
    <tr>
      <td>{{name}}</td>
      <td>{{id}}</td>
      {{#main}}
        <td>{{temp}}</td>
        <td>{{temp_min}}</td>
        <td>{{temp_max}}</td>
        <td>{{humidity}}</td>
      {{/main}}
      <td>{{wind.speed}}</td>
      {{#weather.0}}
        <td>{{main}}</td>
        <td>{{description}}</td>
      {{/weather.0}}
    </tr>
  {{/cities}}
  </table>
</body>

</html>
```

This template works as follows:

- The template is based on an HTML document, and Mustache expands each tag with data from the cities Array.
- A tag can represent a single field, such as: {{temp}}.
- Sections are enclosed within begin (for example, {{#cities}}) and end (for example, {{/cities}}) tags.
  — A section can correspond to an Array (e.g., cities) or an object (e.g., main).
  — A section sets the context for the other tags within that section. For example, the {{temp}} tag inside the {{main}} section could be expressed as {{main.temp}}, and corresponds to *main.temp* in the original JSON input document.

- The field syntax in a tag can refer to an Array index. For example, `{{#weather.0}}` refers to `weather[0]` from the input JSON document.

Next, we'll now show a Unit Test that renders the template with Cities data.

Mustache Unit Test

All tests in this chapter will continue to leverage Mocha/Chai, just as we saw in previous chapters. Before going further, be sure to set up your test environment. If you haven't installed Node yet, visit Appendix A, and install Node.js (see "Install Node.js" on page 320 and "Install npm Modules" on page 325). If you want to follow along with the Node.js project provided in the code examples, cd to *chapter-7/cities-weather-transform-test* and do the following to install all dependencies for the project:

```
npm install
```

If you'd like to set up the Node.js project yourself, follow the instructions in the book's GitHub repository (*https://github.com/tmarrs/json-at-work-examples/tree/master/chapter-7/Project-Setup.md*).

Example 7-4 uses the following Node.js modules:

Mustache
> This is available at *https://www.npmjs.com/package/mustache*. The corresponding GitHub repository can be found at *https://github.com/janl/mustache.js*.

`jsonfile`
> We'll use this module to read the OpenWeatherMap JSON data from a file and parse it. `jsonfile` is available at *https://www.npmjs.com/package/jsonfile*. Here's the `jsonfile` GitHub repository: *https://github.com/jprichardson/node-jsonfile*.

The Unit Test in Example 7-4 shows the example Mustache transformations in action.

Example 7-4. cities-weather-transform-test/test/mustache-spec.js

```
'use strict';

/* Attribution: Cities Weather data provided by OpenWeatherMap API
   ([http://openweathermap.org]) under Creative Commons Share A Like
   License (https://creativecommons.org/licenses/by-sa/4.0).
   Changes were made to the data to work with json-server.
   This does not imply an endorsement by the licensor.

   This code is distributed under Creative Commons Share A Like License.
*/

var expect = require('chai').expect;
var jsonfile = require('jsonfile');
var fs = require('fs');
```

```
var mustache = require('mustache');

describe('cities-mustache', function() {
  var jsonCitiesFileName = null;
  var htmlTemplateFileName = null;


  beforeEach(function() {
    var baseDir = __dirname + '/../..';

    jsonCitiesFileName = baseDir + '/data/cities-weather-short.json';
    htmlTemplateFileName = baseDir +
      '/templates/transform-html.mustache';
  });


  it('should transform cities JSON data to HTML', function(done) {
    jsonfile.readFile(jsonCitiesFileName, function(readJsonFileError,
      jsonObj) {
      if (!readJsonFileError) {
        fs.readFile(htmlTemplateFileName, 'utf8', function(
          readTemplateFileError, templateFileData) {
          if (!readTemplateFileError) {
            var template = templateFileData.toString();
            var html = mustache.render(template, jsonObj);

            console.log('\n\n\nHTML Output:\n' + html);
            done();
          } else {
            done(readTemplateFileError);
          }
        });
      } else {
        done(readJsonFileError);
      }
    });
  });
});
```

This code works as follows:

- beforeEach() runs before any Unit Test and does setup. In this case, it builds the filenames for the input JSON file and the Mustache template.

- In the 'should transform cities JSON data to HTML' Unit Test:
  - jsonfile.readFile() reads and parses the input JSON file into a JavaScript Object (jsonObj).
  - fs.readFile() reads the Mustache template into a JavaScript Object.
  - We then convert the Mustache template to a String.

— `mustache.render()` renders the Mustache template into an HTML document using the values provided by `jsonObj` (which was read in earlier).

Before you run the Unit Test, open a terminal session and run `json-server` on port 5000 from your command line:

```
cd chapter-7/data
```

```
json-server -p 5000 ./cities-weather-short.json
```

Next, run the preceding test from a second terminal session as follows:

```
cd chapter-7/cities-weather-transform-test
```

```
npm test
```

You'll see an HTML document that looks like our HTML target document.

Mustache online tester

The Architect template editor (*http://rowno.github.io/architect/*) is an excellent online tester that makes it easy to iteratively test and develop a Mustache template. This tool is great, because it shows how the result changes as you modify the template. This WYSIWIG (What-You-See-Is-What-You-Get) output enables rapid development and debugging.

In the Architect online tool, select *Mustache.js* in the Engine drop-down, paste the Mustache template, and input JSON into the Template and View text boxes (respectively). You should see the screen in Figure 7-1.

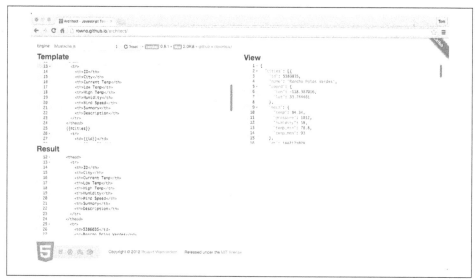

Figure 7-1. Architect: JSON-to-HTML transformation with Mustache

The Architect template editor also works with several other templating engines, including Handlebars (which is covered in the next section), so this is my favorite online template editor.

Remember that this web application is publicly available:

- Any data you paste into this app is visible to others. So don't use this tool with sensitive information (personal, proprietary, and so forth).
- A large amount of data will flood your browser. I've been successful with up to about 10,000 lines of JSON, but after that this application begins to freeze up.

Mustache on the command line

Mustache also works directly from the command line. If you have installed Node.js, do a global installation of the Mustache Node.js module and run it from the command line (within the book example code directory) as follows:

```
npm install -g mustache

cd chapter-7

mustache ./data/cities-weather-short.json \
    ./templates/transform-html.mustache > output.html
```

Mustache on other platforms

A quick glance at the Mustache site (*http://mustache.github.io/*) will show that Mustache enjoys wide cross-platform support, including the following:

- Node.js (*https://www.npmjs.com/package/mustache*)
- Ruby on Rails (*http://github.com/defunkt/mustache*)
- Java (*https://github.com/spullara/mustache.java*)

Mustache scorecard

Table 7-1 shows a scorecard for Mustache based on the evaluation criteria from the beginning of this chapter.

Table 7-1. Mustache scorecard

Mindshare	Y
Dev community	Y
Platforms	JavaScript, Node.js, Java, Ruby on Rails
Intuitive	Y
Standard	N

Overall, Mustache is a powerful and flexible template engine used by many web developers. Although it's not a standard, Mustache has a solid specification.

Let's move on and take a look at Handlebars.

Handlebars

Handlebars is an extension of Mustache, and it also expands the tags in a template file with values from a hash or an object. Handlebars and Mustache are highly compatible, and Mustache templates will usually work with the Handlebars engine. HTML conversion is pretty simple, and we won't see any major differences between Mustache and Handlebars for now. Handlebars adds a few more features to enhance transformation, and we'll cover them in "JSON-to-JSON Transform" on page 206. For more information on Handlebars, see the following:

- Handlebars main site (*http://handlebarsjs.com*) (click the Learn More buttons for further details)
- Handlebars GitHub repository (*https://github.com/wycats/handlebars.js*)

Differences between Handlebars and Mustache

Handlebars extends Mustache by providing additional capabilities, which include the following:

Conditional logic
Handlebars has built-in helpers such as `if` and `unless`. We'll show how to leverage `unless` in "JSON-to-JSON Transform" on page 206.

Helpers
Handlebars allows a developer to register custom helpers to extend Handlebars. Each custom helper provides an additional directive that can be used in a template. For example, you could add a `{{fullName}}` helper that would combine the `firstName` and `lastName` elements for a `speaker`. Helpers are powerful, but we don't cover them further in this book. See the Handlebars website (*http://handlebarsjs.com/#helpers*) and Jasko Koyn's Custom Helpers Handlebars.js Tuto-

rial (*http://jaskokoyn.com/2013/08/08/custom-helpers-handlebars-js-tutorial*) for more information on Handlebars helpers.

The Handlebars GitHub site (*https://github.com/wycats/handlebars.js#differences-between-handlebarsjs-and-mustache*) has a full description of the differences between Handlebars and Mustache.

Handlebars template syntax

Let's use the Handlebars template in Example 7-5 to transform the input JSON to an HTML document.

Example 7-5. templates/transform-html.hbs

```
<!DOCTYPE html>
<html>

  <head>
    <meta charset="UTF-8" />
    <title>OpenWeather - California Cities</title>
    <link rel="stylesheet" href="weather.css">
  </head>
  <body>
    <h1>OpenWeather - California Cities</h1>
    <table class="weatherTable">
      <thead>
        <tr>
          <th>ID</th>
          <th>City</th>
          <th>Current Temp</th>
          <th>Low Temp</th>
          <th>High Temp</th>
          <th>Humidity</th>
          <th>Wind Speed</th>
          <th>Summary</th>
          <th>Description</th>
        </tr>
      </thead>
      {{#each cities}}
      <tr>
        <td>{{id}}</td>
        <td>{{name}}</td>
        {{#main}}
          <td>{{temp}}</td>
          <td>{{temp_min}}</td>
          <td>{{temp_max}}</td>
          <td>{{humidity}}</td>
        {{/main}}
        <td>{{wind.speed}}</td>
        {{#each weather}}
          <td>{{main}}</td>
```

```
        <td>{{description}}</td>
      {{/each}}
    </tr>
    {{/each}}
  </table>
</body>

</html>
```

This template works as follows:

- Handlebars expands each tag with data from the `cities` Array.
- A tag can represent a single field, such as `{{temp}}`.
- Sections are enclosed within begin (e.g., `{{#each cities}}`) and end (e.g., `{{/cities}}`) tags.
  - A section can correspond to an Array (e.g., `cities`) or an object (e.g., `main`).
  - The each tag (e.g., `{{#each cities}}`) is used for arrays (in this case, `cities`).
  - A section sets the context for the other tags within that section. For example, the `{{temp}}` tag inside the `{{main}}` section could be expressed as `{{main.temp}}`, and corresponds to *main.temp* in the original JSON input document.

Handlebars Unit Test

The Unit Test in Example 7-6 uses a Handlebars template to render HTML with the Cities data.

Example 7-6. cities-weather-transform-test/test/handlebars-spec.js

```
'use strict';

/* Attribution: Cities Weather data provided by OpenWeatherMap API
   ([http://openweathermap.org]) under Creative Commons Share A Like
   License (https://creativecommons.org/licenses/by-sa/4.0).
   Changes were made to the data to work with json-server.
   This does not imply an endorsement by the licensor.

   This code is distributed under Creative Commons Share A Like License.
*/

var expect = require('chai').expect;
var jsonfile = require('jsonfile');
var fs = require('fs');
var handlebars = require('handlebars');
```

```
describe('cities-handlebars', function() {
  var jsonCitiesFileName = null;
  var htmlTemplateFileName = null;


  beforeEach(function() {
    var baseDir = __dirname + '/../..';

    jsonCitiesFileName = baseDir + '/data/cities-weather-short.json';
    htmlTemplateFileName = baseDir +
      '/templates/transform-html.hbs';
  });


  it('should transform cities JSON data to HTML', function(done) {
    jsonfile.readFile(jsonCitiesFileName, function(readJsonFileError,
      jsonObj) {
      if (!readJsonFileError) {
        fs.readFile(htmlTemplateFileName, 'utf8', function(
          readTemplateFileError, templateFileData) {
          if (!readTemplateFileError) {
            var template = handlebars.compile(templateFileData);
            var html = template(jsonObj);

            console.log('\n\n\nHTML Output:\n' + html);
            done();
          } else {
            done(readTemplateFileError);
          }
        });
      } else {
        done(readJsonFileError);
      }
    });
  });
});
```

This Handlebars Unit Test is practically identical to its Mustache counterpart, with the following differences:

- We don't need to convert the Handlebars template (that is, read from `fs.read File()`) to a String.
- It takes two steps to render the template:
  - `handlebars.compile()` compiles the template into the `template` variable.
  - `template()` (from the compile) then renders the `jsonObj` (input JSON) into HTML.

When you run the preceding test with `npm test`, you'll see a second HTML document that looks like our HTML target document.

Handlebars online testers

Two excellent online testers make it easy to iteratively test and develop a Handlebars template: TryHandlebars and Architect.

To use TryHandlebars (*http://tryhandlebarsjs.com/*), copy the Handlebars template and JSON into the Handlebars Template and Context text boxes. The result is shown in Figure 7-2.

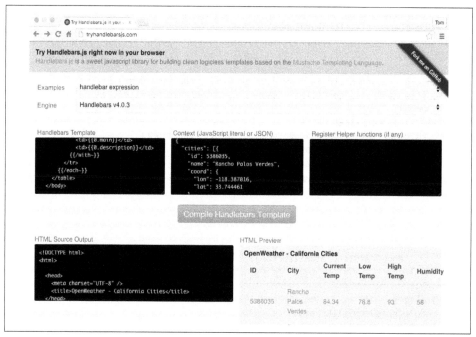

Figure 7-2. Try Handlebars.js: JSON-to-HTML transformation with Handlebars

You can also use the Architect template editor (*http://rowno.github.io/architect*). Select *Handlebars.js* in the Engine drop-down, paste the Handlebars template, and input JSON into the Template and View text boxes (respectively). Click the Compile Handlebars Template button, and you should see the result shown in Figure 7-3.

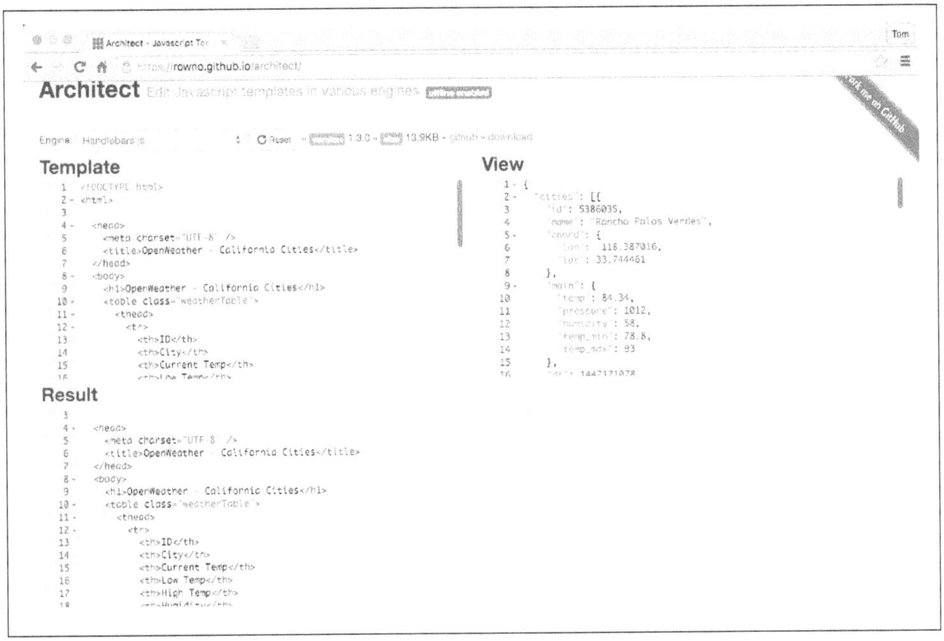

Figure 7-3. Architect: JSON-to-HTML transformation with Handlebars

Handlebars on the command line

Handlebars also works directly from the command line. If you have installed Node.js, do a global installation of the hb-interpolate module (*https://www.npmjs.com/pack age/hb-interpolate*), which is also available on GitHub (*https://github.com/jimlloyd/hb-interpolate*):

```
npm install -g hb-interpolate

cd chapter-7

hb-interpolate -j ./data/cities-weather-short.json \
    -t ./templates/transform-html.hbs > output.html
```

Handlebars on other platforms

Handlebars enjoys wide cross-platform support, including the following:

- Node.js (*https://www.npmjs.com/package/handlebars*)
- Ruby on Rails (*https://github.com/cowboyd/handlebars-rails*)
- Java (*https://github.com/jknack/handlebars.java*)

Handlebars scorecard

Table 7-2 provides a scorecard for Handlebars based on the evaluation criteria from the beginning of this chapter.

Table 7-2. Handlebars scorecard

Mindshare	Y
Dev community	Y
Platforms	JavaScript, Node.js, Java, Ruby on Rails
Intuitive	Y
Standard	N

Handlebars is another excellent engine that is used by many web developers. Just like Mustache, Handlebars isn't a standard, and it too has a solid specification and works across multiple platforms.

JSON-to-HTML Transformation Evaluations—The Bottom Line

Mustache and Handlebars are both excellent choices for converting JSON to HTML, and you'll be fine with either library.

We've covered JSON-to-HTML conversion, and now it's time to cover JSON-to-JSON transformation.

JSON-to-JSON Transform

If you've worked with APIs for any length of time in a professional setting, you've come to realize that APIs don't always work the way you want them to. The JSON response from an API is often the most overlooked part of an API's design, and the data provided by an API is often difficult to use. Even if the data is well-designed, you may not want to use all of it or you may want to convert it to another JSON structure that is better suited to the consuming application (or other applications in your system).

Similar to the discussion in Chapter 6, you could do the following:

- Parse the JSON data from an API and manipulate the resulting hash structure programmatically
- Write custom code to convert between an input JSON document and another JSON structure

But these approaches are tedious and difficult. There's no need to write this type of utility code, because libraries are available to do most of the work for you.

The Issues

The biggest issue I've seen in the area of JSON-to-JSON transformation is the lack of standards (official or de facto). In the previous chapter, for example, even though JSONPath is not an official standard, it is a de facto standard. JSONPath is a concept and query language with wide acceptance and implementations on multiple platforms. But with the JSON Transform libraries, it was difficult to find something that was more than just a single-language/platform implementation. I was looking for products that could transcend individual platforms and serve a larger, more universal purpose in the community. It was a journey to find the best solutions, but a few JSON Transform libraries are better than a one-off solution, and I hope you find them useful for your projects.

JSON-to-JSON Transform Libraries

Several libraries (callable from an application) can transform JSON documents. We'll look into the following libraries:

- JSON Patch
- JSON-T
- Mustache
- Handlebars

If you're in a hurry, Handlebars is the best choice for JSON-to-JSON transformation (see "Handlebars" on page 221 and "JSON-to-JSON Transformation Evaluations— The Bottom Line" on page 223). Otherwise, let's walk through the various JSON-to-JSON transformation techniques so you can see why.

Honorable Mention

Several JSON Transform libraries are available, but we can't cover all of them. Here are three additional libraries that are worth a look:

Jolt (http://bazaarvoice.github.io/jolt)
    Jolt works only in Java environments.

Json2Json (https://github.com/joelvh/json2json)
    Json2Json is only available for Node.js.

`jsonapter` *(https://github.com/amida-tech/jsonapter)*
    `jsonapter` transforms JSON data in a declarative manner that leverages an external template with transformation rules. The template is analogous to XSL, but that's where the similarities stop. `jsonapter` and its template rules are in pure

JavaScript, but XSL had its own separate templating language. Unfortunately, jso napter works only with JavaScript and Node.js.

Target JSON Output

Refer to "Test Input Data" on page 191 earlier in this chapter. Even though there are only three elements in the cities array, the data is overly complex for our use. We don't want to use all of these fields, so let's simplify the structure as follows:

- Keep the cities array along with id and name.
- Make a completely new, flattened weather object.
- Add other weather-related fields from other structures to weather:
  — main.temp, main.humidity, main.temp_min, main.temp_max
  — wind.speed
  — weather.0.main and weather.0.description
- Rename fields for the sake of clarity.

Given these transformation rules, the output should look like Example 7-7.

Example 7-7. data/cities-weather-short-transformed.json

```
{
  "cities": [
    {
      "id": "5386035",
      "name": "Rancho Palos Verdes",
      "weather": {
        "currentTemp": 84.34,
        "lowTemp": 78.8,
        "hiTemp": 93,
        "humidity": 58,
        "windSpeed": 4.1,
        "summary": "Clear"
        "description": "Sky is Clear"
      }
    },
    {
      "id": "5392528",
      "name": "San Pedro",
      "weather": {
        "currentTemp": 84.02,
        "lowTemp": 78.8,
        "hiTemp": 91,
        "humidity": 58,
        "windSpeed": 4.1,
        "summary": "Clear"
```

```
      "description": "Sky is Clear"
    }
  },
  {
    "id": "3988392",
    "name": "Rosarito",
    "weather": {
      "currentTemp": 82.47,
      "lowTemp": 78.8,
      "hiTemp": 86,
      "humidity": 61,
      "windSpeed": 4.6,
      "summary": "Clouds"
      "description": "scattered clouds"
    }
  }
  ]
}
```

We'll evaluate each of the JSON Transform libraries based on how easy it is to convert the sample JSON input data to the target JSON output.

JSON Patch

JSON Patch is an IETF standard (*http://tools.ietf.org/html/rfc6902*) that specifies a data format for operations that transform a single resource. JSON Patch works in conjunction with the HTTP PATCH standard (*http://tools.ietf.org/html/rfc5789*). The purpose of HTTP PATCH is to modify a resource produced by an API. In short, HTTP PATCH changes a *portion* of a resource, whereas HTTP PUT *replaces* the resource entirely.

JSON Patch is supposed to be used as part of an HTTP Request, and not the Response. JSON Patch is really meant for an API Producer, and not the Consumer. But the context of this chapter is from the API Consumer's point of view, and we'll see how far we can go with JSON Patch to transform the data in an HTTP Response.

JSON Patch syntax

Table 7-3 shows the main JSON Patch operations that could be used with the Open-WeatherMap data.

Table 7-3. JSON Patch operations

JSON Patch operation	Description
Add - { "op": "add", "path": "/wind", "value": { "direction": "W" } }	Adds a value to either an existing Object or an Array. It can't create a completely new Object in a document.
Remove - { "op": "remove", "path": "/main" }	Removes the main Object.

JSON Patch operation	Description
Replace - { "op": "replace", "path": "/weather/0/main", "value": "Rain" }	Replaces a value in the document. This is the same as doing a remove followed by an add.
Copy - { "op": "copy", "from": "/main/temp", "path": "/weather/0/temp" }	Copies a value from one field to another.
Move - { "op": "move", "from": "/main/temp", "path": "/weather/0/temp" }	Moves the temp key/value pair from the main Object to the weather Array.

For a full description of JSON Patch, visit the main Patch site (*http://jsonpatch.com/*). Each value for path and from is a JSON Pointer, which was covered in Chapter 6.

JSON Patch Unit Test

The Unit Test in Example 7-8 shows the example transformations in action. This code uses the JSON Patch Node.js module (*https://www.npmjs.com/package/json-patch*). Patch has a corresponding GitHub repository (*https://github.com/bruth/jsonpatch-js*).

The Unit Test in Example 7-8 shows how to use JSON Patch to transform the Cities weather data to the target JSON data structure.

Example 7-8. cities-weather-transform-test/test/json-patch-spec.json

```
'use strict';

/* Attribution: Cities Weather data provided by OpenWeatherMap API
   ([http://openweathermap.org]) under Creative Commons Share A Like
   License (https://creativecommons.org/licenses/by-sa/4.0).
   Changes were made to the data to work with json-server.
   This does not imply an endorsement by the licensor.

   This code is distributed under Creative Commons Share A Like License.
*/

var expect = require('chai').expect;
var jsonfile = require('jsonfile');
var jsonpatch = require('json-patch');

var citiesTemplate = [
  {
    op: 'remove',
    path: '/coord'
  },
  {
    op: 'remove',
    path: '/dt'
  },
  {
    op: 'remove',
    path: '/clouds'
```

```
  },
  {
    op: 'remove',
    path: '/weather/0/id'
  },
  {
    op: 'remove',
    path: '/weather/0/icon'
  },
  {
    op: 'move',
    from: '/main/temp',
    path: '/weather/0/currentTemp'
  },
  {
    op: 'move',
    from: '/main/temp_min',
    path: '/weather/0/lowTemp'
  },
  {
    op: 'move',
    from: '/main/temp_max',
    path: '/weather/0/hiTemp'
  },
  {
    op: 'move',
    from: '/main/humidity',
    path: '/weather/0/humidity'
  },
  {
    op: 'move',
    from: '/weather/0/main',
    path: '/weather/0/summary'
  },
  {
    op: 'move',
    from: '/wind/speed',
    path: '/weather/0/windSpeed'
  },
  {
    op: 'remove',
    path: '/main'
  },
  {
    op: 'remove',
    path: '/wind'
  }
];

describe('cities-json-patch', function() {
  var jsonFileName = null;
  var jsonCitiesFileName = null;
```

```
beforeEach(function() {
  var baseDir = __dirname + '/../../data';

  jsonCitiesFileName = baseDir + '/cities-weather-short.json';
});

it('should patch all cities - fail', function(done) {
  jsonfile.readFile(jsonCitiesFileName, function(fileReadError,
    jsonObj) {
    if (!fileReadError) {
      try {
        var output = jsonpatch.apply(jsonObj, citiesTemplate);

        console.log('\n\n\n\Original JSON');
        console.log(jsonObj);
        console.log('\n\n\n\Patched JSON');
        console.log(JSON.stringify(output, null, 2));
        done();
      } catch (transformError) {
        console.error(transformError);
        done(transformError);
      }
    } else {
      console.error(fileReadError);
      done(fileReadError);
    }
  });
});

...

});
```

In the example code, the test runs an example JSON Patch transformation. To run this test from the command line, do the following:

```
cd cities-weather-transform-test

npm test
```

As you'll notice, the `should patch all cities - fail` test fails as follows:

```
cities-json-patch
{ [PatchConflictError: Value at coord does not exist]
message: 'Value at coord does not exist',
name: 'PatchConflictError' }
  1) should patch all cities - fail
```

In this example, JSON Patch can't find the following path to */coord* because the underlying JSON Pointer works only with individual objects, and not collections.

Example 7-9 is a second test that *almost* works.

Example 7-9. cities-weather-transform-test/test/json-patch-spec.json

```
...

describe('cities-json-patch', function() {
  var jsonFileName = null;
  var jsonCitiesFileName = null;

  beforeEach(function() {
    var baseDir = __dirname + '/../../data';

    jsonCitiesFileName = baseDir + '/cities-weather-short.json';
  });

  ...

  it('should patch all cities - success (kind of)', function(done) {
    jsonfile.readFile(jsonCitiesFileName, function(fileReadError,
      jsonObj) {
      if (!fileReadError) {
        try {
          console.log('\n\n\n\Original JSON');
          console.log(jsonObj);
          var output = [];

          for (var i in jsonObj['cities']) {
            output.push(jsonpatch.apply(jsonObj['cities'][i],
              citiesTemplate));
          }

          console.log('\n\n\n\Patched JSON');
          console.log(JSON.stringify(output, null, 2));
          done();
        } catch (transformError) {
          console.error(transformError);
          done(transformError);
        }
      } else {
        console.error(fileReadError);
        done(fileReadError);
      }
    });
  });

});
```

Although the should patch all cities - success (kind of) test runs, it doesn't *quite* work for the following reasons:

- We want to create a new weather Object rather than use the existing Array, but JSON Patch doesn't allow for that.

- The test code iterates over the input JSON and transforms each element in the cities array, and then collects the results in the output Array. This is needed because JSON Patch can work only on a single resource (an Object) rather than a collection (an Array).

JSON Patch on other platforms

Because JSON Patch is a standard, it enjoys cross-platform support (besides just Node.js), including the following:

- Java (*https://github.com/fge/json-patch*)
- Ruby (*https://github.com/guillec/json-patch*)

See *http://jsonpatch.com/#libraries* for more platform and library support.

JSON Patch scorecard

Table 7-4 shows a scorecard for JSON Patch based on the evaluation criteria from the beginning of this chapter.

Table 7-4. JSON Patch scorecard

Mindshare	Y
Dev community	Y
Platforms	JavaScript, Node.js, Java, Ruby on Rails
Intuitive	N
Standard	Y - RFC 6902

JSON Patch limitations

JSON Patch has the following limitations:

- JSON Patch doesn't allow you to add completely new data structures. It can only modify existing structures and their data.
- JSON Patch is designed only to change a single Object, and isn't designed to work with Arrays. This is because JSON Patch uses JSON Pointer to search for data, where each query returns only a single field from a JSON document.

JSON Patch is not meant to transform the JSON data from an API's HTTP Response, but it was worth a try. JSON Patch is really designed to work with HTTP PATCH, which specifies how to use JSON to patch portions of a resource's data through an HTTP Request. JSON Patch is a great fit when you need to implement HTTP PATCH for an API.

But better libraries are available to transform JSON to other JSON data structures, so let's move on and try JSON-T.

JSON-T

JSON-T was one of the early JSON transform libraries, and it was developed in 2006 by Stefan Goessner (who also created JSONPath). JSON-T is similar to XSLT for XML, and uses a template that contains transformation rules.

JSON-T syntax

JSON-T uses transformation rules defined in a JavaScript Object Literal, where each rule is a key/value pair. Rules are in the following form:

```
var transformRules = {
  'ruleName': 'transformationRule',
  'ruleName': function
  ...
};
```

Note the following in the preceding form:

- Each `ruleName` or `transformationRule` must be enclosed by single (`''`) or double (`""`) quotes.
- Each `transformationRule` has one or more conversion expressions surrounded by curly braces, like this: `{cities}`.
- A conversion expression can evaluate to another `ruleName` or to a field in the document—an Array, Object, or key/value pair.

The following example shows the JSON-T transformation rules that could be used to transform the OpenWeatherMap data:

```
var transformRules = {
  'self': '{ "cities": [{cities}] }',
  'cities[*]': '{ "id": "{$.id}", "name": "{$.name}", ' +
    '"weather": { "currentTemp": {$.main.temp}, "lowTemp": {$.main.temp_min}, ' +
    '"hiTemp": {$.main.temp_max}, "humidity": {$.main.humidity}, ' +
    '"windSpeed": {$.wind.speed}, "summary": "{$.weather[0].main}", ' +
    '"description": "{$.weather[0].description}" } },'
};
```

This example works as follows:

- `self` is the top-level rule that specifies how to format the new JSON document, and `{cities}` refers to the `cities[*]` rule.
- `cities[*]` specifies how to format the `cities` Array:

— The star syntax in the `cities[*]` rule indicates that the rule applies to the cities Array elements.

— The * resolves to each Array index.

— `{$.}` is shorthand notation. The `{$.name}` rule tells JSON-T to pull data from the name field of each cities Array element. Here's the longer notation: `cities[*].name`.

For complete documentation on transformation rules, see "Basic Rules" on the main JSON-T site (*http://goessner.net/articles/jsont/*).

JSON-T Unit Test

The Unit Test in Example 7-10 shows how to use JSON-T, and leverages the jsont Node.js module (*https://github.com/tlrobinson/jsont*).

Example 7-10. cities-weather-transform-test/test/jsont-spec.js

```
'use strict';

/* Attribution: Cities Weather data provided by OpenWeatherMap API
   ([http://openweathermap.org]) under Creative Commons Share A Like
   License (https://creativecommons.org/licenses/by-sa/4.0).
   Changes were made to the data to work with json-server.
   This does not imply an endorsement by the licensor.

   This code is distributed under Creative Commons Share A Like License.
*/

var expect = require('chai').expect;
var jsonfile = require('jsonfile');
var jsonT = require('../lib/jsont').jsonT;

describe('cities-jsont', function() {
  var jsonCitiesFileName = null;

  var transformRules = {
    'self': '{ "cities": [{cities}] }',
    'cities[*]': '{ "id": "{$.id}", "name": "{$.name}", ' +
      '"weather": { "currentTemp": {$.main.temp}, "lowTemp": {$.main.temp_min}, ' +
      '"hiTemp": {$.main.temp_max}, "humidity": {$.main.humidity}, ' +
      '"windSpeed": {$.wind.speed}, "summary": "{$.weather[0].main}", ' +
      '"description": "{$.weather[0].description}" } },'
  };

  ...

  beforeEach(function() {
    var baseDir = __dirname + '/../../data';
```

```
    jsonCitiesFileName = baseDir + '/cities-weather-short.json';
  });

  it('should transform cities JSON data', function(done) {
    jsonfile.readFile(jsonCitiesFileName, function(readFileError,
      jsonObj) {
      if (!readFileError) {
        var jsonStr = jsonT(jsonObj, transformRules);

        jsonStr = repairJson(jsonStr);
        console.log(JSON.stringify(JSON.parse(jsonStr), null, 2));
        done();
      } else {
        done(readFileError);
      }
    });
  });
});
```

Notice that the preceding test invokes the repairJson() function in order to produce
valid JSON:

```
function repairJson(jsonStr) {
  var repairedJsonStr = jsonStr;

  var repairs = [
    [/,\s*}/gi, ' }'],
    [/,\s*\]/gi, ' ]']
  ];

  for (var i = 0, len = repairs.length; i < len; ++i) {
    repairedJsonStr = repairedJsonStr.replace(repairs[i][0], repairs[i][1]);
  }

  return repairedJsonStr;
}

// Modify the spec as follows:

...
jsonStr = repairJson(jsonStr);
console.log(JSON.stringify(JSON.parse(jsonStr), null, 2));
...
```

Without any modification, JSON-T produces a trailing comma after the last element
of the cities Array, so the transformed JSON would be invalid "as is." To fix this, the
repairJson() function in the preceding example uses a Regular Expression (Regex)
to eliminate the final comma before the closing curly object bracket (}) or Array
brace (]). Although most languages have Regex functionality, this is bad because you

have to add custom code to correct the output. You shouldn't have to write your own infrastructure.

JSON-T on other platforms

In addition to Node.js, JSON-T runs on the following platforms:

In the browser
> JSON-T runs as a JavaScript file, *jsont.js* (*http://goessner.net/download/prj/jsont/jsont.js*).

Ruby
> JSON-T can run as a pure Ruby implementation (*https://rubygems.org/gems/jsont/versions/0.1.3*).

I haven't been able to find a pure Java implementation of JSON-T.

JSON-T scorecard

Table 7-5 shows a scorecard for JSON-T based on the evaluation criteria from the beginning of this chapter.

Table 7-5. JSON-T scorecard

Mindshare	Y
Dev community	Y
Platforms	JavaScript, Node.js, Ruby on Rails
Intuitive	N
Standard	N

JSON-T limitations

JSON-T has the following limitations:

- Overly complex syntax.
- No Java implementation.
- Can't handle an escaped String within a String. For example, JSON-T takes the String, `"escapedString": "I have a \"string within\" a string"` and converts it to the following invalid String: `"escapedString": "I have a "string within " a string"`. Again, this requires a Regular Expression to fix the problem.
- Can't handle the last element in an Array or Object.

JSON-T is a small improvement over JSON Patch because JSON-T can process an entire document. But JSON-T still requires a developer to write additional code to make it work. JSON-T is a step in the right direction, but it still won't work in a real development environment. JSON-T is good at converting JSON to HTML, but it's not designed to convert from one JSON document to another JSON structure.

Let's move on and check out Mustache.

Mustache

In the previous section, we saw how Mustache can easily convert from JSON to HTML. We'll now see how well it can convert the Cities data to the target JSON output document.

Example 7-11 is a Mustache template to do the conversion (template details were described in the JSON-to-HTML section on Mustache).

Example 7-11. templates/transform-json.mustache

```
{
  "cities": [
    {{#cities}}
      {
        "id": "{{id}}",
        "name": "{{name}}",
        "weather": {
          {{#main}}
          "currentTemp": {{temp}},
          "lowTemp": {{temp_min}},
          "hiTemp": {{temp_max}},
          "humidity": {{humidity}},
          {{/main}}
          "windSpeed": {{wind.speed}},
          {{#weather.0}}
          "summary": "{{main}}"
          "description": "{{description}}"
          {{/weather.0}}
        }
      },
    {{/cities}}
  ]
}
```

Let's run this template in the Architect template editor (*http://rowno.github.io/archi tect/*). Select *Mustache.js* in the Engine drop-down, paste the Mustache template, and input JSON into the Template and View text boxes (respectively). You should see the result in Figure 7-4.

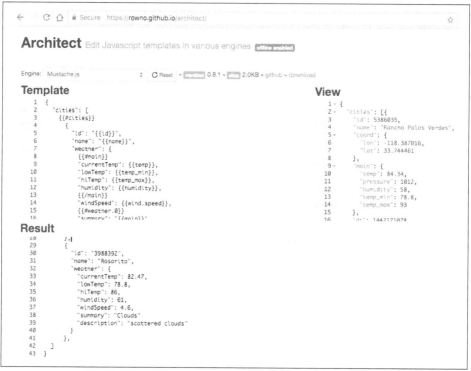

Figure 7-4. Architect: JSON-to-JSON transformation with Mustache

Take a look at line 41 of the resulting JSON (in the Result text box) and you'll see the trailing comma, which is invalid JSON. You can confirm that the resulting JSON is invalid by pasting it into JSONLint:

Results

```
Error: Parse error on line 11:
...ummary": "Clear"              "description": "Sky
----------------------^
Expecting 'EOF', '}', ':', ',', ']', got 'STRING'
```

Mustache limitations

Mustache doesn't work for JSON-to-JSON transformation because (just like JSON-T) it can't determine when it has reached the last element in an Array or Object in the input JSON.

Let's move on to Handlebars.

Handlebars

As we saw previously, Handlebars does a good job of converting JSON to HTML, and the template in Example 7-12 shows how to convert the Cities JSON data into the target JSON output.

Example 7-12. templates/transform-json.hbs

```
{
  "cities": [
    {{#each cities}}
      {
        "id": "{{id}}",
        "name": "{{name}}",
        "weather": {
          {{#main}}
          "currentTemp": {{temp}},
          "lowTemp": {{temp_min}},
          "hiTemp": {{temp_max}},
          "humidity": {{humidity}},
          {{/main}}
          "windSpeed": {{wind.speed}},
          {{#each weather}}
          "summary": "{{main}}",
          "description": "{{description}}"
          {{/each}}
        }
      }{{#unless @last}},{{/unless}}
    {{/each}}
  ]
}
```

This template is similar to the one shown in the JSON-to-HTML section on Handlebars, but with one notable difference. The following line does exactly what we need: it emits a comma after each element *unless* it's the last element:

```
{{#unless @last}},{{/unless}}
```

Here's how it works:

- `{{#unless}}` is a built-in Handlebars helper that renders the enclosing block only if the condition returns `false`.
- `@last@` is a built-in Handlebars variable that returns `false` if an element is the last in an Array, and `true` if the current element is at the end of the Array.

For more information on `{{#unless}}` and `@last@`, visit the Handlebars website (*http://handlebarsjs.com/builtin_helpers.html*).

Let's run the template in the Architect template editor (*http://rowno.github.io/archi tect/*). Select *Handlebars.js* in the Engine drop-down, paste the Handlebars template, and input JSON into the Template and View text boxes (respectively). You should see the result shown in Figure 7-5.

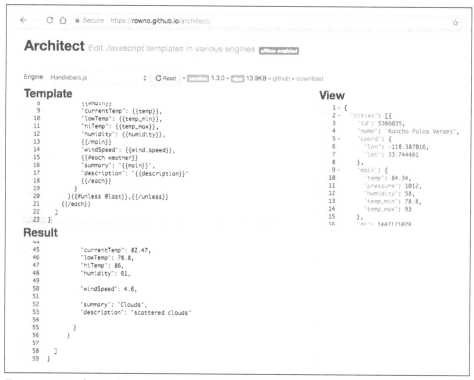

Figure 7-5. Architect: JSON-to-JSON transformation with Handlebars

Take a look at line 56 of the resulting JSON (in the Result text box) and you'll see that there is *no* trailing comma so this should be valid. You can confirm that the resulting JSON is valid by pasting it into JSONLint, as shown in Figure 7-6.

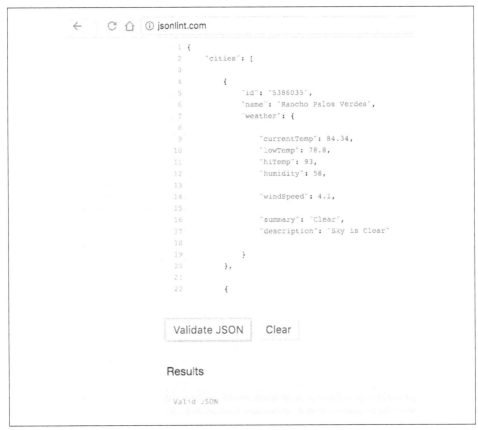

Figure 7-6. JSONLint validation of JSON transformed with Handlebars

This is exactly what we're looking for. As noted earlier, Handlebars differs from Mustache in that Handlebars has just enough conditional logic to make the JSON-to-JSON transformation work properly.

JSON-to-JSON Transformation Evaluations—The Bottom Line

Based on the evaluation criteria and overall usability, Handlebars is my overwhelming choice for JSON-to-JSON transformation for the following reasons:

- It's the only library that works "as is." The conditional logic makes it possible.
- It has solid cross-platform support.
- The template language is rich enough to meet most transformation needs.
- It's declarative, yet allows for custom logic with custom helpers.
- Excellent online tools facilitate development.

We've covered JSON-to-JSON conversion, and now it's time to cover JSON-XML transformation.

JSON-XML Transformation

Often, developers and architects need to integrate with legacy systems that still use XML. To have a clean separation of concerns, it's important to add a thin adapter at the boundaries of your system that encapsulates the translation between XML and JSON.

JSON-XML Transformation Conventions

It's easy to convert XML elements (e.g., `<weather>`) to/from JSON, but it's difficult to convert XML attributes to/from JSON. This is a lossy conversion, which means that you can't convert the JSON back to the original XML, and vice versa because JSON doesn't have a standard way to represent attributes. Remember that JSON's core constructs are Objects, Arrays, and key/value pairs.

For example, an XML attribute provides metadata that describes an element, and looks like this:

```
<weather temp="84.34" pressure="1012" humidity="58"
        temp_min="78.8" temp_max="93"/>
```

In this XML snippet, the `temp`, `pressure`, `humidity`, `temp_min`, and `temp_max` attributes describe the `weather` element. Back in the days when XML was in vogue (roughly 1998–2008), many XML Schema designers leveraged XML attributes to:

- Reduce the overall payload of messages going over the wire
- Simplify the conversion between XML and their native platform (e.g., Java, JS, Ruby, or C#)

We'd like to see how to directly convert between XML and JSON, and several well-known conventions (specifications) describe how to do this:

- Badgerfish
- Parker
- JsonML
- Spark
- GData
- Abdera

This chapter focuses on Badgerfish and Parker because they're well-known. A full discussion and in-depth comparison of these XML-JSON conversion convention is beyond the scope of this book, but you can find further details at the Open311 wiki (*http://wiki.open311.org/JSON_and_XML_Conversion*).

To compare the Badgerfish and Parker conventions, we'll start by showing a sample input XML document based on the OpenWeatherMap data. Then, we'll compare how both conventions would convert from XML to JSON. Example 7-13 provides the input XML.

Example 7-13. data/cities-weather-short.xml

```xml
<?xml version="1.0" encoding="UTF-8" ?>
<cities>
  <city>
    <id>5386035</id>
    <name>Rancho Palos Verdes</name>
    <coord>
      <lon>-118.387016</lon>
      <lat>33.744461</lat>
    </coord>
    <main temp="84.34" pressure="1012" humidity="58" temp_min="78.8" temp_max="93"/>
    <dt>1442171078</dt>
    <wind>
      <speed>4.1</speed>
      <deg>300</deg>
    </wind>
    <clouds>
      <all>5</all>
    </clouds>
    <weather>
      <id>800</id>
      <main>Clear</main>
      <description>Sky is Clear</description>
      <icon>02d</icon>
    </weather>
  </city>
  <city>
    <id>5392528</id>
    <name>San Pedro</name>
    <coord>
      <lon>-118.29229</lon>
      <lat>33.735851</lat>
    </coord>
    <main temp="84.02" pressure="1012" humidity="58" temp_min="78.8" temp_max="91"/>
    <dt>1442171080</dt>
    <wind>
      <speed>4.1</speed>
      <deg>300</deg>
    </wind>
```

```
<clouds>
    <all>5</all>
</clouds>
<weather>
  <id>800</id>
  <main>Clear</main>
  <description>Sky is Clear</description>
  <icon>02d</icon>
</weather>
</city>
<city>
  <id>3988392</id>
  <name>Rosarito</name>
  <coord>
    <lon>-117.033333</lon>
    <lat>32.333328</lat>
  </coord>
  <main temp="82.47" pressure="1012" humidity="61" temp_min="78.8" temp_max="86"/>
  <dt>1442170905</dt>
  <wind>
    <speed>4.6</speed>
    <deg>240</deg>
  </wind>
  <clouds>
    <all>32</all>
  </clouds>
  <weather>
    <id>802</id>
    <main>Clouds</main>
    <description>scattered clouds</description>
    <icon>03d</icon>
  </weather>
</city>
</cities>
```

Badgerfish

Badgerfish has an excellent online tester that makes it easy to convert from the input
XML to JSON (per the Badgerfish convention). The Badgerfish Online Tester (*http://
dropbox.ashlock.us/open311/json-xml*) is shown in Figure 7-6.

Figure 7-7. Badgerfish online tester—convert XML to JSON

Paste the input XML into the text box just below the Convert XML to JSON label, click the "Translate XML above to JSON below button" and you'll see very compact JSON in the resulting text box. You can use JSONLint (*http://jsonlint.com*) or your favorite text editor (which includes a JSON beautifier plug-in), and you'll see the (more readable) JSON output shown in Example 7-14.

Example 7-14. data/cities-weather-short-badgerfish.json

```
{
  "cities": {
    "city": [{
      "id": {
        "$1": 5386035
      },
      "name": {
        "$1": "Rancho Palos Verdes"
      },
      "coord": {
        "lon": {
          "$1": "-118.387016"
        },
        "lat": {
          "$1": "33.744461"
        }
      },
      "main": {
        "@temp": "84.34",
        "@pressure": 1012,
        "@humidity": 58,
        "@temp_min": "78.8",
        "@temp_max": 93
      },
      "dt": {
        "$1": 1442171078
      },
```

```
    "wind": {
      "speed": {
        "$1": "4.1"
      },
      "deg": {
        "$1": 300
      }
    },
    "clouds": {
      "all": {
        "$1": 5
      }
    },
    "weather": {
      "id": {
        "$1": 800
      },
      "main": {
        "$1": "Clear"
      },
      "description": {
        "$1": "Sky is Clear"
      },
      "icon": {
        "$1": "02d"
      }
    }
  }, {
  "id": {
    "$1": 5392528
  },
  "name": {
    "$1": "San Pedro"
  },
  "coord": {
    "lon": {
      "$1": "-118.29229"
    },
    "lat": {
      "$1": "33.735851"
    }
  },
  "main": {
    "@temp": "84.02",
    "@pressure": 1012,
    "@humidity": 58,
    "@temp_min": "78.8",
    "@temp_max": 91
  },
  "dt": {
    "$1": 1442171080
  },
```

```json
    "wind": {
      "speed": {
        "$1": "4.1"
      },
      "deg": {
        "$1": 300
      }
    },
    "clouds": {
      "all": {
        "$1": 5
      }
    },
    "weather": {
      "id": {
        "$1": 800
      },
      "main": {
        "$1": "Clear"
      },
      "description": {
        "$1": "Sky is Clear"
      },
      "icon": {
        "$1": "02d"
      }
    }
  }, {
    "id": {
      "$1": 3988392
    },
    "name": {
      "$1": "Rosarito"
    },
    "coord": {
      "lon": {
        "$1": "-117.033333"
      },
      "lat": {
        "$1": "32.333328"
      }
    },
    "main": {
      "@temp": "82.47",
      "@pressure": 1012,
      "@humidity": 61,
      "@temp_min": "78.8",
      "@temp_max": 86
    },
    "dt": {
      "$1": 1442170905
    },
```

```
    "wind": {
      "speed": {
        "$1": "4.6"
      },
      "deg": {
        "$1": 240
      }
    },
    "clouds": {
      "all": {
        "$1": 32
      }
    },
    "weather": {
      "id": {
        "$1": 802
      },
      "main": {
        "$1": "Clouds"
      },
      "description": {
        "$1": "scattered clouds"
      },
      "icon": {
        "$1": "03d"
      }
    }
  }]
  }
}
```

The core rules of the Badgerfish convention include the following:

- Element names become Object properties.

- The textual content of an element goes into the $ property of an Object with the same name. For example, <name>Rancho Palos Verdes</name> becomes "name": { "$1": "Rancho Palos Verdes" }.

- Nested elements become nested properties. For example, the following XML

```
<wind>
  <speed>4.1</speed>
  <deg>300</deg>
</wind>
```

becomes

```
"wind": {
  "speed": {
    "$1": "4.1"
  },
  "deg": {
```

```
    "$1": 300
  }
}
```

- Multiple elements with the same name at the same level become Array elements. The following XML

```
<city>
</city>
<city>
</city>
```

becomes

```
"city": [ { ... } ]
```

- Attributes go in properties whose names begin with @. For example, the following XML

```
<main temp="84.02" pressure="1012" humidity="58"
      temp_min="78.8" temp_max="91"/>
```

becomes

```
"main": {
  "@temp": "84.34",
  "@pressure": 1012,
  "@humidity": 58,
  "@temp_min": "78.8",
  "@temp_max": 93
}
```

We've glossed over a lot of details, but Badgerfish has excellent documentation and resources. For further information, see the following:

- Badgerfish site (*http://badgerfish.ning.com*)
- Badgerfish documentation (*http://www.sklar.com/badgerfish*)
- Badgerfish online tester (*http://dropbox.ashlock.us/open311/json-xml*)

Parker

Parker provides a simple conversion, but it ignores XML attributes, so you will lose the attribute data when converting to JSON. Following the Parker convention yields the JSON document in Example 7-15 (based on the input XML).

Example 7-15. data/cities-weather-short-parker.json

```
{
  "cities": [{
    "id": 5386035,
```

```
  "name": "Rancho Palos Verdes",
  "coord": {
    "lon": -118.387016,
    "lat": 33.744461
  },
  "main": null,
  "dt": 1442171078,
  "wind": {
    "speed": 4.1,
    "deg": 300
  },
  "clouds": {
    "all": 5
  },
  "weather": [{
    "id": 800,
    "main": "Clear",
    "description": "Sky is Clear",
    "icon": "02d"
  }]
}, {
  "id": 5392528,
  "name": "San Pedro",
  "coord": {
    "lon": -118.29229,
    "lat": 33.735851
  },
  "main": null,
  "dt": 1442171080,
  "wind": {
    "speed": 4.1,
    "deg": 300
  },
  "clouds": {
    "all": 5
  },
  "weather": [{
    "id": 800,
    "main": "Clear",
    "description": "Sky is Clear",
    "icon": "02d"
  }]
}, {
  "id": 3988392,
  "name": "Rosarito",
  "coord": {
    "lon": -117.033333,
    "lat": 32.333328
  },
  "main": null,
  "dt": 1442170905,
  "wind": {
```

```
      "speed": 4.6,
      "deg": 240
    },
    "clouds": {
      "all": 32
    },
    "weather": [{
      "id": 802,
      "main": "Clouds",
      "description": "scattered clouds",
      "icon": "03d"
    }]
  }]
}
```

The core rules of the Parker convention include the following:

- Element names become Object properties.
- Attributes are ignored.
- Nested elements become nested properties.

The Parker convention is simple, but has the following issues:

- It is lossy because it ignores XML attributes when you convert to JSON.
- There is a lack of documentation and supporting tools.

The Issues with JSON-XML Transformation Conventions

The preceding XML-JSON transformation conventions have the following limitations:

- None are considered to be a widely accepted standard.
- They lack cross-platform support and full implementations.
- Documentation is not always complete.
- Data conversion can be lossy (Parker).
- Data conversion can introduce changes in the data structure (Badgerfish).

XML-JSON Transform—The Bottom Line

With these shortcomings in mind, I suggest No Convention (none of the above) to convert the following:

XML-to-JSON

Parse (unmarshal) the XML into Objects/Hashes on your current platform by using a well-known library (we'll use `xml2js` for our Node.js-based examples). Then, convert the Objects/Hashes from your platform into JSON with `JSON.stringify()` if you're using JavaScript. Chapters 3 and 4 show how to convert Ruby and Java, respectively, to JSON.

JSON-to-XML

Parse the JSON into data structures on your platform using a common library. `JSON.parse()` works great for JavaScript. Chapters 3 and 4 show to parse JSON into Ruby and Java. Then, generate an XML document from your data structure (this is also known as *marshaling*). Again, we'll leverage `xml2js` from a Node.js-based Mocha/Chai test.

Rather than being concerned with a particular convention/style of conversion, focus on the following:

- Do what works best for you.
- Use the libraries you already know and have on hand.
- Test the conversion results to make sure that you're not losing any data.
- Keep it simple.
- Encapsulate everything and make sure that it fits well with the rest of your enterprise application architecture.

In short, choose the best library that you can find on your platform and work with or around the limitations.

Parsing/generating XML libraries

XML has been around for a long time, and each major platform has a solid implementation, including the following:

Node.js

We'll use `xml2js` (*https://www.npmjs.com/package/xml2js*).

Ruby

There are several good libraries, and two of the best are LibXml (*https://xml4r.github.io/libxml-ruby*) and Nokogiri (*http://www.nokogiri.org*).

Java

Java Architecture for XML Binding (JAXB) (*https://jaxb.java.net/tutorial*) has been a mainstay for years in the Java community.

JSON-XML Transformation Unit Test

The Unit Test suite in Example 7-16 has methods to test JSON-to-XML and XML-to-JSON conversion, and uses the following technologies:

xml2js
> To convert XML to/from JavaScript data structures, you can use xml2js (*https://www.npmjs.com/package/xml2js*), which is also available on GitHub (*https://github.com/Leonidas-from-XIV/node-xml2js*).

JSON.parse() / JSON.stringify()
> To convert JSON to/from JavaScript structures. You can find more information about JSON.parse() / JSON.stringify() at MDN (*https://mzl.la/2s8UCRU*) and in Chapter 3.

Example 7-16. cities-weather-transform-test/test/json-xml-spec.js

```
'use strict';

/* Attribution: Cities Weather data provided by OpenWeatherMap API
   ([http://openweathermap.org]) under Creative Commons Share A Like
   License (https://creativecommons.org/licenses/by-sa/4.0).
   Changes were made to the data to work with json-server.
   This does not imply an endorsement by the licensor.

   This code is distributed under Creative Commons Share A Like License.
*/

var expect = require('chai').expect;
var jsonfile = require('jsonfile');
var fs = require('fs');
var xml2js = require('xml2js');


describe('json-xml', function() {
  var jsonCitiesFileName = null;
  var xmlCitiesFileName = null;

  beforeEach(function() {
    var baseDir = __dirname + '/../..';

    jsonCitiesFileName = baseDir + '/data/cities-weather-short.json';
    xmlCitiesFileName = baseDir +
      '/data/cities-weather-short.xml';
  });

  it('should transform cities JSON data to XML', function(done) {
    jsonfile.readFile(jsonCitiesFileName, function(readJsonFileError,
      jsonObj) {
      if (!readJsonFileError) {
```

```
      var builder = new xml2js.Builder();
      var xml = builder.buildObject(jsonObj);

      console.log('\n\n\nXML Output:\n' + xml);
      done();
    } else {
      done(readJsonFileError);
    }
  });
});

it('should transform cities XML data to JSON', function(done) {
  fs.readFile(xmlCitiesFileName, 'utf8', function(
    readXmlFileError, xmlData) {
    if (!readXmlFileError) {
      var parser = new xml2js.Parser();

      parser.parseString(xmlData, function(error, xmlObj) {
        if (!error) {
          console.log('\n\n\nJSON Output:\n' +
            JSON.stringify(xmlObj, null, 2));

          done();
        } else {
          done(error);
        }
      });
    } else {
      done(readXmlFileError);
    }
  });
});
});
```

The preceding code works as follows:

- beforeEach() runs before any Unit Test and does setup. In this case, it builds the filenames for the input JSON file and the output XML file.

- In the 'should transform cities JSON data to XML' Unit Test:

  — jsonfile.readFile() reads and parses the input JSON file into a JavaScript Object (jsonObj).

  — xml2js.Builder() creates an Object that can convert from JSON to XML.

  — builder.buildObject(jsonObj) converts the JavaScript Object (from the input JSON file) into an XML String.

- In the 'should transform cities XML data to JSON' Unit Test:

  — fs.readFile() reads the XML file into a String.

- `xml2js.Parser()` creates an XML parser.
- `parser.parseString()` parses the XML String (from the input XML file) into a JavaScript Object (`xmlObj`).
- `JSON.stringify()` converts the `xmlObj` JavaScript Object into a JSON String.

What We Covered

We've shown several JSON Transform libraries to do the following:

- Convert JSON to HTML
  - Either Mustache or JSON will work just fine.
- Transform JSON to other, cleaner JSON structures
  - Choose Handlebars.
- Convert between XML and JSON
  - Don't worry about the XML/JSON conventions.
  - Use an XML library that works well on your platform.
- Write Unit Tests that transform the content of JSON documents returned by a Web API

Use these JSON Transform techniques to convert JSON data from external APIs into data formats that are compatible with your applications.

What's Next?

Now that we've covered the JSON Ecosystem (Schema, Search, and Transform), we'll move to the final section on JSON in the enterprise; this part of the book covers the following topics:

- Hypermedia
- MongoDB (NoSQL)
- Messaging with Kafka

In Chapter 8, we'll discuss Hypermedia with JSON in order to show how to interact with an API.

PART III

JSON in the Enterprise

JSON and Hypermedia

Imagine building an application in HTML for use in a web browser. You can add forms, links, and buttons by using standard HTML, and the browser renders your new controls without requiring a new release of the browser. In the "olden days," it didn't work this way. If we released a new version of our server-side application with new functionality, we often had to release a new version of the client code to pair with it. Browsers changed this expectation.

We now live in a world where "rich clients" are coming back in the form of apps on people's devices. We could just have phones access web pages, but for various reasons, people (and companies) want native apps as icons that they can touch on their devices. So how can we get rich native apps back, while still benefitting from the configurability of the browser? Hypermedia. We send not only the data, but also the actions the user can take on the data, along with a representation of how to trigger that action.

So far, the RESTful API calls and JSON responses in this book have been isolated (without reference to other calls). Each JSON response from the Speakers API has just contained data about the speaker, but without providing any information about other related resources and actions.

Hypermedia enables a REST API to guide its Consumers on the following:

- Links to other related resources (e.g., other APIs). For example, a Conference API could provide links to the Reservation, Speaker, or Venue APIs so that Consumers could learn more about the conference and the speakers, and purchase a ticket.

- Semantics on the data returned by an API. This metadata documents the data in the JSON response, and defines the meaning of the data elements.

- Additional actions that they can take on the current resource exposed by the API. For example, a Speakers API could provide more than just CRUD operations. How about a set of links that lead and guide a speaker through the speaker proposal process (in order to speak at a conference)?

Hypermedia groups resources together and guides a Consumer through a series of calls to achieve a business result. Think of Hypermedia as the API equivalent of a web-based shopping cart that leads the Consumer through the buying process and (hopefully) to an eventual purchase. A Hypermedia format provides a standard way for Consumers to interpret and process the link-related data elements from an API response.

In this chapter, we'll show how to compare these well-known JSON-based Hypermedia formats:

- Siren
- JSON-LD
- Collection+JSON
- json:api
- HAL

Comparing Hypermedia Formats

We'll use the Speaker data from previous chapters to drive the discussion of Hypermedia formats. The following invocation to the fictitious myconference Speakers API might return:

```
GET http://myconference.api.com/speakers/123456

{
    "id": "123456",
    "firstName": "Larson",
    "lastName": "Richard",
    "email": "larson.richard@myconference.com",
    "tags": [
        "JavaScript",
        "AngularJS",
        "Yeoman"
    ],
    "age": 39,
    "registered": true
}
```

To see a list of a speaker's presentations, make another API call:

```
GET http://myconference.api.com/speakers/123456/presentations

[
  {
    "id": "1123",
    "speakerId": "123456",
    "title": "Enterprise Node",
    "abstract": "Many developers just see Node as a way to build web APIs ...",
    "audience": [
      "Architects",
      "Developers"
    ]
  },
  {
    "id": "2123",
    "speakerId": "123456",
    "title": "How to Design and Build Great APIs",
    "abstract": "Companies now leverage APIs as part of their online ...",
    "audience": [
      "Managers",
      "Architects",
      "Developers"
    ]
  }
]
```

Let's see how to represent the Speaker and Presentation APIs using several Hypermedia formats.

Defining Key Terms

Before we go further, let's define a couple of key terms related to REST:

Resource
Anything that holds data—an Object, a Document, or a Service (e.g., Stock Quote). A resource can be related to other resources. A resource is an endpoint that has a URI.

Representation
The current state of a resource, expressed in JSON or XML.

My Opinion on Hypermedia

All architects and developers have opinions that shape the way they evaluate a particular technology. Before we review and compare each Hypermedia format, I'll let you know my opinion on Hypermedia. Hypermedia is powerful and provides rich metadata to the data returned by an API, but it is controversial. Many people love it, and other people hate it, and I'm somewhere between these two groups.

Many people in the REST and Hypermedia communities believe that adding metadata on operations and semantic data definitions to a JSON payload is helpful. I respect everyone's opinion, but I believe in the use of links to other resources only for these reasons:

- Additional information on operations and data definitions is unnecessary if you document your API properly in the first place. Why should the JSON data returned from each API call return information on actions and data types? This seems like clutter when you have the following situations:
  - OpenApi (*https://openapis.org/*) (formerly Swagger), RAML (*http://raml.org/*), and API Blueprint (*https://apiblueprint.org/*) can all provide this information in an API's documentation.
  - JSON Schema describes the data types for the JSON data representation.
- Hypermedia adds complexity to the JSON payload returned by an API. With richer/more functional Hypermedia formats, the following are true:
  - The original data representation is altered and difficult to interpret. Most of the formats shown in this chapter alter or embed the original data representation of the resource, which makes it harder for Consumers to understand and process.
  - You have to spend more time and effort to explain how to use your API, and Consumers will move on to something simpler.
  - The payload is larger and takes up more network bandwidth.
- Simple links to other related resources are great because they guide an API Consumer through the use of your API(s) without altering the original JSON data representation.

Siren

Structured Interface for Representing Entities (Siren) was developed in 2012. It was designed to represent data from Web APIs, and works with both JSON and XML. You can find Siren on GitHub (*https://github.com/kevinswiber/siren*). Siren's Internet Assigned Numbers Authority (IANA) (*http://www.iana.org/assignments/media-types/media-types.xhtml*) media type is `application/vnd.siren+json`.

The key concepts in Siren are as follows:

Entities
   An Entity is a resource that is accessible with a URI. It has properties and Actions.

Actions

Actions that can be taken on an Entity.

Links

Navigational links to other Entities.

Example 8-1 shows the Speaker data in Siren format based on the following HTTP Request:

```
GET http://myconference.api.com/speakers/123456
Accept: application/vnd.siren+json
```

Example 8-1. data/speaker-siren.json

```json
{
  "class": ["speaker"],
  "properties": {
    "id": "123456",
    "firstName": "Larson",
    "lastName": "Richard",
    "email": "larson.richard@myconference.com",
    "tags": [
      "JavaScript",
      "AngularJS",
      "Yeoman"
    ],
    "age": 39,
    "registered": true
  },
  "actions": [
    {
      "name": "add-presentation",
      "title": "Add Presentation",
      "method": "POST",
      "href": "http://myconference.api.com/speakers/123456/presentations",
      "type": "application/x-www-form-urlencoded",
      "fields": [
        {
          "name": "title",
          "type": "text"
        },
        {
          "name": "abstract",
          "type": "text"
        },
        {
          "name": "audience",
          "type": "text"
        }
      ]
    }
  ],
```

```
  "links": [
    { "rel": ["self"],
      "href": "http://myconference.api.com/speakers/123456"
    },
    {
      "rel": ["presentations"],
      "href": "http://myconference.api.com/speakers/123456/presentations"
    }
  ]
}
```

In this example, the `speaker` Entity is defined as follows:

- `class` indicates the class of the resource (in this case, `speaker`).

- `properties` is an Object that holds the representation of the resource. It's the real data payload from an API response.

- `actions` describes the Actions that can be taken on a `speaker`. In this case, the `actions` indicate that you can add a `presentation` to a `speaker`.

- `links` provides links to `self` (the current resource) and `presentations`, a URI that returns the list of the `speaker`'s presentations.

Siren provides excellent metadata for describing the available actions on an Entity (resource). Siren has classes (types) to describe the data, but does not provide data definitions (semantics) like JSON-LD.

JSON-LD

JavaScript Object Notation for Linking Data (JSON-LD) (*https://www.w3.org/TR/json-ld-api*) became a W3C standard in 2014. It was designed as a data-linking format to be used with REST APIs, and it works with NoSQL databases such as MongoDB and CouchDB. You can find more information at the main JSON-LD site (*http://json-ld.org*), and you can find it on GitHub (*https://github.com/json-ld/json-ld.org*). The JSON-LD media type is `application/ld+json`, and *.jsonld* is the file extension. JSON-LD has an active community and large working group because of its status with the W3C.

Example 8-2 shows the Speaker data in JSON-LD format based on the following HTTP Request:

```
GET http://myconference.api.com/speakers/123456
Accept: application/vnd.ld+json
```

Example 8-2. data/speaker.jsonld

```json
{
  "@context": {
    "@vocab": "http://schema.org/Person",
    "firstName": "givenName",
    "lastName": "familyName",
    "email": "email",
    "tags": "http://myconference.schema.com/Speaker/tags",
    "age": "age",
    "registered": "http://myconference.schema.com/Speaker/registered"
  },
  "@id": "http://myconference.api.com/speakers/123456",
  "id": "123456",
  "firstName": "Larson",
  "lastName": "Richard",
  "email": "larson.richard@myconference.com",
  "tags": [
    "JavaScript",
    "AngularJS",
    "Yeoman"
  ],
  "age": 39,
  "registered": true,
  "presentations": "http://myconference.api.com/speakers/123456/presentations"
}
```

In this example, the `@context` Object provides the overall context for the Speaker data representation. In this case, `@context` does more than merely list the fields. Rather, `@context` (in conjunction with `@vocab`) seeks to provide unambiguous semantic meaning for each data element that comprises the `speaker` Object. Here are the specifics:

- The Schema.org site provides unambiguous definitions for commonly used data elements such as age and Person (*http://schema.org/Person*).

- `@vocab` sets the base type to Person and allows you to extend it with other fields (e.g., `tags` or `registered`) for the `speaker`.

- `@id` is essentially the URI, the unique ID for accessing a particular `speaker`.

Notice that the core JSON representation of the `speaker` remains unchanged, which is a major selling point if you have an existing API. This additive approach makes it easier to adopt JSON-LD gradually, without breaking your API Consumers. The existing JSON representation is undisturbed, which enables you to iteratively add the semantics of data linking to your API's data representation.

Note that *http://myconference.schema.com* does not exist. Rather, it's shown for the sake of the example. If you need a definition that doesn't exist on Schema.org, you're free to create one on your own domain. Just be sure that you provide good documentation.

Example 8-3 shows a speaker's list of presentations in JSON-LD format based on the following HTTP Request:

```
GET http://myconference.api.com/speakers/123456/presentations
Accept: application/vnd.ld+json
```

Example 8-3. data/presentations.jsonld

```
{
  "@context": {
    "@vocab": "http://myconference.schema.com/",
    "presentations": {
      "@type": "@id",
      "id": "id",
      "speakerId": "speakerId",
      "title": "title",
      "abstract": "abstract",
      "audience": "audience"
    }
  },
  "presentations": [
    {
      "@id": "http://myconference.api.com/speakers/123456/presentations/1123",
      "id": "1123",
      "speakerId": "123456",
      "title": "Enterprise Node",
      "abstract": "Many developers just see Node as a way to build web APIs or ...",
      "audience": [
        "Architects",
        "Developers"
      ]
    }, {
      "@id": "http://myconference.api.com/speakers/123456/presentations/2123",
      "id": "2123",
      "speakerId": "123456",
      "title": "How to Design and Build Great APIs",
      "abstract": "Companies now leverage APIs as part of their online strategy ...",
      "audience": [
        "Managers",
        "Architects",
        "Developers"
      ]
    }
  ]
}
```

In this example, @context indicates that all the data is related to the concept of pre
sentations. In this case, we need to define presentations inline because the
http://myconference.schema.com/presentations Object doesn't exist. If the
Object did exist, the @context would look like this:

```
"@context": "http://myconference.schema.com/presentations"
```

You can try out the preceding example on the JSON-LD Playground (*http://json-ld.org/playground*). This is an excellent online tester that validates JSON-LD documents. Use this tool to validate your data format before writing the code for your API.

JSON-LD by itself does not provide information on operations, nor does it provide
semantics on the data representations. HYDRA is an add-on to JSON-LD that provides a vocabulary to specify client-server communication.

Here's where to find more information on HYDRA:

- Main site (*http://www.markus-lanthaler.com/hydra/*)
- W3C community (*https://www.w3.org/community/hydra*)

Example 8-4 shows the list of presentations in JSON-LD format enhanced with
HYDRA operations:

```
GET http://myconference.api.com/speakers/123456/presentations
Accept: application/vnd.ld+json
```

Example 8-4. data/presentations-operations.jsonld

```
{
  "@context": [
    "http://www.w3.org/ns/hydra/core", {
      "@vocab": "http://myconference.schema.com/",
      "presentations": {
        "@type": "@id",
        "id": "id",
        "speakerId": "speakerId",
        "title": "title",
        "abstract": "abstract",
        "audience": "audience"
      }
    }
  ],
  "presentations": [
    {
      "@id": "http://myconference.api.com/speakers/123456/presentations/1123",
      "id": "1123",
      "speakerId": "123456",
      "title": "Enterprise Node",
      "abstract": "Many developers just see Node as a way to build web APIs or ...",
      "audience": [
```

```
          "Architects",
          "Developers"
        ]
    }, {
        "@id": "http://myconference.api.com/speakers/123456/presentations/2123",
        "id": "2123",
        "speakerId": "123456",
        "title": "How to Design and Build Great APIs",
        "abstract": "Companies now leverage APIs as part of their online strategy ...",
        "audience": [
          "Managers",
          "Architects",
          "Developers"
        ]
    }
    ],
    "operation": {
      "@type": "AddPresentation",
      "method": "POST",
      "expects": {
        "@id": "http://schema.org/id",
        "supportedProperty": [
          {
            "property": "title",
            "range": "Text"
          }, {
            "property": "abstract",
            "range": "Text"
          }
        ]
      }
    }
  }
}
```

Note the following in this example:

- operation indicates that you can add a presentation with a POST.

- @context points to the HYDRA domain to add the operation keyword.

- @vocab adds in the *http://myconference.schema.com/* domain and the presenta
  tions definition.

JSON-LD by itself is great, because it provides links to other related resources without
altering the original data representation. In other words, JSON-LD does not introduce breaking changes to your API Consumers. For the sake of simplicity, use JSON-
LD without the overhead of HYDRA.

Collection+JSON

Collection+JSON was created in 2011, focuses on handling data items in a collection, and is similar to the Atom Publication/Syndication formats. You can find more information at the main Collection+JSON site (*http://amundsen.com/media-types/collection/*), and on GitHub (*https://github.com/collection-json/spec*). The Collection+JSON media type is `application/vnd.collection+json`.

To be valid, a Collection+JSON response must have a top-level `collection` Object that holds the following:

- A `version`
- An `href` with a URI that points to `self` (the original resource that was requested)

Example 8-5 shows the Speaker data in Collection+JSON format based on the following HTTP request:

```
GET http://myconference.api.com/speakers/123456
Accept: application/vnd.collection+json
```

Example 8-5. data/speaker-collection-json-links.json

```
{
  "collection": {
    "version": "1.0",
    "href": "http://myconference.api.com/speakers",
    "items": [
      {
        "href": "http://myconference.api.com/speakers/123456",
        "data": [
          { "name": "id", "value": "123456" },
          { "name": "firstName", "value": "Larson" },
          { "name": "lastName", "value": "Richard" },
          { "name": "email", "value": "larson.richard@myconference.com" },
          { "name": "age", "value": "39" },
          { "name": "registered", "value": "true" }
        ],
        "links": [
          {
            "rel": "presentations",
            "href": "http://myconference.api.com/speakers/123456/presentations",
            "prompt": "presentations"
          }
        ]
      }
    ]
  }
}
```

Note the following in this example:

- The `collection` Object encapsulates the Speaker data.
- The `items` Array contains all objects in the Speaker collection. Because we queried by ID, there's only one Object in the collection.
- The `data` Array contains name/value pairs for each data element that comprises a Speaker.
- The `links` Array provides link relationships to resources related to the speaker. Each link is composed of:
  — A `rel` key that describes the relation.
  — An `href` that provides a hyperlink to the `presentations` for this speaker.
  — A `prompt` that could be used by HTML forms to reference the speaker collection.

Collection+JSON also provides the ability to read, write, and query items in a collection, but a full discussion of Collection+JSON is outside the scope of this book. Visit *http://amundsen.com/media-types/collection/examples/* for examples, and *http://amundsen.com/media-types/tutorials/collection/tutorial-01.html* for a tutorial.

Collection+JSON does a nice job of providing link relations, but it completely changes the structure of the Speaker data by converting it to key/value pairs inside the `data` Array.

json:api

`json:api` was developed in 2013 and provides conventions for standardizing the format of JSON requests/responses to/from an API. Although `json:api`'s main focus is on API request/response data, it also includes Hypermedia. You can find more information at the main `json:api` site (*http://jsonapi.org/*) and on GitHub (*https://github.com/json-api/json-api*). The `json:api` media type is `application/vnd.api+json`.

A valid `json:api` document *must* have one of the following elements at the top level:

data
> The data representation for the resource. This contains resource Objects, each of which must have a `type` (specifies the data type) and `id` (unique resource ID) field.

errors
> An Array of error Objects that shows an error code and message for each error encountered by the API.

`meta`
    Contains nonstandard metadata (e.g., copyright and authors, etc.).

Optional top-level elements include the following:

`links`
    An Object that holds link relations (hyperlinks) to resources related to the primary resource.

`included`
    An Array of embedded resource Objects that are related to the primary resource.

Example 8-6 shows a list of Speakers in `json:api` format based on the following HTTP Request:

```
GET http://myconference.api.com/speakers
Accept: application/vnd.api+json
```

Example 8-6. data/speakers-jsonapi-links.json

```
{
  "links": {
    "self": "http://myconference.api.com/speakers",
    "next": "http://myconference.api.com/speakers?limit=25&offset=25"
  },
  "data": [
    {
      "type": "speakers",
      "id": "123456",
      "attributes": {
        "firstName": "Larson",
        "lastName": "Richard",
        "email": "larson.richard@myconference.com",
        "tags": [
          "JavaScript",
          "AngularJS",
          "Yeoman"
        ],
        "age": 39,
        "registered": true
      }
    },
    {
      "type": "speakers",
      "id": "223456",
      "attributes": {
        "firstName": "Ester",
        "lastName": "Clements",
        "email": "ester.clements@myconference.com",
        "tags": [
          "REST",
```

```
            "Ruby on Rails",
            "APIs"
        ],
        "age": 29,
        "registered": true
    }
  },
  ...
 ]
}
```

This example works as follows:

- The links Array provides link relationships to resources related to the speaker. In this case, each element contains the URI to the related resource. Note that there are no restrictions/qualifications on the link names, but self is commonly understood as the current resource, and next paginate.

- The data Array contains a list of the resource objects, each of which has a type (e.g., speakers) and id to meet the requirements of the json:api format definition. The attributes object holds the key/value pairs that make up each speaker Object.

Example 8-7 shows how to embed all presentation Objects for a speaker with json:api:

```
GET http://myconference.api.com/speakers/123456
Accept: application/vnd.api+json
```

Example 8-7. data/speaker-jsonapi-embed-presentations.json

```
{
  "links": {
    "self": "http://myconference.api.com/speakers/123456"
  },
  "data": [
    {
      "type": "speaker",
      "id": "123456",
      "attributes": {
        "firstName": "Larson",
        "lastName": "Richard",
        "email": "larson.richard@myconference.com",
        "tags": [
          "JavaScript",
          "AngularJS",
          "Yeoman"
        ],
        "age": 39,
        "registered": true
```

```
      }
    }
  ],
  "included": [
    {
      "type": "presentations",
      "id": "1123",
      "speakerId": "123456",
      "title": "Enterprise Node",
      "abstract": "Many developers just see Node as a way to build web APIs or ...",
      "audience": [
        "Architects",
        "Developers"
      ]
    }, {
      "type": "presentations",
      "id": "2123",
      "speakerId": "123456",
      "title": "How to Design and Build Great APIs",
      "abstract": "Companies now leverage APIs as part of their online ...",
      "audience": [
        "Managers",
        "Architects",
        "Developers"
      ]
    }
  ]
}
```

In this example, the included Array (part of the json:api specification) specifies the embedded presentations for the speaker. Although embedding resources reduces the number of API calls, it introduces tight data coupling between resources because the speaker needs to know the format and content of the presentation data.

Example 8-8 provides a better way to show relationships between resources with links:

```
GET http://myconference.api.com/speakers/123456
Accept: application/vnd.api+json
```

Example 8-8. data/speaker-jsonapi-link-presentations.json

```
{
  "links": {
    "self": "http://myconference.api.com/speakers/123456",
    "presentations": "http://myconference.api.com/speakers/123456/presentations"
  },
  "data": [
    {
      "type": "speaker",
      "id": "123456",
```

```
    "attributes": {
      "firstName": "Larson",
      "lastName": "Richard",
      "email": "larson.richard@myconference.com",
      "tags": [
        "JavaScript",
        "AngularJS",
        "Yeoman"
      ],
      "age": 39,
      "registered": true
    }
  }
 ]
}
```

In this example, the `links` Array shows that the `speaker` has `presentations` and provides a URI, but the `speaker` resource (and API) doesn't know about the data in the `presentation` resource. Plus, there's less data for the Consumer to process. This loose coupling enables the `presentation` data to change without impacting the Speakers API.

`json:api` has a rich feature set including standardized error messages, pagination, content negotiation, and policies for Creating/Updating/Deleting resources. In the past, I've borrowed portions of the `json:api` specification to create API style guides. Plus, there are excellent libraries for most platforms (*http://jsonapi.org/implementa tions/*) that simplify working with `json:api`. The `data` Array and its resource Objects (which require a `type` and `id`) alter the JSON data representation, but the rest of the Object remains the same. A full discussion of `json:api` is outside the scope of this book; visit the JSON API page for examples (*http://jsonapi.org/examples*), and the full specification (*http://jsonapi.org/format*).

HAL

Hypertext Application Language (HAL) became an IETF standard in 2012 (*https:// tools.ietf.org/html/draft-kelly-json-hal-08*). It was designed as a way to link resources using hyperlinks, and works with either JSON or XML. You can find more information at the main HAL site (*http://stateless.co/hal_specification.html*) and on GitHub (*https://github.com/mikekelly/hal_specification*). The HAL media types are `applica tion/hal+json` and `application/hal+xml`.

HAL's format is simple, readable, and doesn't alter the original data representation. HAL is a popular media type, and is based on the following:

Resource Objects

Resources contain links (contained in a _links Object), other resources, and embedded resources (e.g., an Order contains items) contained in an _embedded Object.

Links

Links provide target URIs that lead to other external resources.

Both the _embedded and _links objects are optional, but one must be present as the top-level object so that you have a valid HAL document.

Example 8-9 shows the Speaker data in HAL format based on the following HTTP Request:

```
GET http://myconference.api.com/speakers/123456
Accept: application/vnd.hal+json
```

Example 8-9. data/speaker-hal.json

```
{
  "_links": {
    "self": {
      "href": "http://myconference.api.com/speakers/123456"
    },
    "presentations": {
      "href": "http://myconference.api.com/speakers/123456/presentations"
    }
  },
  "id": "123456",
  "firstName": "Larson",
  "lastName": "Richard",
  "email": "larson.richard@myconference.com",
  "tags": [
    "JavaScript",
    "AngularJS",
    "Yeoman"
  ],
  "age": 39,
  "registered": true
}
```

This example works as follows:

- The _links object contains link relations, each of which shows the semantic meaning of a link.

  — href is required within a link relation. The value of an href must be a valid URI (see RFC 3986 (*https://tools.ietf.org/html/rfc3986*)) or URI Template (see RFC 6570 (*https://tools.ietf.org/html/rfc6570*)).

- The link relations are as follows:

  — self is a link to the current speaker resource (self).

  — presentations are the presentations that this speaker will deliver. In this case, the presentations Object describes the relationship between the current resource and the http://myconference.api.com/speakers/123456/presen tations hyperlink (through the href key).

  — Note that next and find are *not* HAL keywords. HAL allows you to have custom names for link objects.

Let's make the example more interesting by getting a list of speakers, as shown in Example 8-10.

```
GET http://myconference.api.com/speakers
Accept: application/vnd.hal+json
```

Example 8-10. data/speakers-hal-links.json

```
{
  "_links": {
    "self": {
      "href": "http://myconference.api.com/speakers"
    },
    "next": {
      "href": "http://myconference.api.com/speakers?limit=25&offset=25"
    },
    "find": {
      "href": "http://myconference.api.com/speakers{?id}", "templated": true
    }
  },
  "speakers": [
    {
      "id": "123456",
      "firstName": "Larson",
      "lastName": "Richard",
      "email": "larson.richard@myconference.com",
      "tags": [
        "JavaScript",
        "AngularJS",
        "Yeoman"
      ],
      "age": 39,
      "registered": true
    },
    {
      "id": "223456",
      "firstName": "Ester",
      "lastName": "Clements",
      "email": "ester.clements@myconference.com",
```

```
     "tags": [
       "REST",
       "Ruby on Rails",
       "APIs"
     ],
     "age": 29,
     "registered": true
   },
   ...
 ]
}
```

This example works as follows:

- In addition to self, here are the following link relations:
  - next indicates the next set of speaker resources. In other words, this is a way to provide pagination for an API. In this case, the limit parameter indicates that 25 speaker Objects will be returned in each API call. The offset parameter indicates that we're at the 26th Object in the list. This convention is similar to Facebook's pagination style.
  - find provides a hyperlink to find an individual speaker with a templated link, where {?id} indicates to the caller that they can find the speaker by id in the URI. The templated key indicates that this is a templated link.
- The JSON data representation remains unchanged.

Returning to our first example, let's embed all presentation Objects for a speaker, as shown in Example 8-11:

```
GET http://myconference.api.com/speakers/123456
Accept: application/vnd.hal+json
```

Example 8-11. /data/speaker-hal-embed-presentations.json

```
{
  "_links": {
    "self": {
      "href": "http://myconference.api.com/speakers/123456"
    },
    "presentations": {
      "href": "http://myconference.api.com/speakers/123456/presentations"
    }
  },
  "_embedded": {
    "presentations": [
      {
        "_links": {
          "self": {
            "href": "http://myconference.api.com/speakers/123456/presentations/1123"
```

```
          }
        },
        "id": "1123",
        "title": "Enterprise Node",
        "abstract": "Many developers just see Node as a way to build web APIs ...",
        "audience": [
          "Architects",
          "Developers"
        ]
      },
      {
        "_links": {
          "self": {
            "href": "http://myconference.api.com/speakers/123456/presentations/2123"
          }
        },
        "id": "2123",
        "title": "How to Design and Build Great APIs",
        "abstract": "Companies now leverage APIs as part of their online ...",
        "audience": [
          "Managers",
          "Architects",
          "Developers"
        ]
      }
    ]
  },
  "id": "123456",
  "firstName": "Larson",
  "lastName": "Richard",
  "email": "larson.richard@myconference.com",
  "tags": [
    "JavaScript",
    "AngularJS",
    "Yeoman"
  ],
  "age": 39,
  "registered": true
}
```

In this example, instead of the presentations link relation, we're using the _embed ded Object to embed the presentation Objects for a speaker. Each presentation Object in turn has a _links Object for related resources.

At first glance, embedding related resources looks reasonable, but I prefer link relations instead for the following reasons:

- Embedded resources increase the size of the payload.

- The _embedded Object alters the data representation.

- It couples the Speakers and Presentation APIs. The Speakers API now has to know about the data structure of the presentations. With a simple `presentations` link relation, the Speakers API knows only that there is a related API.

HAL (minus the embedded resources) is lightweight and provides links to other resources without altering the data representation.

Conclusions on Hypermedia

Here's the bottom line on Hypermedia: keep it simple. Maintain the original structure of the resource representation. Provide solid documentation for your API as part of the design process, and much of the need for Hypermedia (actions, documentation, data typing) is already taken care of. For me, the most useful parts of Hypermedia are the links to other resources. Proponents of full Hypermedia may vehemently disagree (and that's OK), but here's my rebuttal:

- If your API is difficult to understand, people won't want to use it.
- The original JSON representation is the most important thing. Don't alter the structure of the resource just for the sake of adhering to a Hypermedia format.

With these considerations in mind, I choose a minimal HAL structure (links only, without embedded resources) as my Hypermedia format. With these caveats, HAL is excellent because it

- Is the simplest possible thing that can work
- Is a standard
- Enjoys wide community support
- Has solid cross-platform libraries
- Doesn't alter my JSON data representation
- Doesn't impose requirements for data semantics and operations
- Does just what I want, and not a bit more

`json:api` (with links rather than embedded resources) is my second choice for Hypermedia because it standardizes JSON requests/responses in addition to providing Hypermedia capabilities, and still respects the integrity and intent of the original JSON data representation. Of the Hypermedia formats that alter the JSON data representation, `json:api` appears to have the least impact. Because of its wide cross-platform support, you can reduce the formatting work by leveraging a `json:api` library for your programming language (this shortens and simplifies development). `json:api` deserves strong consideration if you need more than just Hypermedia, and you want to standardize JSON requests/responses across all the APIs in your enterprise (but API design is outside the scope of this book).

JSON-LD (without HYDRA) is my third favorite Hypermedia format because it's simple and doesn't change the JSON data representation. Although the data semantics are not hard to add to an existing API, I don't see a need for this, because good API documentation combined with JSON Schema does a better job of defining the meaning and structure of the data.

Recommendations for Working with Hypermedia

You may disagree with my opinion on Hypermedia, but imagine you're the architect or team lead and you're asking your team to use all aspects of Hypermedia to develop an API. Would your developers see Hypermedia as being useful or burdensome? Harkening back to the original days of eXtreme Programming (XP), do the simplest thing that could possibly work. Use the right tools and techniques for the job, and take the following approach:

- Document your API properly with OpenApi/Swagger or RAML.
- Define your data constructs by using JSON Schema.
- Choose HAL, json:api, or JSON-LD as your Hypermedia format, and start out with simple links to related resources.
- Evaluate how well the development process is going:
  — What's the team velocity?
  — How testable is the API?
- Ask your API Consumers for feedback. Can they
  — Easily understand the data representation?
  — Read and consume the data?
- Iterate and evaluate early and often.

Then, see whether you need to add in the operations and data definitions; you probably won't.

Practical Issues with Hypermedia

Here are some things to think about when you consider adding Hypermedia to an API:

- Hypermedia is not well understood in the community. When I speak on this topic, many developers haven't heard of it, know little about it, or don't know what it's used for. Some education is required even with the simplest Hypermedia format.

- Lack of standardization. We've covered five of the leading formats, but there are more. Only two (HAL and JSON-LD) in this chapter are backed by a standards body. So there's no consensus in the community.

- Hypermedia (regardless of the format) requires additional serialization/deserialization by both the API Producer and Consumer. So, be sure to choose a widely used Hypermedia format that provides cross-platform library support. This makes life easier for developers. We'll cover this in the next section when we test with HAL.

Testing with HAL in the Speakers API

As in previous chapters, we'll test against a Stub API (that provides a JSON response) that doesn't require us to write any code.

Test Data

To create the stub, we'll use the Speaker data from earlier chapters as our test data, which is available on GitHub (*https://github.com/tmarrs/json-at-work-examples/tree/master/chapter-8/data*), and deploy it as a RESTful API. Again, we'll leverage the json-server Node.js module to serve up the *speakers.json* file as a Web API. If you need to install json-server, refer to "Install npm Modules" on page 325 in Appendix A.

Here's how to run json-server on port 5000 from your local machine:

```
cd chapter-8/data

json-server -p 5000 ./speakers-hal-server-next-rel.json
```

Visit *http://localhost:5000/speakers* in Postman (which we used in earlier chapters), select GET as the HTTP verb, and click the Send button. You should see all the speakers from our Stub API, as shown in Figure 8-1.

Figure 8-1. Speakers data in HAL format served by json-server and viewed with Postman

This URI is also viewable from your browser.

Note that we had to massage the Speaker data to work with `json-server` for this example. Example 8-12 shows the updated structure that works with HAL.

Example 8-12. data/speakers-hal-server-next-rel.json

```
{
  "speakers": {
    "_links": {
      "self": {
        "href": "http://myconference.api.com/speakers"
      },
      "next": {
        "href": "http://myconference.api.com?limit=25&offset=25"
      },
      "find": {
        "href": "http://myconference.api.com/speakers{?id}",
        "templated": true
      }
    },
    "speakers": [{
      "id": "123456",
      "firstName": "Larson",
      "lastName": "Richard",
      "email": "larson.richard@myconference.com",
      "tags": [
```

```
        "JavaScript",
        "AngularJS",
        "Yeoman"
      ],
      "age": 39,
      "registered": true
    }, {
      "id": "223456",
      "firstName": "Ester",
      "lastName": "Clements",
      "email": "ester.clements@myconference.com",
      "tags": [
        "REST",
        "Ruby on Rails",
        "APIs"
      ],
      "age": 29,
      "registered": true
    }]
  }
}
```

In this example, the outer `speakers` Object is needed so that `json-server` will serve up the file with the proper URI: *http://localhost:5000/speakers*. The rest of the data (`links` Object and `speakers` Array) remain the same.

HAL Unit Test

Now that we have the API in place, let's create a Unit Test. We will continue to leverage Mocha/Chai (within Node.js), just as we saw in previous chapters. Before going further, be sure to set up your test environment. If you haven't installed Node.js yet, then refer to Appendix A, and install Node.js (see "Install Node.js" on page 320 and "Install npm Modules" on page 325). If you want to follow along with the Node.js project provided in the code examples, `cd` to *chapter-8/myconference* and do the following to install all dependencies for the project:

```
npm install
```

If you'd like to set up the Node.js project yourself, follow the instructions in the book's GitHub repository (*https://github.com/tmarrs/json-at-work-examples/tree/master/chapter-8/Project-Setup.md*).

Here are the npm modules in our Unit Test:

Unirest
   We've used this in previous chapters to invoke RESTful APIs.

halfred

A HAL parser available at *https://www.npmjs.com/package/halfred*. The corresponding GitHub repository can be found at *https://github.com/basti1302/halfred*.

The following Unit Test shows how to validate the HAL response from the (Stub) Speakers API.

Example 8-13. speakers-hal-test/test/hal-spec.js

```
'use strict';

var expect = require('chai').expect;
var unirest = require('unirest');
var halfred = require('halfred');

describe('speakers-hal', function() {
  var req;

  beforeEach(function() {
    halfred.enableValidation();
    req = unirest.get('http://localhost:5000/speakers')
      .header('Accept', 'application/json');
  });

  it('should return a 200 response', function(done) {
    req.end(function(res) {
      expect(res.statusCode).to.eql(200);
      expect(res.headers['content-type']).to.eql(
        'application/json; charset=utf-8');
      done();
    });
  });

  it('should return a valid HAL response validated by halfred', function(
    done) {
    req.end(function(res) {
      var speakersHALResponse = res.body;

      var resource = halfred.parse(speakersHALResponse);
      var speakers = resource.speakers;
      var speaker1 = null;

      console.log('\nValidation Issues: ');
      console.log(resource.validationIssues());
      expect(resource.validationIssues()).to.be.empty;
      console.log(resource);
      expect(speakers).to.not.be.null;
      expect(speakers).to.not.be.empty;
      speaker1 = speakers[0];
      expect(speaker1.firstName).to.not.be.null;
      expect(speaker1.firstName).to.eql('Larson');
```

```
      done();
    });
  });
});
```

This Unit Test runs as follows:

- beforeEach(function() runs before each test, and does the following:
  — Sets up the halfred library to validate HAL by invoking halfred.enableVali
    dation()
  — Invokes the Stub API at the following URI: *http://localhost:5000/speakers*
- The 'should return a 200 response' test ensures that the Stub API has a suc-
  cessful HTTP response.
- The 'should return a valid HAL response validated by halfred' test is
  the main test, and does the following:
  — Invokes halfred.parse() to parse the HAL response from the Stub API. This
    call returns a halfred Response object that contains the HAL links and the
    remaining JSON payload. Please see the halfred documentation for more
    information
  — Uses chai to check for validation errors in the HAL response by testing
    resource.validationIssues(). We'll see this call in action when we test with
    invalid data in our second run of the Unit Test that follows
  — Uses chai to ensure that the Response object still contains the original speak
    ers Array in the payload

When you run the Unit Test with npm test, it will pass because the Stub API produces valid HAL data. You should see the following:

```
> mocha test


speakers-hal
  ✓ should return a 200 response

Validation Issues:
[]
Resource {
  _links: { self: [ [Object] ], next: [ [Object] ], find: [ [Object] ] },
  _curiesMap: {},
  _curies: [],
  _resolvedCuriesMap: {},
  _embedded: {},
  _validation: [],
  speakers:
   [ { id: '123456',
       firstName: 'Larson',
       lastName: 'Richard',
       email: 'larson.richard@myconference.com',
       tags: [Object],
       age: 39,
       registered: true },
     { id: '223456',
       firstName: 'Ester',
       lastName: 'Clements',
       email: 'ester.clements@myconference.com',
       tags: [Object],
       age: 29,
       registered: true } ],
  _original:
   { _links: { self: [Object], next: [Object], find: [Object] },
     speakers: [ [Object], [Object] ] } }
  ✓ should return a valid HAL response validated by halfred


2 passing (62ms)
```

Now that we've shown how to validate HAL data, we'll change the data served up by
the Stub API so that it responds with invalid HAL data. Let's remove the link to self
in the _links object as shown in Example 8-14.

Example 8-14. data/speakers-hal-server-next-rel-invalid.json

```
{
  "speakers": {
    "_links": {
      "next": {
        "href": "http://myconference.api.com?limit=25&offset=25"
      },
      "find": {
        "href": "http://myconference.api.com/speakers{?id}",
        "templated": true
      }
    },
    ...
  }
}
```

Remember that the HAL specification requires the `_links` object to contain a reference to `self`. Restart `json-server` with the invalid HAL data as follows:

```
cd chapter-8/data

json-server -p 5000 ./speakers-hal-server-next-rel-invalid.json
```

Rerun the test, and you should see that `halfred` catches the HAL validation issue and that the test now fails:

```
> mocha test


  speakers-hal
    ✓ should return a 200 response

Validation Issues:
[ { path: '$._links',
    message: 'Resource does not have a self link' } ]
    1) should return a valid HAL response validated by halfred


  1 passing (64ms)
  1 failing

  1) speakers-hal should return a valid HAL response validated by halfred:
     Uncaught AssertionError: expected [ Array(1) ] to be empty
      at test/hal-spec.js:36:48
      at Request.handleRequestResponse [as _callback] (node_modules/unirest/index.js:463:26)
      at Request.self.callback (node_modules/request/request.js:187:22)
      at Request.<anonymous> (node_modules/request/request.js:1044:10)
      at IncomingMessage.<anonymous> (node_modules/request/request.js:965:12)
      at endReadableNT (_stream_readable.js:905:12)

npm ERR! Test failed.  See above for more details.
```

Server-Side HAL

We've shown how to use HAL from the client side with Unit Tests, but the server-side was deployed as a Stub (using `json-server` and a JSON file that follows the HAL specification). We have limited server-side coverage throughout this book to keep the focus on JSON. But here are some server-side libraries that will enable your RESTful APIs to render HAL-based responses:

Java
Spring HATEOS provides HAL support for Spring-based RESTful APIs in Java. You can find a good tutorial in the Spring documentation (*https://spring.io/ guides/gs/rest-hateoas*).

Ruby on Rails

The `roar` gem (*https://github.com/apotonick/roar*) provides HAL support for Ruby on Rails.

JavaScript/NodeJS

`express-hal` (*https://www.npmjs.com/package/express-hal*) adds HAL to Express-based NodeJS RESTful APIs.

Regardless of your development platform and which Hypermedia format you choose, be sure to do a spike implementation to test a library before committing to it as a solution. It's important to ensure that the library is easy to use and that it doesn't get in the way.

Going Deeper with Hypermedia

We've just scratched the surface with Hypermedia in this chapter. Here are a couple resources that will take you further:

- *RESTful Web APIs*, by Leonard Richardson et al. (O'Reilly)
- *REST in Practice: Hypermedia and Systems Architecture*, by Jim Webber et al. (O'Reilly)

What We Covered

We've shown how JSON and Hypermedia work together by doing the following:

- Comparing some of the well-known JSON-based Hypermedia formats
- Discussing considerations for adding Hypermedia to an API
- Leveraging HAL to support testing with the Speakers API

What's Next?

Now that we've shown how JSON works with Hypermedia, we'll move on to Chapter 9 to show how JSON works with MongoDB.

JSON and MongoDB

MongoDB is a NoSQL database that enables developers to persist data in document form. This document-based approach works well with JSON, which is also document-oriented. The MongoDB data model is hierarchical, and supports rich data types similar to those we've seen in typical JSON documents. Just like JSON documents, MongoDB documents integrate well with Object-Oriented platforms because documents are compatible with Objects, so developers can move data in/out of the database with little or no extra mapping logic. This approach is intuitive to developers and reduces development effort needed to access the database.

In this chapter, we'll show how to do the following:

- Import a JSON document into MongoDB
- Perform core CRUD operations with MongoDB
- Export MongoDB data to a JSON document
- Access MongoDB as a Mock/Stub RESTful API (without writing code)

This chapter focuses on using JSON with MongoDB and provides just enough information to work with the database. This chapter doesn't cover how to develop applications with MongoDB because that would fill an entire book. For a full description of the rich functionality provided by MongoDB, I recommend reading *MongoDB in Action*, 2nd Ed by Kyle Banker et al. (Manning).

What About BSON?

You may have seen references to Binary JSON (BSON) in the MongoDB documentation. *BSON* is a binary data format that MongoDB uses internally to serialize JSON documents. See the following for further details:

- BSON specification (*http://bsonspec.org/*)
- MongoDB (*https://www.mongodb.com/json-and-bson*)

You can also use BSON to add richer data types to a JSON document.

But for our purposes in this chapter:

- JSON is all you need to know to access the database.
- JSON is the external interface to MongoDB, and BSON is used only internally by MongoDB.

MongoDB Setup

Before we go any further, let's install MongoDB. Refer to "Install MongoDB" on page 331 in Appendix A. With MongoDB in place, you'll be able to run and build on the examples in this chapter.

MongoDB Server and Tools

MongoDB comprises the following:

- The MongoDB server, `mongod`.
- The command shell, which is written in JavaScript.
- Database drivers, which enable developers to access MongoDB from their platform. 10gen, the creator of MongoDB, provides support for many languages, including Java, Ruby, JavaScript, Node.js, C++, C#/.Net, and many others. Check the MongoDB site (*https://docs.mongodb.com/ecosystem/drivers*) for the official supported drivers.
- Command-line tools:
  — `mongodump` and `mongorestore` are backup and restore utilities.
  — `mongoexport` and `mongoimport` are utilities to export/import CSV, TSV, and JSON data to/from MongoDB.
  — `mongostat` monitors database performance (e.g., number of connections and memory usage).

MongoDB Server

The mongod process is similar to other database servers; it accepts connections and processes commands for Create/Read/Update/Delete (CRUD) operations on the data. Let's start mongod from the (macOS and Linux) command line:

```
mongod &
```

If MongoDB was installed properly, the log from the initial startup should look similar to this:

```
2016-06-29T11:05:37.960-0600 I CONTROL   [initandlisten] MongoDB starting : pid...
2016-06-29T11:05:37.961-0600 I CONTROL   [initandlisten] db version v3.2.4
2016-06-29T11:05:37.961-0600 I CONTROL   [initandlisten] git version: e2ee9ffcf...
2016-06-29T11:05:37.961-0600 I CONTROL   [initandlisten] allocator: system
2016-06-29T11:05:37.961-0600 I CONTROL   [initandlisten] modules: none
2016-06-29T11:05:37.961-0600 I CONTROL   [initandlisten] build environment:
2016-06-29T11:05:37.961-0600 I CONTROL   [initandlisten]     distarch: x86_64
2016-06-29T11:05:37.961-0600 I CONTROL   [initandlisten]     target_arch: x86_64
2016-06-29T11:05:37.961-0600 I CONTROL   [initandlisten] options: { config: "/u...
2016-06-29T11:05:37.962-0600 I -         [initandlisten] Detected data files in...
2016-06-29T11:05:37.963-0600 W -         [initandlisten] Detected unclean shutd...
2016-06-29T11:05:37.973-0600 I JOURNAL   [initandlisten] journal dir=/usr/local...
2016-06-29T11:05:37.973-0600 I JOURNAL   [initandlisten] recover begin
2016-06-29T11:05:37.973-0600 I JOURNAL   [initandlisten] info no lsn file in jo...
2016-06-29T11:05:37.973-0600 I JOURNAL   [initandlisten] recover lsn: 0
2016-06-29T11:05:37.973-0600 I JOURNAL   [initandlisten] recover /usr/local/var...
2016-06-29T11:05:37.974-0600 I JOURNAL   [initandlisten] recover applying initi...
2016-06-29T11:05:37.976-0600 I JOURNAL   [initandlisten] recover cleaning up
2016-06-29T11:05:37.976-0600 I JOURNAL   [initandlisten] removeJournalFiles
2016-06-29T11:05:37.977-0600 I JOURNAL   [initandlisten] recover done
2016-06-29T11:05:37.996-0600 I JOURNAL   [durability] Durability thread started
2016-06-29T11:05:37.996-0600 I JOURNAL   [journal writer] Journal writer thread...
2016-06-29T11:05:38.329-0600 I NETWORK   [HostnameCanonicalizationWorker] Start...
2016-06-29T11:05:38.330-0600 I FTDC      [initandlisten] Initializing full-time...
2016-06-29T11:05:38.330-0600 I NETWORK   [initandlisten] waiting for connection...
2016-06-29T11:05:39.023-0600 I FTDC      [ftdc] Unclean full-time diagnostic da...
```

Out of the box, mongod listens on port 27017, but you can change the port as follows:

```
mongod --port <your-port-number>
```

To stop the server, type the following from the command line:

```
kill <pid>
```

Here, <pid> is the Process ID (PID) of the mongod process. *Never* use kill -9 because this could corrupt the database.

Importing JSON into MongoDB

Now that we have the server up and running, let's import our Speaker data into the database. We'll leverage the `mongoimport` tool to upload the *speakers.json* file into MongoDB. Even though we've been using the same Speaker data throughout the book, we need to remove the following outer root document and the Array name:

```
{
  "speakers": [
  ]
}
```

The *speakers.json* file now looks like Example 9-1.

Example 9-1. speakers.json

```
[
  {
    "fullName": "Larson Richard",
    "tags": [
      "JavaScript",
      "AngularJS",
      "Yeoman"
    ],
    "age": 39,
    "registered": true
  }, {
    "fullName": "Ester Clements",
    "tags": [
      "REST",
      "Ruby on Rails",
      "APIs"
    ],
    "age": 29,
    "registered": true
  }, {
    "fullName": "Christensen Fisher",
    "tags": [
      "Java",
      "Spring",
      "Maven",
      "REST"
    ],
    "age": 45,
    "registered": false
  }
]
```

This change was needed because we don't want to insert the contents of the JSON file as an entire document. If we did that, the result would be a single `speakers` Array document in the database. Instead, we want a simple collection of individual `speaker` documents, each of which corresponds to a `speaker` Object from the input file.

When you execute `mongoimport` from the command line, you should see this:

```
json-at-work => mongoimport --db=jsaw --collection=speakers --upsert --jsonArray --file=speakers.json
2016-06-30T10:33:50.202-0600    connected to: localhost
2016-06-30T10:33:50.207-0600    imported 3 documents
json-at-work => mongo
MongoDB shell version: 3.2.4
connecting to: test
> use jsaw
switched to db jsaw
> db.speakers.find()
{ "_id" : ObjectId("577549ee061561f7f9be9725"), "fullName" : "Larson Richard", "tags" : [ "JavaScript", "AngularJS", "Ye
oman" ], "age" : 39, "registered" : true }
{ "_id" : ObjectId("577549ee061561f7f9be9726"), "fullName" : "Ester Clements", "tags" : [ "REST", "Ruby on Rails", "APIs
" ], "age" : 29, "registered" : true }
{ "_id" : ObjectId("577549ee061561f7f9be9727"), "fullName" : "Christensen Fisher", "tags" : [ "Java", "Spring", "Maven",
"REST" ], "age" : 45, "registered" : false }
>
```

In this example, we used the following:

- `mongoimport` to import the `speakers` JSON file into the `speakers` collection in the `jsaw` database.
- `mongo` to access MongoDB, and select all documents from the `speakers` collection. See the next section for further details.

Table 9-1 shows how basic MongoDB concepts relate to relational databases.

Table 9-1. MongoDB and relational databases

MongoDB	Relational
Database	Database instance
Collection	Table
Document	Row

MongoDB Command Shell

Now that the MongoDB server is up and running with some data, it's time to access the database and start working with the Speaker data. The `mongo` shell (which was shown in the previous example) provides MongoDB access from the command line. Start `mongo` as follows:

```
json-at-work => mongo
MongoDB shell version: 3.2.4
connecting to: test
>
```

mongo defaults to the test database. We'll use another database called jsaw (JSON at Work) to keep the Speaker data separate:

```
json-at-work => mongo
MongoDB shell version: 3.2.4
connecting to: test
> use jsaw
switched to db jsaw
>
```

The use command switches context to the jsaw database so that all future commands will affect only that database. But you may be wondering how the jsaw database was created. This happens in two ways:

- Through the mongoimport tool. The --db=jsaw and --collection-speakers command-line options from the initial import created the speakers collection in the jsaw database.

- By inserting a document into a collection from the mongo shell. We'll show how to do this in the next section.

To exit the shell, type exit at the prompt. This ends the shell session and returns control back to the command line.

Basic CRUD with mongo

We've worked with some basic operations with the mongo shell, and now we'll use it for CRUD operations to modify the Speaker data. The MongoDB query language used in the shell is based on JavaScript, which makes it easy to access JSON-based documents.

Query documents

Here's how to get all documents in the speakers collection (which was just imported into MongoDB):

```
json-at-work => mongo jsaw
MongoDB shell version: 3.2.4
connecting to: jsaw
> db.speakers.find()
{ "_id" : ObjectId("577549ee061561f7f9be9725"), "fullName" : "Larson Richard", "tags" : [ "JavaScript", "AngularJS", "Yeoman" ]
, "age" : 39, "registered" : true }
{ "_id" : ObjectId("577549ee061561f7f9be9726"), "fullName" : "Ester Clements", "tags" : [ "REST", "Ruby on Rails", "APIs" ], "a
ge" : 29, "registered" : true }
{ "_id" : ObjectId("577549ee061561f7f9be9727"), "fullName" : "Christensen Fisher", "tags" : [ "Java", "Spring", "Maven", "REST"
], "age" : 45, "registered" : false }
>
```

Here's a breakdown of the shell command (`db.speakers.find()`):

- Shell commands start with `db`.
- `speakers` is the collection name.
- The `find()` without a query parameter returns all documents from the `speakers` collection.

Going back to the shell output, notice that the data returned *looks* like JSON, and it's *so* close. Copy the output from the shell and paste it into JSONLint (*https://json lint.com/*). Click the Validate JSON button, and you'll see that it complains about the `_id` field. MongoDB inserted the `_id` field (an Object ID that serves as a Primary Key) when `mongoimport` imported the Speakers data from the JSON input file and created the `speakers` collection. The output from the MongoDB shell is not valid JSON because of the following:

- It lacks the surrounding Array brackets (`[]`).
- The `ObjectId(...)` is not a valid JSON value. Valid values include Numbers, Booleans, and double-quoted Strings.
- There are no commas to separate the `speaker` documents.

We've shown how to import valid JSON into MongoDB, and later we'll show how to export MongoDB collections as valid JSON after going through the remaining CRUD operations.

To return only those speakers who are present on REST, add a query to the `find()` method:

```
json-at-work => mongo jsaw
MongoDB shell version: 3.2.4
connecting to: jsaw
> db.speakers.find({tags:'REST'})
{ "_id" : ObjectId("577549ee061561f7f9be9726"), "fullName" : "Ester Clements", "tags" : [ "REST", "Ruby on Rails", "APIs" ], "a
ge" : 29, "registered" : true }
{ "_id" : ObjectId("577549ee061561f7f9be9727"), "fullName" : "Christensen Fisher", "tags" : [ "Java", "Spring", "Maven", "REST"
], "age" : 45, "registered" : false }
>
```

In this example, we added a query, `{tags:'REST'}`, which returns only `speaker` documents that contain the value `'REST'` in their `tags` Array. The MongoDB query language is based on JavaScript Object Literal syntax. *JavaScript: The Definitive Guide 6th Ed.* by David Flanagan (O'Reilly) can help you improve your knowledge of JavaScript Objects.

Use the following command to get the number of documents in the `speakers` collection:

```
> db.speakers.count()
3
```

Create a document

The following example shows how to add a new document to the `speakers` collection:

```
json-at-work => mongo jsaw
MongoDB shell version: 3.2.4
connecting to: jsaw
> db.speakers.insert({
...     fullName: 'Carl ClojureDev',
...     tags: ['Clojure', 'Functional Programming'],
...     age: 45,
...     registered: false
... })
WriteResult({ "nInserted" : 1 })
> db.speakers.find()
{ "_id" : ObjectId("577549ee061561f7f9be9725"), "fullName" : "Larson Richard", "tags" : [ "JavaScript", "AngularJS", "Yeoman" ]
, "age" : 39, "registered" : true }
{ "_id" : ObjectId("577549ee061561f7f9be9726"), "fullName" : "Ester Clements", "tags" : [ "REST", "Ruby on Rails", "APIs" ], "a
ge" : 29, "registered" : true }
{ "_id" : ObjectId("577549ee061561f7f9be9727"), "fullName" : "Christensen Fisher", "tags" : [ "Java", "Spring", "Maven", "REST"
], "age" : 45, "registered" : false }
{ "_id" : ObjectId("577584327a0be85396f1daed"), "fullName" : "Carl ClojureDev", "tags" : [ "Clojure", "Functional Programming"
], "age" : 45, "registered" : false }
>
```

This example uses the `insert()` function with a JavaScript Object Literal containing the key/value pairs for the new `speaker` document.

Update a document

Our new speaker, Carl ClojureDev, has decided to add Scala to his technical repertoire. To add this language to the `tags` Array, do the following:

```
json-at-work => mongo jsaw
MongoDB shell version: 3.2.4
connecting to: jsaw
> db.speakers.find({fullName: 'Carl ClojureDev'})
{ "_id" : ObjectId("577584327a0be85396f1daed"), "fullName" : "Carl ClojureDev", "tags" : [ "Clojure" ], "age" : 45, "registered
" : false }
> db.speakers.update({fullName: 'Carl ClojureDev'},
... { $push:
...     { tags: 'Scala' }
... })
WriteResult({ "nMatched" : 1, "nUpserted" : 0, "nModified" : 1 })
> db.speakers.find({fullName: 'Carl ClojureDev'})
{ "_id" : ObjectId("577584327a0be85396f1daed"), "fullName" : "Carl ClojureDev", "tags" : [ "Clojure", "Scala" ], "age" : 45, "r
egistered" : false }
>
```

This example uses the `update()` function as follows:

- The `{fullName: 'Carl ClojureDev'}` query finds the `speaker` document to update.

- The $push operator adds 'Scala' to the tags Array. This is similar to the push() function in JavaScript.

Note that many other operators support the update() function, such as $set, but be careful because it sets a field to a completely new value.

Delete a document

Finally, let's delete the *Carl Clojuredev* speaker from the collection:

```
json-at-work => mongo jsaw
MongoDB shell version: 3.2.4
connecting to: jsaw
> db.speakers.find({fullName: 'Carl ClojureDev'})
{ "_id" : ObjectId("5775906647776536ff96a2fc"), "fullName" : "Carl ClojureDev", "tags" : [ "Clojure", "Scala", "Functional Prog
ramming" ], "age" : 45, "registered" : false }
> db.speakers.remove({fullName: 'Carl ClojureDev'})
WriteResult({ "nRemoved" : 1 })
> db.speakers.find({fullName: 'Carl ClojureDev'})
> db.speakers.find()
{ "_id" : ObjectId("577549ee061561f7f9be9725"), "fullName" : "Larson Richard", "tags" : [ "JavaScript", "AngularJS", "Yeoman" ]
, "age" : 39, "registered" : true }
{ "_id" : ObjectId("577549ee061561f7f9be9726"), "fullName" : "Ester Clements", "tags" : [ "REST", "Ruby on Rails", "APIs" ], "a
ge" : 29, "registered" : true }
{ "_id" : ObjectId("577549ee061561f7f9be9727"), "fullName" : "Christensen Fisher", "tags" : [ "Java", "Spring", "Maven", "REST"
], "age" : 45, "registered" : false }
>
```

Here we use the remove() function with the {fullName: 'Carl ClojureDev'} query to delete only that document. Subsequent calls to find() show that this document was deleted without affecting the rest of the documents in the speakers collection.

Exporting from MongoDB to a JSON Document

Now that we're comfortable with the MongoDB server and shell, let's export the data to a valid JSON document. Use the mongoexport tool as follows, and you should see this:

```
json-at-work => mongoexport --db=jsaw --collection=speakers --pretty --jsonArray
2016-06-30T12:58:32.270-0600    connected to: localhost
[{
        "_id": {
                "$oid": "577549ee061561f7f9be9725"
        },
        "fullName": "Larson Richard",
        "tags": [
                "JavaScript",
                "AngularJS",
                "Yeoman"
        ],
        "age": 39,
        "registered": true
},
{
```

```
    "_id": {
        "$oid": "577549ee061561f7f9be9726"
    },
    "fullName": "Ester Clements",
    "tags": [
        "REST",
        "Ruby on Rails",
        "APIs"
    ],
    "age": 29,
    "registered": true
},
{

    "_id": {
        "$oid": "577549ee061561f7f9be9727"
    },
    "fullName": "Christensen Fisher",
    "tags": [
        "Java",
        "Spring",
        "Maven",
        "REST"
    ],
    "age": 45,
    "registered": false
}]
```

```
2016-06-30T12:58:32.271-0600    exported 3 records
```

The mongoexport command in the above example pulls the data from the speakers collection in the jsaw database and pretty-prints a JSON array to Standard Output. This is a good start, but we need to remove the MongoDB Object ID (_id) so we have valid JSON and can use the data outside MongoDB. Other tools are needed to filter out the _id field because the mongoexport utility will always output the _id.

We can get the JSON format we want by combining tools, and jq is just the right tool for the job. As you'll recall from Chapter 6, jq is an amazing command-line utility that not only searches JSON but also has excellent filtering capabilities. jq doesn't provide the full-blown JSON Transform capabilities of Handlebars (see Chapter 7), but it's more than adequate for our needs. By piping the output from mongoexport to jq, you should see the following:

```
json-at-work => mongoexport --db=jsaw --collection=speakers --pretty --jsonArray | jq '[.[] | del(._id)]'
2016-06-30T13:09:56.236-0600    connected to: localhost
2016-06-30T13:09:56.237-0600    exported 3 records
[
  {
    "fullName": "Larson Richard",
    "tags": [
      "JavaScript",
      "AngularJS",
      "Yeoman"
    ],
    "age": 39,
    "registered": true
  },
  {
    "fullName": "Ester Clements",
    "tags": [
      "REST",
      "Ruby on Rails",
      "APIs"
    ],
    "age": 29,
    "registered": true
  },
  {
    "fullName": "Christensen Fisher",
    "tags": [
      "Java",
      "Spring",
      "Maven",
      "REST"
    ],
    "age": 45,
    "registered": false
  }
]
json-at-work => 
```

The output is everything we're looking for: a valid JSON Array of speaker Objects without the MongoDB Object ID. Here's a breakdown of the command line:

- The mongoexport command is as follows:
  - --db=jsaw --collection=speakers specifies the speakers collection in the jsaw database.
  - --pretty --jsonArray ensures that the output is a pretty-printed JSON array.
- The mongoexport output goes to Standard Output and gets piped to jq.
- The jq expression [.[] | del(._id)] works as follows:
  - The outer array brackets ([]) ensure that the JSON Array, Objects, and Fields/Keys are preserved in the final output.
  - The .[] tells jq to look at the whole Array.
  - The pipe to the del(._id) command tells jq to delete the _id field from the output.

- The jq output goes to Standard Output, which could serve as input to a file.

This is a practical example of the power of jq. Although the jq syntax is a bit terse, it's a great addition to your JSON toolbelt. For more details on jq, refer to Chapter 6. You can also visit the jq manual (*https://stedolan.github.io/jq/manual*).

What About Schema?

MongoDB is schemaless, which means that the database neither validates data nor does it requires a Schema in order to store data. But the data stored in each document still has a structure that applications expect so that they can reliably work with collections and documents. Object Document Mappers (ODMs) provide additional features on top of MongoDB:

- A Schema that validates the data and enforces a common data structure
- Object modeling
- Object-based data access

There is no single, cross-platform ODM for MongoDB. Rather, each platform has its own library. Node.js developers typically use Mongoose (*http://mongoosejs.com/index.html*). Here's a brief example of how to specify a speaker Schema, create a model, and insert a speaker into the database:

```
var mongoose = require('mongoose');
var Schema = mongoose.Schema;
mongoose.connect('mongodb://localhost/jsaw');

// Specify the Speaker schema.

var speakerSchema = new Schema({
  fullName:  String,
  tags: [String],
  age: Number,
  registered: Boolean
});

// Create the Speaker model.

var Speaker = mongoose.model('Speaker', speakerSchema);

var speaker = new Speaker({
  fullName: 'Carl ClojureDev',
  tags: ['Clojure', 'Functional Programming'],
  age: 45,
  registered: false
});
```

```
speaker.save(function (err) {
  if (err) {
    console.log(err);
  } else {
    console.log('Created Speaker: ' + speaker.fullName);
  }
});
```

A Mongoose model is a constructor based on a Schema, and it encapsulates the details of accessing a MongoDB collection. A Mongoose document is an instance of a model, and provides access to a MongoDB document. A Mongoose Schema is not the same thing as a JSON Schema. The `json-schema-to-mongoose` (*https://www.npmjs.com/package/json-schema-to-mongoose*) Node.js module can convert a JSON Schema to an equivalent Mongoose Schema, but this is left as an exercise for you. In addition to creating a document, Mongoose also provides the ability to read (`find()`), update (`save()` or `update()`), and delete (`remove()`) a document.

Other platforms have their own ODMs for accessing MongoDB:

Java
> Spring users can leverage Spring Data (*http://www.springsource.org/spring-data/mongodb*), which provides POJO mapping to MongoDB. Hibernate OGM (*http://hibernate.org/ogm*) provides Java Persistence API (JPA) support for NoSQL databases, including MongoDB.

Ruby
> Mongoid (*http://bit.ly/2rvO0Z0*), which is officially supported by MongoDB.

RESTful API Testing with MongoDB

The MEAN Stack is outside the scope of this book, so we can't do justice to the topic in this chapter and stay focused on JSON. Let's do something different with MongoDB, and leverage it as a Mock/Stub RESTful API instead. Mock/Stub RESTful APIs are great:

- There's no coding involved, which frees developers from the drudgery of developing and maintaining infrastructure code. Instead, developers can focus on useful code that delivers business value—the business logic of the API.

- It pushes the API development team to create an initial design for their API *before* they start coding. This is also known as "API First" design. By doing it this way, developers are less likely to expose the implementation details of domain Objects and databases because they are designing to an interface (because the Stub API has no implementation).

- API consumers have a viable Stub version of an API without having to wait for the completion of the real API.

- API developers now have enough time to develop the API properly without having to rush to "get something out the door" to support their consumers.

- API developers can gain early feedback on the usability of the API from their consumers and use this information to iteratively update their design and implementation.

Test Input Data

We'll continue to use the Speaker data that we imported earlier in this chapter.

Providing a RESTful Wrapper for MongoDB

According to the MongoDB documentation (*https://docs.mongodb.com/ecosystem/tools/http-interfaces/*), there are several solid REST interfaces (that run as separate servers in front of MongoDB), including these:

Crest
> Based on Node.js, Crest provides full CRUD (HTTP GET, PUT, POST, and DELETE) capabilities. You can find details at the GitHub repository (*https://github.com/cordazar/crest*).

RESTHeart
> This is Java-based, provides full CRUD functionality, and is available at *http://www.restheart.org*.

DrowsyDromedary
> Based on Ruby, this server provides full CRUD capabilities. You can find it on GitHub (*https://github.com/zuk/DrowsyDromedary*).

Simple REST API
> This is provided by default as part of MongoDB, but it works only with HTTP GET, and doesn't provide full REST capabilities (PUT, POST, and DELETE). For further information, see the Simple REST API documentation at the RESTHeart site (*https://docs.mongodb.com/ecosystem/tools/http-interfaces/#simple-rest-api*).

Either Crest, RESTHeart, or DrowsyDromedary will meet our needs here because they can all handle CRUD requests from Consumers by supporting all major HTTP verbs. Let's go with Crest because it's simple to install and set up. Refer to Appendix A, and install Crest (see "Install npm Modules" on page 325). Then, navigate to the *crest* directory on your local machine and start the Crest server by typing node server on the command line. You should see the following:

```
node server

DEBUG: util.js is loaded
```

```
DEBUG: rest.js is loaded
crest listening at http://:::3500
```

Then, open your browser and enter the following URL: *http://localhost:3500/jsaw/speakers*. This tells Crest to do a `GET` (read/find) on the `speakers` collection in the `jsaw` database on MongoDB. You should see the screen in Figure 9-1.

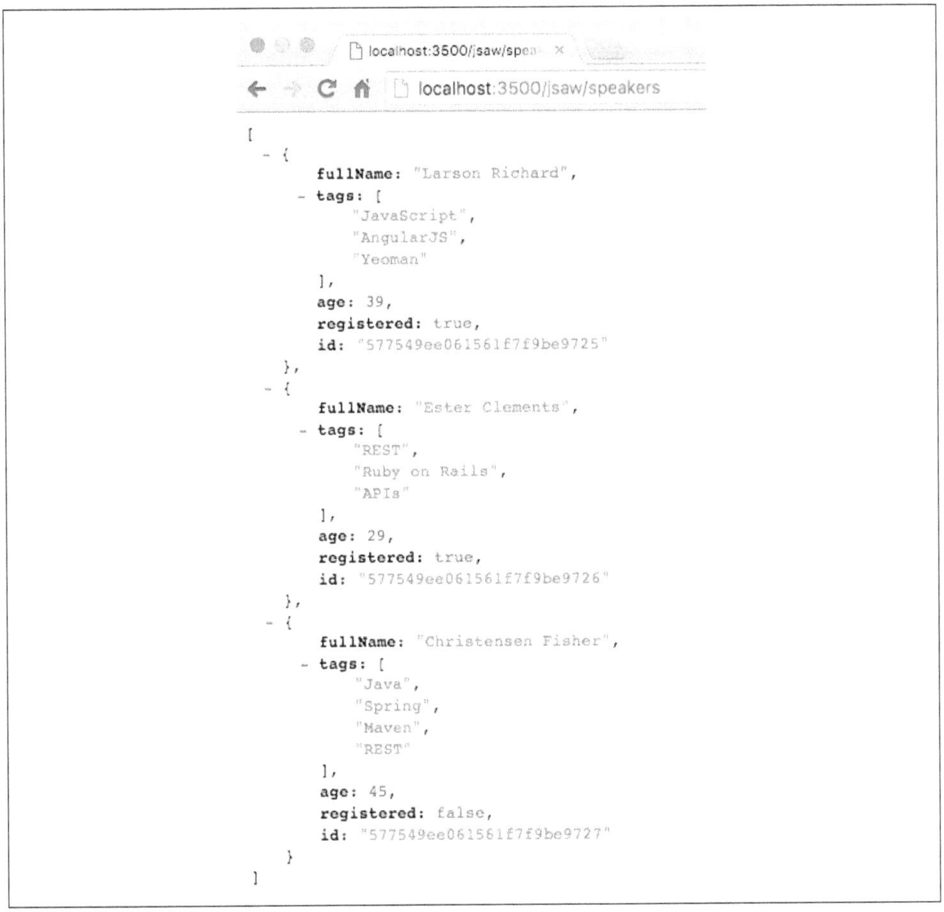

Figure 9-1. Speakers data served by MongoDB/Crest and viewed from the browser

This is a good start, but you can't do full API testing with your browser because it can only send an HTTP `GET` request. Let's use Postman (from earlier chapters) to fully exercise the Crest/MongoDB-based Speakers API. Enter the *http://localhost:3500/jsaw/speakers* URL, select `GET` as the HTTP verb, and click the Send button. You should see the screen in Figure 9-2.

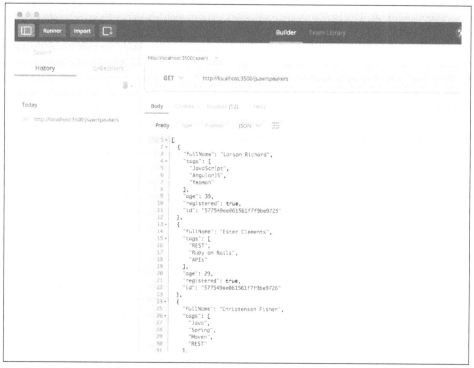

Figure 9-2. Speakers data served by MongoDB/Crest and viewed from Postman

This is what we saw before in the browser, but now we have the ability to modify the data represented by the API. Let's delete one of the `speaker` Objects. First, copy the `id` for one of the `speaker` Objects, and add it to the URL *http://localhost:3500/jsaw/speakers/id* (where `id` is the Object ID that you copied). Then (in Postman) choose `DELETE` as the HTTP verb, and click the Send button. You should see the following in the HTTP Response:

```
{
  "ok": 1
}
```

Now, go back and do another `GET` on *http://localhost:3500/jsaw/speakers* and you should see that Crest invoked MongoDB to delete the selected `speaker`.

We now have a fully functional Stub REST API that accesses MongoDB and produces valid JSON output, without the need to write code or set up big infrastructure. Use this style of workflow to streamline your API Design and testing, and watch your team's productivity soar.

What We Covered

In this chapter, we've shown the basics of how JSON and MongoDB work together by covering these topics:

- Importing a JSON document into MongoDB
- Performing core CRUD operations with MongoDB
- Exporting MongoDB data to a JSON document
- Accessing MongoDB as a Mock/Stub RESTful API (without writing code)

What's Next?

Now that we've shown the synergy between JSON and MongoDB, we'll move on to the final stage of our Enterprise JSON journey and put everything together as we describe how JSON works with Apache Kafka in Chapter 10.

JSON Messaging with Kafka

Apache Kafka is a popular distributed scalable messaging system that enables hetero-genous applications (those that run on multiple platforms) to communicate asyn-chronously by passing messages. Kafka was originally developed by the LinkedIn engineering team as part of a major rearchitecture effort. After the company moved from monolithic applications to Microservices, they created Kafka to fill the need for a universal data pipeline capable of processing large message volumes in order to integrate the services and applications across their enterprise. In 2011, LinkedIn open sourced Kafka to the Apache Foundation. Today, many companies successfully lever-age Kafka as the central messaging platform in their enterprise architecture strategy. You can find more information about Kafka on the Apache Kafka main page (*http:// kafka.apache.org*).

Kafka differs from other messaging systems (e.g., Java Message Service, or JMS) in that it is not tied to a particular platform. Although Kafka was written in Java, Pro-ducers and Consumers can be written in different languages. To demonstrate this, we'll have a Node.js-based Consumer and a Consumer written in Bourne Shell in our end-to-end example.

Kafka supports both binary and text messages. The most popular text formats are plain/flat text, JSON, and Apache Avro. The Kafka APIs (used by Producers and Con-sumers) communicate over TCP. In this chapter, we'll use Kafka as a traditional mes-saging system with JSON-based messages, and show how to do the following:

- Produce/consume JSON messages with Kafka from the command line
- Design and implement a small end-to-end example that leverages Kafka with JSON

Kafka Use Cases

Typical Kafka use cases include the following:

Traditional messaging
Applications publish messages that are consumed by other applications. Kafka uses an asynchronous (i.e., the sender doesn't wait for a response) publish/subscribe (or pub/sub) messaging model that decouples Producers from Consumers.

Analytics and stream processing
Applications publish real-time usage information (e.g., clicks, visitors, sessions, page views, and purchases) to Kafka Topics. Then a streaming application such as Apache Spark/Spark Streaming reads messages from the various topics, transforms the data (e.g., map/reduce), and sends it to a data store such as Hadoop (via Flume). You can add analytics tools (e.g., data visualization) on top of the target data store.

Operational and application performance netrics
Applications can publish statistics (e.g., message counts, number of transactions, response time, HTTP status codes, and counts) for review by operations personnel to monitor and track performance, usage, and potential issues.

Log aggregation
Applications across an enterprise can publish their log messages to a Kafka Topic, which makes them available to log management applications—e.g., the ELK (ElasticSearch, Logstash, Kibana) stack (*http://oreil.ly/2sprtks*). Kafka could be used in front of Logstash to receive large data volumes and allow Logstash to perform more-expensive operations at its own pace without losing messages.

Kafka Concepts and Terminology

Here are some of the key concepts in Kafka's architecture:

Producer
Publishes messages to a Topic.

Consumer
Registers for or Subscribes to a Topic and reads messages as they become available.

Topic
A named channel, a message feed/stream for a category of messages. In our example, `new-proposals-recvd` contains messages that represent new speaker session proposals at MyConference. You can also think of a Topic as a stream of

business events, including orders and product returns. A Topic is divided into one or more Partitions.

Broker
A Kafka server that manages one or more Topics.

Cluster
Contains one or more Brokers.

Partition
In a distributed environment, a Topic is replicated across multiple Partitions (each of which is managed by a separate Broker).

Offset
A unique ID for a message within a Partition. This is how Kafka maintains the ordering and sequencing of messages.

This is all you need to know in order to produce/consume JSON messages for this chapter. Many other important areas are not covered in this book in order to maintain brevity and focus, including Durability, Consumer Groups, Delivery Guarantees, and Replication. Kafka is a big topic that warrants its own book, and you can find more information in *Kafka: The Definitive Guide*, by Neha Narkhede et al. (O'Reilly).

For our example, we will have a single Broker (Kafka server), and each Topic will have a single Partition.

The Kafka Ecosystem—Related Projects

Kafka is a general-purpose messaging system that integrates with other message-processing systems to build larger, more powerful messaging applications. Kafka's ecosystem includes, but is not limited to the following:

Apache Spark (http://spark.apache.org/)/Spark Streaming (https://spark.apache.org/streaming/)
Used for stream processing (see "Kafka Use Cases" on page 290).

HiveKa (https://github.com/HiveKa/HiveKa)
Provides integration with Hive to create a SQL-like interface to Kafka Topics.

ElasticSearch (http://bit.ly/2rhV2B5)
The standalone Consumer pulls data from Kafka Topics and loads it into Elastic-Search.

Kafka Manager (https://github.com/yahoo/kafka-manager)
A management console for Kafka that enables administrators to work with Kafka Clusters, Topics, Consumers, and so forth.

Flume (http://flume.apache.org/)

Moves large amounts of data from a channel (e.g., a Kafka topic) to the Hadoop Distributed File System (HDFS).

Avro (https://avro.apache.org/)

A data serialization alternative to pure JSON that provides richer data structures. Avro is not a standard, but has its own Schemas (which have no relationship to JSON Schema) that are written in JSON. Avro is an alternative to JSON that provides richer data structures and a more compact data format. Avro started as part of Hadoop, and eventually became its own project.

This list is just a small sample of other systems that work with Kafka. See the Kafka Ecosystem page (*https://cwiki.apache.org/confluence/display/KAFKA/Ecosystem*) for a full description of the Kafka Ecosystem.

Kafka Environment Setup

Before we look at the command-line interface, let's install Kafka and Apache Zoo-Keeper to run and build all the examples in this chapter. Refer to "Install Apache Kafka" on page 334 in Appendix A, and install Kafka and ZooKeeper.

Now it's time to configure Kafka so that it allows us to delete Topics (this setting is turned off by default). Edit the *KAFKA-INSTALL-DIR/KAFKA_VERSION/libexec/config/server.properties* file (where *KAFKA-INSTALL-DIR* is the directory where your installation procedure installed Kafka, and *KAFKA_VERSION* is the installed Kafka version) as follows:

```
# Switch to enable topic deletion or not, default value is false
delete.topic.enable=true
```

Why Do I Need ZooKeeper?

At this point, you may be wondering why you need ZooKeeper in addition to Kafka. The short answer is that ZooKeeper is required in order to run Kafka. In other words, Kafka (as a distributed application) is designed to run within the ZooKeeper environment. ZooKeeper is a server that coordinates distributed processes by managing the following: naming, status information, configuration, location information, synchronization, failover, etc. The naming registry uses a hierarchical namespace that is similar to a filesystem.

ZooKeeper is used by several well-known projects, including Kafka, Storm, Hadoop MapReduce, HBase, and Solr (Cloud Edition), and so forth. To learn more, visit the ZooKeeper main page (*https://zookeeper.apache.org/*).

Kafka Command-Line Interface (CLI)

Kafka comes with a built-in CLI that enables developers to experiment with Kafka without leaving the command line. We'll demonstrate how to start Kafka, publish JSON messages, and then shutdown the Kafka infrastructure.

To use the convenience scripts and avoid lots of typing, please be sure to visit the *chapter-10/scripts* directory (from the code examples) and change the file permissions so that all scripts will be executable:

```
chmod +x *.sh
```

How to Publish a JSON Message with the CLI

Here are the steps (in the required order) to start Kafka and then publish/consume messages:

1. Start ZooKeeper.
2. Start the Kafka server.
3. Create a Topic.
4. Start a Consumer.
5. Publish a message to a Topic.
6. Consume a message.
7. Clean up and shut down Kafka:

    - Stop the Consumer.
    - Delete a Topic.
    - Shutdown Kafka.
    - Stop ZooKeeper.

Start ZooKeeper

As mentioned earlier, Kafka requires ZooKeeper. To start ZooKeeper, run the following command in a new terminal:

```
./start-zookeeper.sh
```

Example 10-1 shows the script.

Example 10-1. scripts/start-zookeeper.sh

```
zkServer start
```

You should see the following:

```
json-at-work => ./start-zookeeper.sh
ZooKeeper JMX enabled by default
Using config: /usr/local/etc/zookeeper/zoo.cfg
Starting zookeeper ... STARTED
```

Start Kafka

Now it's time to start a Kafka server (from a new terminal):

```
./start-kafka.sh
```

The script looks like Example 10-2

Example 10-2. scripts/start-kafka.sh

```
kafka-server-start /usr/local/etc/kafka/server.properties
```

In this script, the *server.properties* file has configuration settings for Kafka. We edited this file earlier to enable the ability to delete topics.

The Kafka server should now be running. This command prints a lot of logging messages, and you should see the following when the server reaches the steady state:

```
[2016-12-31 16:42:01,371] INFO Creating /brokers/ids/0 (is it secure? false) (kafka.utils.ZKCheckedEphemeral)
[2016-12-31 16:42:01,375] INFO Result of znode creation is: OK (kafka.utils.ZKCheckedEphemeral)
[2016-12-31 16:42:01,377] INFO Registered broker 0 at path /brokers/ids/0 with addresses: PLAINTEXT -> EndPoint(10.229.1
04.161,9092,PLAINTEXT) (kafka.utils.ZkUtils)
[2016-12-31 16:42:01,385] INFO Kafka version : 0.10.1.0 (org.apache.kafka.common.utils.AppInfoParser)
[2016-12-31 16:42:01,385] INFO Kafka commitId : 3402a74efb23d1d4 (org.apache.kafka.common.utils.AppInfoParser)
[2016-12-31 16:42:01,386] INFO [Kafka Server 0], started (kafka.server.KafkaServer)
```

Create a Topic

Next, let's create the `test-proposals-recvd` Topic to receive new speaker session proposals. To create the Topic, run the script as follows (from a new terminal):

```
./create-topic.sh test-proposals-recvd
```

The script runs the `kafka-topics` command as shown in Example 10-3.

Example 10-3. scripts/create-topic.sh

```
...

kafka-topics --zookeeper localhost:2181 --create \
          --topic $1 --partitions 1 \
          --replication-factor 1
```

This script works as follows:

- $1 is the command-line variable that has the Topic name (in this case, test-proposals-recvd).
- We kept things simple by using only a single partition (an ordered sequence of records) and one replica for the Topic. A Partition can be replicated across multiple servers for fault tolerance and load balancing. In a production configuration, you would have multiple replicas to support large message volumes.

When you run the preceding script, you should see this:

```
json-at-work => ./create-topic.sh test-proposals-recvd
Created topic "test-proposals-recvd".
```

List Topics

Let's make sure that the new Topic was created properly by running the following script:

```
./list-topics.sh
```

The script uses the kafka-topics command as shown in Example 10-4.

Example 10-4. scripts/list-topics.sh

```
kafka-topics --zookeeper localhost:2181 --list
```

You should see that the test-proposals-recvd Topic was created:

```
json-at-work => ./list-topics.sh
__consumer_offsets
test-proposals-recvd
```

The __consumer_offsets is a low-level, internal Kafka implementation detail—pay no attention to it. We're concerned only with the Topic that we created.

Start a Consumer

Now that we have a Topic, it's time to produce and consume messages. First, we'll create a Consumer that subscribes to the test-proposals-recvd topic with the following script:

```
./start-consumer.sh test-proposals-recvd
```

This script uses the kafka-console-consumer command as shown in Example 10-5.

Example 10-5. scripts/start-consumer.sh

```
...

kafka-console-consumer --bootstrap-server localhost:9092 \
                       --topic $1
```

In this script, $1 is the command-line variable that has the Topic name (in this case, test-proposals-recvd) that the Consumer is listening on.

You should see that the Consumer is now polling/waiting for a new message, so there's no output yet:

```
json-at-work ⇒ ./start-consumer.sh test-proposals-recvd
```

Publish a JSON Message

It's now time to publish a JSON message to our topic with the following script (in a new terminal):

```
./publish-message.sh '{ "message": "This is a test proposal." }' test-proposals-recvd
```

Example 10-6 provides the script.

Example 10-6. scripts/publish-message.sh

```
...

echo $MESSAGE_FROM_CLI | kafka-console-producer \
        --broker-list localhost:9092 \
        --topic $TOPIC_NAME_FROM_CLI

...
```

Note the following in this script:

- We use echo to print the JSON message to Standard Output and pipe it to the kafka-console-producer command.

- $MESSAGE_FROM_CLI is the command-line variable that has the JSON message to publish.

- $TOPIC_NAME_FROM_CLI is the command-line variable that has the Topic name (in this case, test-proposals-recvd).

When you publish the message, you should see the following:

```
json-at-work => ./publish-message.sh '{ "message": "This is a test proposal." }' test-proposals-recvd
```

The message doesn't show in this terminal window.

Consume a JSON Message

When you revisit the terminal window where you started the Consumer, you should see that the Consumer has read and printed the message from the `test-proposals-recvd` Topic:

```
json-at-work => ./start-consumer.sh test-proposals-recvd
{ "message": "This is a test proposal." }
```

We now have a simple CLI-based example with Kafka that produces and consumes JSON messages. Now let's clean up.

Clean Up and Shut Down Kafka

Here are the steps to clean up and shut down Kafka:

1. Stop the Consumer.
2. Delete a Topic (optional).
3. Stop Kafka.
4. Stop ZooKeeper.

Stop the Consumer

Just hit Ctrl-C in the terminal window where you started the Consumer and you should see the following:

```
json-at-work => ./start-consumer.sh test-proposals-recvd
{ "message": "This is a test proposal." }
^CProcessed a total of 1 messages
```

Delete a Topic

We'll now delete the `test-proposals-recvd` Topic with the following script (this is optional):

```
./delete-topic.sh test-proposals-recvd
```

Example 10-7 shows the script.

Example 10-7. scripts/delete-topic.sh

```
...

kafka-topics --zookeeper localhost:2181 --delete --topic $1
```

In this script, `$1` is the command-line variable that has the Topic name (in this case, `test-proposals-recvd`).

You should see the following on your screen:

```
json-at-work => ./delete-topic.sh test-proposals-recvd
Topic test-proposals-recvd is marked for deletion.
Note: This will have no impact if delete.topic.enable is not set to true.
```

Stop Kafka

To stop Kafka, just press Ctrl-C in the terminal window where you started Kafka or you can do a graceful shutdown as follows:

```
./stop-kafka.sh
```

Example 10-8 shows the script.

Example 10-8. scripts/stop-kafka.sh

```
kafka-server-stop
```

This script uses the `kafka-server-stop` command to stop the Kafka server. The controlled/graceful shutdown takes a while and produces a lot of log messages. If you return to the terminal window where you started the Kafka server, you should see the following message at the end:

```
[2016-12-31 18:40:06,981] INFO [GroupCoordinator 0]: Shutdown complete. (kafka.coordinator.GroupCoordinator)
[2016-12-31 18:40:06,988] INFO Terminate ZkClient event thread. (org.I0Itec.zkclient.ZkEventThread)
[2016-12-31 18:40:06,990] INFO Session: 0x159573c11390007 closed (org.apache.zookeeper.ZooKeeper)
[2016-12-31 18:40:06,990] INFO EventThread shut down for session: 0x159573c11390007 (org.apache.zookeeper.ClientCnxn)
[2016-12-31 18:40:06,992] INFO [Kafka Server 0], shut down completed (kafka.server.KafkaServer)
```

If you deleted the `test-proposals-recvd` Topic in the previous section, it won't exist when you restart Kafka. If you did not delete this Topic, it will be there upon a Kafka restart.

Stop ZooKeeper

Let's finish up by stopping ZooKeeper. Type the following from the command line:

```
./stop-zookeeper.sh
```

Example 10-9 shows the script.

Example 10-9. scripts/stop-zookeeper.sh

```
zkServer stop
```

At this point, all the Kafka-related infrastructure should be stopped, and you should see the following:

```
json-at-work => ./stop-zookeeper.sh
ZooKeeper JMX enabled by default
Using config: /usr/local/etc/zookeeper/zoo.cfg
Stopping zookeeper ... STOPPED
```

Kafka Libraries

Kafka enjoys wide support across the major application development platforms, including the following libraries:

Java
> Spring is widely used for integration within the Java community, and provides support through the Spring Kafka library (*http://bit.ly/2sp3LEW*).

Ruby
> Karafka is a gem you can find on GitHub (*https://github.com/karafka/karafka*).

JS
> kafka-node is a module we'll use for the end-to-end example in the next section. You can find more information on kafka-node on npm (*https://www.npmjs.com/package/kafka-node*) and GitHub (*https://github.com/SOHU-Co/kafka-node*).

End-to-End Example—Speaker Proposals at MyConference

We've shown how to use Kafka at the command line, and we'll now combine that with Node.js-based applications that consume and produce messages. For our final example, we're going to create an application that enables speakers to submit proposals to speak at MyConference (a fictitious company). Each speaker will submit a proposal, which is reviewed by a member of the MyConference proposal team. The speaker is then notified by email on the MyConference reviewer's decision.

Test Data

We'll continue to use the Speaker data that we've used in previous chapters, but we need to add a few more elements to make this a fully dressed proposal. Example 10-10 shows the upgraded speaker session proposal.

Example 10-10. data/speakerProposal.json

```json
{
  "speaker": {
    "firstName": "Larson",
    "lastName": "Richard",
    "email": "larson.richard@ecratic.com",
    "bio": "Larson Richard is the CTO of ... and he founded a JavaScript meetup ..."
  },
  "session": {
    "title": "Enterprise Node",
    "abstract": "Many developers just see Node as a way to build web APIs or ...",
    "type": "How-To",
    "length": "3 hours"
  },
  "conference": {
    "name": "Ultimate JavaScript Conference by MyConference",
    "beginDate": "2017-11-06",
    "endDate": "2017-11-10"
  },
  "topic": {
    "primary": "Node.js",
    "secondary": [
      "REST",
      "Architecture",
      "JavaScript"
    ]
  },
  "audience": {
    "takeaway": "Audience members will learn how to ...",
    "jobTitles": [
      "Architects",
      "Developers"
    ],
    "level": "Intermediate"
  },
  "installation": [
    "Git",
    "Laptop",
    "Node.js"
  ]
}
```

In this example, we have the following Objects:

speaker
    The speaker's contact information.

session
    A description of the session, including title and length.

`conference`
> Tells which conference the speaker is applying for. MyConference runs multiple events, so this is important.

`topic`
> Primary and secondary topics covered in the talk.

`audience`
> The audience level (beginner, intermediate, or advanced).

`installation`
> Installation instructions (if any) that the audience should follow before attending the session.

Architecture Components

Here are the components needed for the MyConference application:

Speaker Proposal Producer
> Uses the *publish-message.sh* script to send the JSON-based speaker session proposal on the speaker's behalf to the `new-proposals-recvd` Topic. In the real world, this would be a nice AngularJS application with a solid UX design that invokes a RESTful API, but we'll stick with an extremely simple shell script interface to keep the focus on JSON.

Proposal Reviewer (i.e., Consumer)
> Listens on the `new-proposals-recvd` Topic, accepts/rejects a proposal, and sends a corresponding message to the `proposals-reviewed` Topic for further processing. In an enterprise-level architecture, we would put a RESTful API in front to receive the speaker proposal and then publish the message to the `new-proposals-recvd` Topic. But again, we're not showing an API here to simplify the example.

Speaker Notifier (i.e., Consumer)
> Listens on the `proposals-reviewed` Topic, generates an acceptance/rejection email (based on the reviewer's decision), and sends a notification email to the speaker.

Email Server (emulated)
> Acts as MyConference's Email Server to send notification emails.

Email Client (emulated)
> Serves as the speaker's Email Client to receive notification emails.

For the Email Client and Server, we'll use MailCatcher, a simple email emulator to simplify infrastructure setup.

Figure 10-1 shows the overall flow and the way the components interact.

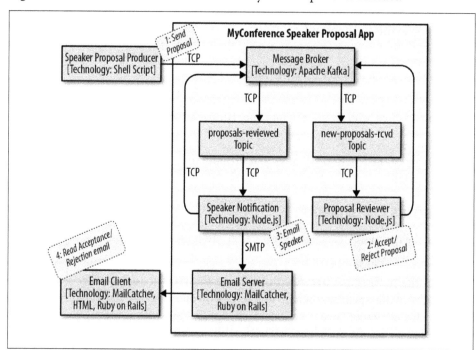

Figure 10-1. MyConference Speaker Proposal architecture—components

The flow of this diagram is as follows:

1. The Speaker uses the Speaker Proposal Producer to send a proposal to the new-proposals-recvd Topic within the MyConference application.

2. The Proposal Reviewer receives a proposal message on new-proposals-recvd Topic, makes a decision, and sends the acceptance/rejection message to the proposals-reviewed Topic.

3. The Speaker Notifier receives an acceptance/rejection message on the proposals-reviewed Topic, creates a notification email message, and sends it.

4. The Speaker reviews the notification email message(s).

It's now time to walk through some code and run the example.

Set Up the Kafka Environment

If you ran through the CLI example, the steps should look familiar (refer to that section if you need to refresh your memory). We'll need four terminal sessions to run the example. Do the following to get started:

1. Create terminal session 1.

   - Start ZooKeeper.
   - Start Kafka.

2. Create terminal session 2.

   - Create the `proposals-reviewed` Topic.
   - Create the `new-proposals-recvd` Topic.

With the core Kafka components in place, let's set up an Email Server to receive acceptance/rejection notification email messages.

Set Up Fake Email Server and Client—MailCatcher

We'll use MailCatcher. A Simple Mail (SMTP) server is a great tool for testing emails without forcing you to send a real email. MailCatcher has the characteristics we need for this example:

- Follows standards—MailCatcher is based on the Simple Mail Transfer Protocol (SMTP) (*https://tools.ietf.org/html/rfc5321*).
- Easy installation.
- Simple startup/shutdown.
- Security is optional. I know this sounds scary, but we don't want to go through the hassle of setting up the user ID/password for an email server. For simple examples and prototyping as we're doing here, this is OK. Of course, for bigger prototypes and real-world situations, you definitely want to secure access to your email server. MailCatcher will work well for bigger examples because it can also accept user credentials.
- Nice web UI that shows email messages sent to the server.

For more information on MailCatcher, visit its website (*https://mailcatcher.me*).

If you haven't installed Ruby on Rails yet, refer to "Install Ruby on Rails" on page 328 in Appendix A, and install it. Install the `mailcatcher` gem on the command line (staying in terminal session 2) as follows (also see "Install Ruby Gems" on page 329 in Appendix A):

```
gem install mailcatcher
```

Start the MailCatcher server as follows, and you should see the following on your screen:

```
json-at-work => mailcatcher
Starting MailCatcher
==> smtp://127.0.0.1:1025
==> http://127.0.0.1:1080
*** MailCatcher runs as a daemon by default. Go to the web interface to quit.
```

MailCatcher runs as a daemon in the background, which enables you to do other things in the current terminal session. We'll visit the MailCatcher web UI after we have some emails to review (see "Review Notification Email Messages with Mail-Catcher" on page 315 later in this chapter).

Set Up Node.js Project Environment

The Proposal Reviewer and Speaker Notifier are both written in Node.js. If you haven't installed Node.js yet, refer to Appendix A, and install Node.js (see "Install Node.js" on page 320 and "Install npm Modules" on page 325). If you want to follow along with the Node.js project provided in the code examples, cd to *chapter-10/myconference* and do the following to install all dependencies for the project:

```
npm install
```

If you'd like to set up the Node.js project yourself, follow the instructions in the book's GitHub repository (*https://github.com/tmarrs/json-at-work-examples/tree/master/chapter-10/Project-Setup.md*).

Speaker Proposal Producer (Send Speaker Proposals)

We'll use the *publish-message.sh* script (that you saw earlier) to send the contents of the *speakerProposal.json* file to the `new-proposals-recvd` Topic. In the same terminal session (2), run the following command from the *scripts* directory:

```
./publish-message.sh -f ../data/speakerProposal.json new-proposals-recvd
```

The Proposal Reviewer accepts/rejects proposals randomly (see the next section for details), so you'll need to run this script three to five times (or more) to get acceptance and rejection and notification messages for the Speaker.

Proposal Reviewer (Consumer/Producer)

The Proposal Reviewer does the following:

- Listens on the `new-proposals-recvd` Topic to receive Speaker session proposals
- Validates the proposal and decides to accept or reject it

- Sends the decision on the proposal to the `proposals-reviewed` Topic for further processing

myconference/proposalReviewer.js includes the full Proposal Reviewer application. Example 10-11 shows the portion of the code (along with setup) that receives the Speaker session proposals on the `new-proposals-recvd` Topic.

Example 10-11. myconference/proposalReviewer.js

```
var kafka = require('kafka-node');

...

const NEW_PROPOSALS_RECEIVED_TOPIC = 'new-proposals-recvd';

...

var consumer = new kafka.ConsumerGroup({
  fromOffset: 'latest',
  autoCommit: true
}, NEW_PROPOSALS_RECEIVED_TOPIC);

// Use incoming JSON message.
// Use JSON.parse() and JSON.stringify() to process JSON.
consumer.on('message', function(message) {
  // console.log('received kafka message', message);
  processProposal(message);
});

consumer.on('error', function(err) {
  console.log(err);
});

process.on('SIGINT', function() {
  console.log(
    'SIGINT received - Proposal Reviewer closing. ' +
    'Committing current offset on Topic: ' +
    NEW_PROPOSALS_RECEIVED_TOPIC + ' ...'
  );

  consumer.close(true, function() {
    console.log(
      'Finished committing current offset. Exiting with graceful shutdown ...'
    );

    process.exit();
  });
});
```

Note the following in this example:

- Use the `kafka-node` npm module to consume/produce Kafka messages. You can find more information on `kafka-node` on the npm site (*https://www.npmjs.com/package/kafka-node*) and on GitHub (*https://github.com/SOHU-Co/kafka-node*).
- Listen on and consume messages from the `new-proposals-recvd` Topic as follows:
  - Instantiate and use the `ConsumerGroup` Object to consume Kafka messages on the `new-proposals-recvd` Topic. The `fromOffset: 'latest'` parameter indicates that we want to receive the latest message on the Topic, and `autoCommit: true` tells the consumer to commit each message automatically after it is consumed (this marks the message as processed).
  - `consumer.on('message' …)` listens for a message and invokes `processProposal()` (more on this later) to process the incoming Speaker proposal that was just received.
  - `consumer.on('error' …)` prints an error message for any errors encountered when processing the message.
  - `process.on('SIGINT' …)` listens for a `SIGINT` (process shutdown), commits the current offset, and does a graceful exit:
    - `consumer.close(…)` commits the current offset. This ensures that the current message is marked as read, and that the Consumer on this Topic will receive the next message on the topic upon restart.

Example 10-12 shows how to validate the Speaker proposal and make a decision.

Example 10-12. myconference/proposalReviewer.js

```
...

var fs = require('fs');
var Ajv = require('ajv');

...

const SPEAKER_PROPOSAL_SCHEMA_FILE_NAME =
  './schemas/speakerProposalSchema.json';

...

function processProposal(proposal) {
  var proposalAccepted = decideOnProposal();
  var proposalMessage = proposal.value;
  var proposalMessageObj = JSON.parse(proposalMessage);
```

```
  console.log('\n\n');
  console.log('proposalMessage = ' + proposalMessage);
  console.log('proposalMessageObj = ' + proposalMessageObj);
  console.log('Decision - proposal has been [' +
    (proposalAccepted ? 'Accepted' : 'Rejected') + ']');

  if (isSpeakerProposalValid(proposalMessageObj) && proposalAccepted) {
    acceptProposal(proposalMessageObj);
  } else {
    rejectProposal(proposalMessageObj);
  }
}


function isSpeakerProposalValid(proposalMessage) {
  var ajv = Ajv({
    allErrors: true
  });

  var speakerProposalSchemaContent = fs.readFileSync(
    SPEAKER_PROPOSAL_SCHEMA_FILE_NAME);

  var valid = ajv.validate(speakerProposalSchemaContent, proposalMessage);

  if (valid) {
    console.log('\n\nJSON Validation: Speaker proposal is valid');
  } else {
    console.log('\n\nJSON Validation: Error - Speaker proposal is invalid');
    console.log(ajv.errors + '\n');
  }

  return valid;
}

function decideOnProposal() {
  return Math.random() >= 0.5;
}

function acceptProposal(proposalMessage) {
  var acceptedProposal = {
    decision: {
      accepted: true,
      timeSlot: {
        date: "2017-11-06",
        time: "10:00"
      }
    },
    proposal: proposalMessage
  };

  var acceptedProposalMessage = JSON.stringify(acceptedProposal);
  console.log('Accepted Proposal = ' + acceptedProposalMessage);
```

```
    publishMessage(acceptedProposalMessage);
}

function rejectProposal(proposalMessage) {
  var rejectedProposal = {
    decision: {
      accepted: false
    },
    proposal: proposalMessage
  };

  var rejectedProposalMessage = JSON.stringify(rejectedProposal);
  console.log('Rejected Proposal = ' + rejectedProposalMessage);
  publishMessage(rejectedProposalMessage);
}
```

. . .

After the Proposal Reviewer receives a Speaker proposal message, `processPro`
`posal()` does the following:

- `decideOnProposal()` randomly chooses to accept or reject the proposal to keep
  things simple. In a real system, an application would put the proposal into someone's work inbox, and a human would review and make a decision.

- `JSON.parse()` parses the proposal message to ensure that it is *syntactically* correct (it follows basic JSON formatting rules).

- `isSpeakerProposalValid()` uses the `ajv` npm module to validate against a JSON
  Schema (*schemas/speakerProposalSchema.json*):

  — Chapter 5 covers JSON Schema if you need to refresh your memory.

  — Validating against a JSON Schema ensures that the incoming message is
    semantically correct (it has all the required fields needed to process a Speaker
    proposal).

  — You can find more information on `ajv` on the npm site (*https://
    www.npmjs.com/package/ajv*) and on GitHub (*https://github.com/epoberezkin/
    ajv*).

- If the Speaker proposal was accepted, `acceptProposal()` does the following:

  — Creates an acceptance object with fields to indicate that the proposal was
    accepted, and the time slot when the speaker will deliver the presentation at
    the conference

  — Uses `JSON.stringify()` to convert the acceptance object to JSON

  — Invokes `publishMessage()` to send the acceptance message to the `proposals-`
    `reviewed` Topic

- If the Speaker proposal was rejected (or its format was invalid), `rejectPro posal()` does the following:
  - — Creates a rejection Object with fields to indicate that the proposal was rejected
  - — Uses `JSON.stringify()` to convert the rejection Object to JSON
  - — Invokes `publishMessage()` to send the rejection message to the `proposals-reviewed` Topic

Example 10-13 shows how to send an acceptance/rejection message on to the `proposals-reviewed` Topic.

Example 10-13. myconference/proposalReviewer.js

```
...

const PROPOSALS_REVIEWED_TOPIC = 'proposals-reviewed';

...

var producerClient = new kafka.Client(),
  producer = new kafka.HighLevelProducer(producerClient);

...

function publishMessage(message) {
  var payloads = [{
    topic: PROPOSALS_REVIEWED_TOPIC,
    messages: message
  }];

  producer.send(payloads, function(err, data) {
    console.log(data);
  });
}

producer.on('error', function(err) {
  console.log(err);
});
```

This code publishes messages to the `proposals-reviewed` Topic as follows:

- Instantiates and uses the `HighLevelProducer` Object to publish messages to the `proposals-reviewed` Topic. The instantiation for `HighLevelProducer` actually happens toward the beginning of the file, but we show it here for convenience.
- `publishMessage()` invokes `producer.send()` to send the message. `pro ducer.on('message' …)` listens for a message and invokes `processProposal()`

(more on this later) to process the incoming Speaker proposal that was just received.

We've only touched on the `kafka-node` Objects used by Producers and Consumers. For further details, visit the `kafka-node` module documentation (*http://bit.ly/2soUUmL*) to learn more about the following:

- `HighLevelProducer`
- `ConsumerGroup`
- `Client`

Now that we've looked at Proposal Reviewer code, create a new terminal session (3) and run the following command (from the *myconference* directory) to start the Proposal Reviewer:

```
node proposalReviewer.js
```

When Speaker proposal messages arrive on the `new-proposals-recvd` Topic, you should see that the Proposal Reviewer logs the proposals it receives and the decisions it makes (on the `proposals-reviewed` Topic):

```
json-at-work => node proposalReviewer.js


proposalMessage = { "speaker": { "firstName": "Larson", "lastName": "Richard", "email": "larson.richard@ecratic.com", "bi
o": "Larson Richard is the CTO of ... and he founded a JavaScript meetup in ..." }, "session": { "title": "Enterprise Nod
e", "abstract": "Many developers just see Node as a way to build web APIs or applications ...", "type": "How-To", "length
": "3 hours" }, "conference": { "name": "Ultimate JavaScript Conference by MyConference", "beginDate": "2017-11-06", "end
Date": "2017-11-10" }, "topic": { "primary": "Node.js", "secondary": [ "REST", "Architecture", "JavaScript" ] }, "audienc
e": { "takeaway": "Audience members will learn how to ...", "jobTitles": [ "Architects", "Developers" ], "level": "Interm
ediate" }, "installation": [ "Git", "Laptop", "Node.js" ] }
proposalMessageObj = [object Object]
Decision - proposal has been [Accepted]


JSON Validation: Speaker proposal is valid
Accepted Proposal = {"decision":{"accepted":true,"timeSlot":{"date":"2017-11-06","time":"10:00"}},"proposal":{"speaker":{
"firstName":"Larson","lastName":"Richard","email":"larson.richard@ecratic.com","bio":"Larson Richard is the CTO of ... an
d he founded a JavaScript meetup in ..."},"session":{"title":"Enterprise Node","abstract":"Many developers just see Node
as a way to build web APIs or applications ...","type":"How-To","length":"3 hours"},"conference":{"name":"Ultimate JavaSc
ript Conference by MyConference","beginDate":"2017-11-06","endDate":"2017-11-10"},"topic":{"primary":"Node.js","secondary
":["REST","Architecture","JavaScript"]},"audience":{"takeaway":"Audience members will learn how to ...","jobTitles":["Arc
hitects","Developers"],"level":"Intermediate"},"installation":["Git","Laptop","Node.js"]}}
{ 'proposals-reviewed': { '0': 12 } }
```

Speaker Notifier (Consumer)

After the decision has been made to accept/reject a proposal, the Speaker Notifier:

- Listens on the `proposals-reviewed` Topic for accepted/rejected proposals
- Formats an acceptance/rejection email
- Sends the acceptance/rejection email

myconference/speakerNotifier.js includes the full Speaker Notifier application. Example 10-14 shows the portion of the code (along with setup) that receives the accepted/rejected proposals on the `proposals-reviewed` Topic.

Example 10-14. myconference/speakerNotifier.js

```
var kafka = require('kafka-node');

...

const PROPOSALS_REVIEWED_TOPIC = 'proposals-reviewed';

...

var consumer = new kafka.ConsumerGroup({
  fromOffset: 'latest',
  autoCommit: true
}, PROPOSALS_REVIEWED_TOPIC);

...

consumer.on('message', function(message) {
  // console.log('received message', message);
  notifySpeaker(message.value);
});

consumer.on('error', function(err) {
  console.log(err);
});

process.on('SIGINT', function() {
  console.log(
    'SIGINT received - Proposal Reviewer closing. ' +
    'Committing current offset on Topic: ' +
    PROPOSALS_REVIEWED_TOPIC + ' ...'
  );

  consumer.close(true, function() {
    console.log(
      'Finished committing current offset. Exiting with graceful shutdown ...'
    );

    process.exit();
  });
});

...
```

The Speaker Notifier listens on and consumes messages from the proposals-reviewed Topic as follows:

- Instantiates and uses the ConsumerGroup Object to consume Kafka messages on the proposals-reviewed Topic. The setup for this consumer is similar to the code in the Proposal Reviewer.

- consumer.on('message' …) listens for a message and invokes notifySpeaker() (more on this later) to process the incoming acceptance/rejection message that was just received.

- consumer.on('error' …) and process.on('SIGINT' …) function in the same manner as the Proposal Reviewer example.

Example 10-15 shows how to process the accepted/rejected proposals and formats a corresponding acceptance/rejection email using Handlebars (which was covered in Chapter 7).

Example 10-15. myconference/speakerNotifier.js

```
...

var handlebars = require('handlebars');
var fs = require('fs');

...

const EMAIL_FROM = 'proposals@myconference.com';
const ACCEPTED_PROPOSAL_HB_TEMPLATE_FILE_NAME =
  './templates/acceptedProposal.hbs';

const REJECTED_PROPOSAL_HB_TEMPLATE_FILE_NAME =
  './templates/rejectedProposal.hbs';

const UTF_8 = 'utf8';

...

function notifySpeaker(notification) {
  var notificationMessage = createNotificationMessage(notification);

  sendEmail(notificationMessage);
}

function createNotificationMessage(notification) {
  var notificationAsObj = JSON.parse(notification);
  var proposal = notificationAsObj.proposal;

  console.log('Notification Message = ' + notification);
```

```
  var mailOptions = {
    from: EMAIL_FROM, // sender address
    to: proposal.speaker.email, // list of receivers
    subject: proposal.conference.name + ' - ' + proposal.session.title, // Subject
    html: createEmailBody(notificationAsObj)
  };

  return mailOptions;
}

function createEmailBody(notification) {
  // Read Handlebars Template file.
  var hbTemplateContent = fs.readFileSync(((notification.decision.accepted) ?
    ACCEPTED_PROPOSAL_HB_TEMPLATE_FILE_NAME :
    REJECTED_PROPOSAL_HB_TEMPLATE_FILE_NAME), UTF_8);

  // Compile the template into a function.
  var template = handlebars.compile(hbTemplateContent);
  var body = template(notification); // Render the template.

  console.log('Email body = ' + body);
  return body;
}
```

...

After the Speaker Notifier receives an acceptance/rejection message, `notify` `Speaker()` does the following:

- Invokes `createNotificationMessage()` to create the notification email to send to the Speaker:
  - Uses `JSON.parse()` to parse the acceptance/rejection message into an Object
  - Invokes `createEmailBody()`:
    - Uses the `handlebars` npm module to generate an acceptance/rejection email message in HTML format from the acceptance/rejection Object.
    - Chapter 7 covers Handlebars if you need to refresh your memory.
    - You can find more information on `handlebars` on the npm site (*https://www.npmjs.com/package/handlebars*) and on GitHub (*https://github.com/wycats/handlebars.js*).
- Invokes `sendEmail()` to send the notification email to the Speaker (see the next example)

Example 10-16 shows how to send an acceptance/rejection email.

Example 10-16. myconference/speakerNotifier.js

```
...

var nodeMailer = require('nodemailer');

...

const MAILCATCHER_SMTP_HOST = 'localhost';
const MAILCATCHER_SMTP_PORT = 1025;

var transporter = nodeMailer.createTransport(mailCatcherSmtpConfig);

...

function sendEmail(mailOptions) {
  // send mail with defined transport object
  transporter.sendMail(mailOptions, function(error, info) {
    if (error) {
      console.log(error);
    } else {
      console.log('Email Message sent: ' + info.response);
    }
  });
}
```

The Speaker Notifier sends email messages to the MailCatcher server as follows:

- Instantiates and uses the `nodemailer` transporter Object to send email. The `MAIL CATCHER_SMTP_...` constants indicate the host and port used by the MailCatcher on your local machine. The instantiation for the `nodemailer` transporter Object actually happens toward the beginning the file, but we show it here for convenience.

- `sendEmail()` invokes `transporter.sendMail()` to send the email message.

- `nodemailer` is a generic npm module that sends email messages by using SMTP. You can find more information on `ajv` on the npm site (*https://www.npmjs.com/package/nodemailer*) and on the `nodemailer` Community Page (*https://community.nodemailer.com*).

Now, create a new terminal session (4) and run the following command (from the *myconference* directory) to start the Speaker Notifier:

```
node speakerNotifier.js
```

When accepted/rejected proposal messages arrive on the `proposals-reviewed` Topic, you should see that the Speaker Notifier logs the accepted/rejected proposals it receives and the email notifications it sends:

```
json-at-work => node speakerNotifier.js
Notification Message = {"decision":{"accepted":true,"timeSlot":{"date":"2017-11-06","time":"10:00"}},"proposal":{"speaker
":{"firstName":"Larson","lastName":"Richard","email":"larson.richard@ecratic.com","bio":"Larson Richard is the CTO of ...
 and he founded a JavaScript meetup in ..."},"session":{"title":"Enterprise Node","abstract":"Many developers just see No
de as a way to build web APIs or applications ...","type":"How-To","length":"3 hours"},"conference":{"name":"Ultimate Jav
aScript Conference by MyConference","beginDate":"2017-11-06","endDate":"2017-11-10"},"topic":{"primary":"Node.js","second
ary":["REST","Architecture","JavaScript"]},"audience":{"takeaway":"Audience members will learn how to ...","jobTitles":["
Architects","Developers"],"level":"Intermediate"},"installation":["Git","Laptop","Node.js"]}}
Email body = <!DOCTYPE html>
<html>
  <body>
    <p>
    Larson,
    </p>
    <p>
    We are pleased to inform you that your talk on <u>Enterprise Node</u>
    has been accepted for the <b>Ultimate JavaScript Conference by MyConference</b>.
    </p>
    <p>
    Your session scheduled for 2017-11-06 at 10:00.
    </p>
    <p>
    Sincerely,<br/>
    The Ultimate JavaScript Conference by MyConference Event Team.
    </p>
  </body>
</html>
Email Message sent: 250 Message accepted
```

Review Notification Email Messages with MailCatcher

To wrap up our example, let's look at the notification messages (generated by the Speaker Notifier) sent to the prospective MyConference speakers.

Visit *http://localhost:1080* on your machine and you'll see the MailCatcher user interface. Figure 10-2 shows the summary page that lists the email messages generated by the MyConference application (using Handlebars).

Figure 10-2. Speaker Notification messages on MailCatcher

Click some of the messages until you see an Acceptance message indicating that the session proposal was accepted, as shown in Figure 10-3.

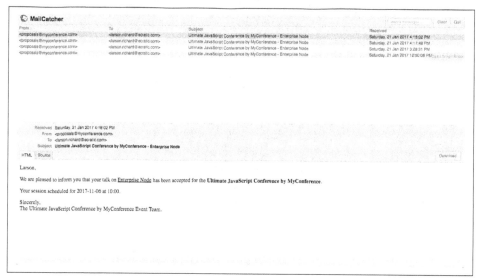

Figure 10-3. Speaker Proposal Acceptance message on MailCatcher

Figure 10-4 shows a sample rejection message.

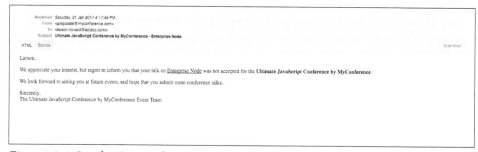

Figure 10-4. Speaker Proposal Rejection message on MailCatcher

The MailCatcher web UI controls work as follows:

- Download the current email message by clicking the Download button. This saves the message as a file (with the extension *.eml*) in EML format, which

  — Follows the MIME 822 standard (*https://www.ietf.org/rfc/rfc0822.txt*)

  — Is compatible with MS Outlook and Outlook Express, Apple Mail, Mozilla Thunderbird, and other email clients

  — Preserves the original HTML format and headers

- Shut down the MailCatcher background process by clicking on the Quit button on the upper-right side of the page

What We Covered

In this chapter, we've shown how to do the following:

- Produce/Consume JSON messages with Kafka from the command line.
- Design and implement a small end-to-end example MyConference application that leverages Kafka Topics, Node.js, and a fake email server to process JSON-based Speaker applications.

Installation Guides

This appendix provides an installation guide and setup instructions to support the code examples in this book.

Install JSON Tools in the Browser

This section shows how to install JSON-based tools in the browser.

Install JSONView in Chrome and Firefox

JSONView pretty-prints JSON in Chrome or Firefox. Follow the installation instructions on the JSONView site (*http://jsonview.com/*) for your browser.

JSONLint

Use JSONLint (*https://jsonlint.com/*) to validate JSON documents online. JSONLint doesn't require an installation.

JSON Editor Online

Use JSON Editor Online (*http://www.jsoneditoronline.org*) to model JSON documents. Since this is a web app, there's nothing to install.

Install Postman

Postman provides the ability to fully test a RESTful API. It can send HTTP GET, POST, PUT, and DELETE requests and set HTTP headers. You can install Postman as a Chrome extension or as a standalone GUI application on macOS, Linux, or Windows. Visit the Postman site (*https://www.getpostman.com/*) for installation instructions.

Install Node.js

This book uses Node.js version `v6.10.2` (*https://nodejs.org/en/download*), which is the current latest stable version as of this writing.

Install Node.js on macOS and Linux with NVM

Although you could use the installation package from the Node.js site (*https://nodejs.org*), it's difficult to change versions. Instead, let's use Node Version Manager (NVM) (*https://github.com/creationix/nvm*). NVM makes it easy to install/uninstall Node.js, and upgrade to newer versions.

Install and configure NVM

First, install NVM by using one of the following methods:

- Install script (*https://github.com/creationix/nvm#install-script*)
- Manual install (*https://github.com/creationix/nvm#manual-install*)

Next, let's make sure that NVM runs properly. Source it from a shell as follows:

```
source ~/.nvm/nvm.sh
```

Now NVM will work properly for the remainder of the installation process.

If you're running bash, do the following so that NVM is automatically sourced (configured):

- In *$HOME/.bashrc*, add these lines:

```
source ~/.nvm/nvm.sh export NVM_HOME=~/.nvm/v6.10.2
```

- In *$HOME/.bashrc_profile*, add this line:

```
[[ -s $HOME/.nvm/nvm.sh ]] && . $HOME/.nvm/nvm.sh # This loads NVM
```

Note that similar steps apply to the Bourne Shell or Korn Shell.

Install Node.js with NVM

Now that NVM is installed, use it to install Node.js:

1. Type `nvm ls-remote` to see what remote (not on your local machine) versions of Node.js are available to install.
2. Install version `v6.10.2` with the following command:

```
nvm install v6.10.2
```

- All Node.js versions are installed in $HOME/.nvm.

3. Set the default Node.js version to be used in any new shell:

```
nvm alias default v6.10.2
```

- Without this, neither the node or npm commands will work properly when you exit the current shell.
- Now, exit your current shell.

From a new shell, upgrade to the latest version of npm:

```
npm update -g npm
```

Then, do the following health checks:

- nvm ls, and you should see ... -> v6.10.2 system default -> v6.10.2
- node -v, which yields v6.10.2
- npm -v, and it looks like 4.6.1

To see a full list of NVM's capabilities, type nvm --help.

When you check out the Node.js Request-Eval-Print-Loop (REPL) (*https://nodejs.org/api/repl.html*), you should see this:

```
json-at-work => node
-> .exit
```

Avoiding sudo with npm

npm may require you to run as sudo, and this can get cumbersome and annoying. This also can be a security risk because packages can contain scripts, and npm is running with root privilege. To avoid this, do the following:

```
sudo chown -R $USER ~/.nvm
```

This works if you installed Node.js with NVM (all Node.js installations go under that directory). This tip was inspired by Isaac Z. Schlueter from How to Node (*http://howtonode.org/introduction-to-npm*).

Taming the REPL—mynode

Out of the box, the default behavior of the REPL leaves a bit to be desired because you see undefined after most lines of JavaScript, hitting the Enter key, breathing, and so forth. This is because JavaScript functions always return something. If nothing is returned, undefined is returned by default. This behavior can be annoying and unproductive. Here's a sample session:

```
json-at-work => node
-> Hit Enter
-> undefined

-> var y = 5
-> undefined
-> .exit
```

To turn off undefined in the REPL, add the following to *.bashrc* (or your setup for Bourne or Korn Shell):

```
source ~/.nvm/nvm.sh

...

alias mynode="node -e \"require('repl').start({ignoreUndefined: true})\""
```

Now, exit the current shell and start a new shell. Rather than redefining node, it's safer to define a new alias (in this case, mynode). This way, node will still work properly from the command line and be able to run JavaScript files. Meanwhile, mynode serves as your new REPL command:

```
json-at-work => mynode
-> var x = 5
-> .exit
```

You now have a Node.js REPL that does what you want—no more annoying unde fined. You're welcome.

Install Node.js on Windows

NVM also works well on Windows thanks to Corey Butler's nvm-windows (*https://github.com/coreybutler/nvm-windows*) application. This is a port of nvm to a Windows environment. I successfully used nvm-windows (*https://github.com/coreybutler/nvm-windows*) on Windows 7.

Install Node.js on Windows with nvm-windows

Here are the steps:

1. Visit the nvm-windows Downloads page (*https://github.com/coreybutler/nvm-windows/releases*).
2. Download the latest *nvm-setup.zip* to your *Downloads* folder.
3. Unzip *nvm-setup.zip* with your favorite zip tool.
4. Run *nvm-setup.exe*, which is a wizard. Accept all defaults and the MIT License agreement:

    a. Download to *C:\Users{username}\AppData\Roaming\nvm*.

b. Click Finish when the install completes.

c. This sets up the necessary environment variables to run Node.js on your Windows machine.

5. Ensure that NVM is on your PATH:

a. Navigate to Control Panel → System → Advanced System Settings.

b. Click Environment Variables on the Advanced System Settings pop up.

c. NVM_HOME should have been added to Env Vars during install: *C:\Users{username}\AppData\Roaming\nvm*

d. NVM_SYMLINK should point to *C:\Program Files\nodejs*

e. Both NVM_HOME and NVM_SYMLINK should be on the PATH.

6. Install Node.js with nvm-windows (*https://github.com/coreybutler/nvm-windows*):

a. Type nvm list available to get a list of available versions.

b. Type nvm install v6.10.2

c. Set the version of Node.js: nvm use v6.10.2

d. Test the install: node -v

Uninstall Node.js

If you have a previous installation of Node.js that isn't quite working properly anymore, you may need to completely uninstall it from your machine. This includes both the node and npm executables.

Uninstall Node.js on macOS

Uninstalls can be complicated, and credit for the Mac uninstall instructions goes to Clay at Hungred Dot Com (*http://hungred.com/how-to/completely-removing-nodejs-npm/*). If Homebrew was used to install Node.js, simply type brew uninstall node at the prompt.

If you didn't use Homebrew, do the following:

- cd to */usr/local/lib* and delete any node executable and node_modules.
- cd to */usr/local/include* and delete any node and the *node_modules* directory.
- cd to */usr/local/bin* and delete any node executable.

You may also need to do the following:

```
rm -rf /usr/local/bin/npm
rm -rf /usr/local/share/man/man1/node.1
```

```
rm -rf /usr/local/lib/dtrace/node.d
rm -rf $USER/.npm
```

Uninstall Node.js on Linux

Credit for the Linux uninstall instructions goes to Stack Overflow (*http://bit.ly/ 2rGq2xs*) and GitHub (*https://github.com/joyent/node/issues/4058*). Do the following:

1. Find the node installation by typing which node. Let's assume it's at */usr/ local/bin/node*.

2. cd to */usr/local*.

3. Execute the following:

```
sudo rm -rf bin/node
sudo rm -rf bin/npm
sudo rm -rf lib/node_modules/npm
sudo rm -rf lib/node
sudo rm -rf share/man/*/node.*
```

Uninstall Node.js on Windows

Credit for the Windows uninstall instructions goes to Team Treehouse (*http:// blog.teamtreehouse.com/install-node-js-npm-windows*). Here are the steps:

1. Open the Windows Control Panel.

2. Choose Programs and Features.

3. Click "Uninstall a program."

4. Select Node.js, and click the Uninstall link.

Install Yeoman

Yeoman (*http://yeoman.io*) consists of the following:

- yo (for Scaffolding)
- Either npm (*https://www.npmjs.com*) or bower (*https://bower.io*) (for Package Management)
- Either gulp (*http://gulpjs.com*) or grunt (*https://gruntjs.com*) (for the Build System)

For the code examples in this book, you'll need both gulp (*http://gulpjs.com*) and grunt-cli (*https://github.com/gruntjs/grunt-cli*) for the Build System. Although gulp (*http://gulpjs.com*) is used as the primary build tool, you still need grunt-cli (*https:// github.com/gruntjs/grunt-cli*) to run some of the gulp tasks.

I chose bower (*https://bower.io*) for Package Management.

Here are the installation steps:

- Install yo:
  - — npm install -g yo
  - — Test the yo installation: yo --version
- Install bower (*https://bower.io*):
  - — npm install -g bower
  - — Test the bower installation: bower --version
- Install gulp (*http://gulpjs.com*):
  - — npm install -g gulp-cli
  - — Test the gulp installation: gulp --version
- Install grunt-cli (*https://github.com/gruntjs/grunt-cli*):
  - — npm install -g grunt-cli
  - — Test the grunt-cli installation: grunt --version

Refer to the Yeoman setup page (*http://yeoman.io/codelab/setup.html*) for more information.

Install the generator-webapp Yeoman generator

See the generator-webapp GitHub page (*http://bit.ly/2rhUvz8*). Install the generator as follows:

```
npm install -g generator-webapp
```

Install npm Modules

We use the following npm modules at the command line, so we install them globally:

- jsonlint
- json
- ujs-jsonvalidate
- http-server
- json-server
- jq-tutorial

Install jsonlint

This is the npm equivalent of the JSONLint site (*https://jsonlint.com/*) used to validate a JSON document. You can find `jsonlint` in the GitHub repository (*https://github.com/zaach/jsonlint*).

To install:

```
npm install -g jsonlint
```

To validate a JSON document:

```
jsonlint basic.json
```

Install json

`json` (*https://github.com/trentm/json*) provides the ability to work with JSON (e.g., pretty-printing) from the command line. It's similar to `jq` (*http://stedolan.github.io/jq/*), but not as powerful.

To install:

```
npm install -g json
```

Visit the `json` GitHub repository (*https://github.com/trentm/json*) for usage instructions. `json` is available as an npm module (*https://www.npmjs.com/package/json*).

Install ujs-jsonvalidate

This is the npm equivalent of the JSON Validate site (*http://jsonvalidate.com/*) used to validate a JSON document against a JSON Schema. `ujs-jsonvalidate` can be found in the GitHub repository (*http://bit.ly/2riiFJM*).

To install:

```
npm install -g ujs-jsonvalidate
```

To validate a JSON document:

```
validate basic.json basic-schema.json
```

Install http-server

`http-server` is a simple Web Server that serves up files in the current directory structure on the local host system as static content. I like `http-server` because it has solid documentation, and the command-line options and shutdown are intuitive. Here's the `http-server` in the GitHub Repository (*https://github.com/indexzero/http-server*) and `http-server` in the npm repository (*https://www.npmjs.com/package/http-server*).

To install:

```
npm install -g http-server
```

To run:

```
http-server -p 8081
```

To access:

```
http://localhost:8081
```

To shut down: press Ctrl-C

Install json-server

`json-server` is a Stub REST server that takes a JSON file and exposes it as a RESTful service. You can find `json-server` in the GitHub repository (*https://github.com/typi code/json-server*).

To install:

```
npm install -g json-server
```

To run:

```
json-server -p 5000 ./speakers.json
```

To access:

```
http://localhost:5000/speakers
```

Install Crest

Crest is a small REST server that provides a RESTful wrapper for MongoDB. You can find Crest in the GitHub Repository (*https://github.com/cordazar/crest*). The global `npm` installation would be the simplest way to install Crest, but this is broken. Instead, do a `git clone` as follows:

1. `cd` to the directory where your other development projects reside. We'll call this directory *projects*:

   ```
   cd projects
   ```

2. Clone the repository:

   ```
   git clone git://github.com/Cordazar/crest.git
   ```

3. Navigate to the *crest* directory:

   ```
   cd crest
   ```

4. Update the *config.json* file to remove the `username` and `password`. Of course, this isn't secure, but you can re-add these fields and set them to proper values later; just make sure that the settings match your MongoDB password. We just want to get started quickly. The *config.json* file should now look like this:

```
{
  "db": { "port": 27017, "host": "localhost" },
  "server": { "port": 3500, "address": "0.0.0.0" },
  "flavor": "normal",
  "debug": true
}
```

5. Be sure to install and start MongoDB first.

6. In a separate tab or command shell, start Crest by typing `node server` on the command line. You should see the following:

```
node server

DEBUG: util.js is loaded
DEBUG: rest.js is loaded
crest listening at http://:::3500
```

Install jq-tutorial

`jq-tutorial` (*https://www.npmjs.com/package/jq-tutorial*) is an npm module that provides a nice `jq` tutorial from the command line. Install it as follows:

```
npm install -g jq-tutorial
```

Then run it from the command line:

```
jq-tutorial
```

Install Ruby on Rails

There are several ways to install Ruby on Rails:

- Rails Installer (*http://railsinstaller.org*)
- ruby-install (*https://github.com/postmodern/ruby-install*)
- Ruby Version Manager (RVM) (*https://rvm.io/*) + the `rails` gem
- rbenv (*https://github.com/sstephenson/rbenv*) + the `rails` gem

Install Rails on macOS and Linux

I prefer RVM for macOS and Linux because it's easy to upgrade to switch between Ruby versions. Install RVM by visiting the RVM site (*https://rvm.io/*) and following the installation instructions (*https://rvm.io/rvm/install*).

Use RVM to install Ruby as follows:

1. See the available versions of Ruby:

```
rvm list known
```

2. Install Ruby v2.4.0 as follows:

```
rvm install 2.4.0
```

3. Check the Ruby version, and you should see something like this:

```
ruby -v
ruby 2.4.0
```

4. After installing Ruby, you can install Rails as follows:

```
gem install rails
```

5. Check the Rails version, and it should look like this:

```
rails -v
Rails Rails 5.0.2
```

And you're done.

You can easily upgrade to new versions of Ruby and Rails by following these steps:

1. Install a new version of Ruby (2.x for example):

```
rvm install 2.x
```

2. Use the new version:

```
rvm use 2.x
```

3. Install the rails gem as shown previously.

Install Rails on Windows

Use Rails Installer (*http://railsinstaller.org*) for a Windows environment, and do the following:

- Download the installer for Windows.
- Run the installer and follow the defaults.

I've used Rails Installer (*http://railsinstaller.org*) on Windows 7, and it worked properly. The Rails Installer (*http://railsinstaller.org*) page has excellent information on RoR tutorials and how to get help with installation issues.

Install Ruby Gems

We use the following Ruby gems outside Rails, so we install them globally:

- multijson

- oj
- awesome_print
- activesupport
- minitest
- mailcatcher

Install multi_json

`multi_json` (*https://github.com/intridea/multi_json*) provides a wrapper that invokes the most common JSON gems on behalf of the caller by choosing the fastest JSON gem that has been loaded in an application's environment. Install it as follows:

```
gem install multi_json
```

Install oj

Optimized JSON (`oj`) (*https://github.com/ohler55/oj*), is considered by many to be the fastest Ruby-based JSON processor available. Install it as follows:

```
gem install oj
```

Install awesome_print

`awesome_print` (*https://github.com/awesome-print/awesome_print*) pretty-prints a Ruby object and is used for debugging purposes. Install it as follows:

```
gem install awesome_print
```

Install activesupport

`activesupport` (*https://github.com/rails/rails/tree/master/activesupport*) provides functionality that has been extracted from Rails. ActiveSupport's JSON module provides the ability to convert keys between camel case and snake case. Install it as follows:

```
gem install activesupport
```

Install mailcatcher

`mailcatcher` (*https://mailcatcher.me*) is a simple mail (SMTP) server. It's a great tool for testing emails without forcing you to send a real email. Install it as follows:

```
gem install mailcatcher
```

Install MongoDB

See the MongoDB installation documentation (*https://docs.mongodb.com/manual/installation/*) and follow the instructions to install and start MongoDB on your platform.

Install the Java Environment

Our Java environment depends on the following:

- Java SE
- Gradle

Install Java SE

We're using Java Standard Edition (SE) 8 for this book, so visit the Oracle Java SE 8 download site (*http://bit.ly/1X9h0Ea*).

You'll see the term *JDK* (for *Java Developer Kit*) on that page. JDK is the old name for Java SE. Just look for Java SE Development Kit, accept the license agreement, and do the proper download for your operating system. After you've downloaded and run the installer, you'll want to set up your Java command-line environment for your operating system.

Follow the instructions that follow for you system. Then run this:

```
java -version
```

You should see something similar to this

```
java version "1.8.0_72"
Java(TM) SE Runtime Environment (build 1.8.0_72-b15)
Java HotSpot(TM) 64-Bit Server VM (build 25.72-b15, mixed mode)
```

Java setup on macOS

In *.bashrc*, do the following to set up JAVA_HOME and add it to your PATH:

```
...

export
JAVA_HOME=/Library/Java/JavaVirtualMachines/jdk1.x.y.jdk/Contents/Home #
x and y are the minor and patch versions

...

export PATH=...:$\{JAVA_HOME}/bin:...
```

Java setup on Linux

In *.bashrc*, do the following to set up JAVA_HOME and add it to your PATH:

```
...

export JAVA_HOME=/usr/java/jdk1.x.y/bin/java # x and y are the minor and
patch versions

...

export PATH=...:$\{JAVA_HOME}/bin:...
```

Then, refresh your environment:

```
source ~/.bashrc
```

Credit for Java setup on Linux goes to nixCraft (*http://www.cyberciti.biz/faq/linux-unix-set-java_home-path-variable/*).

Java setup on Windows

The Java Windows Installer usually puts the JDK in one of the following directories: *C:\Program Files\Java* or *C:\Program Files (x86)\Java*.

Then, do the following:

1. Right-click the My Computer icon on your desktop and select Properties.
2. Click the Advanced tab.
3. Click the Environment Variables button.
4. Under System Variables, click New.
5. Enter the variable name as JAVA_HOME.
6. Enter the variable value as the installation path for the Java Development Kit (see where the installer put the JDK directory).
7. Click OK.
8. Click Apply Changes.

Credit for the Java setup on Windows goes to Robert Sindall (*http://www.robertsindall.co.uk/blog/setting-java-home-variable-in-windows/*).

Install Gradle

Gradle (*http://www.gradle.org*) is used for building source and test code. Visit the Gradle Installation Guide (*https://gradle.org/install*) and follow the instructions for your operating system. After you've completed the installation, run `gradle -v` from the command line and you should see something like this:

```
gradle -v
```

```
Gradle 3.4.1
```

On macOS, I succesfully used Homebrew to install Gradle (*https://gradle.org/ install#with-homebrew*).

Install jq

jq (*http://stedolan.github.io/jq/*) provides JSON-based command-line processing. To install it, just follow the download instructions on the jq GitHub repository (*http:// stedolan.github.io/jq/download/*).

jq works with and depends on cURL.

Install cURL

cURL (*http://curl.haxx.se/*) provides the ability to communicate over multiple proto-cols, including HTTP. Use this to make HTTP calls to RESTful APIs from the com-mand line.

Install cURL on macOS

Just as with Linux, cURL may already be installed on your Mac. Check it as follows:

```
curl --version
```

If it's already there, there's nothing else to do. Otherwise, you'll need to install it. I use Homebrew (*http://brew.sh/*) as my package installer on macOS, so use the following command to install cURL on a Mac:

```
brew install curl
```

Install cURL on Linux

Check whether cURL is already installed by entering the following command:

```
curl --version
```

If it isn't there, do the following from the command line:

```
sudo apt-get install curl
```

This should work on Ubuntu or Debian.

Install cURL on Windows

To install cURL on Windows, do the following:

1. Visit the cURL Download Wizard (*http://curl.haxx.se/dlwiz/*).

2. Select the type of package: curl executable.

3. Select the Operating System: either Windows/Win32 or Win64.

4. Select the Flavor: either Cygwin (if you use Cygwin (*https://www.cygwin.com/*)) or Generic (if you don't use Cygwin (*https://www.cygwin.com/*)).

5. Select the Win32 version (only if you selected Windows/Win32 previously): Unspecified.

Credit for the cURL Windows installation instructions goes to Stack Overflow (*http://bit.ly/2r6Yrqx*).

Install Apache Kafka

We use Apache Kafka (*http://kafka.apache.org/*) in Chapter 10 for JSON-based messaging. Kafka depends on Apache ZooKeeper (*http://zookeeper.apache.org/*) so you'll need to install ZooKeeper, too. Before going any further, be sure to install the Java Environment on your machine (because Kafka is based on Java).

Install Kafka on macOS

Homebrew (*http://brew.sh/*) is the easiest way to install Kafka on macOS. Do the following from the command line:

```
brew install kafka
```

This installs both Kafka and ZooKeeper. You're done.

Install Kafka on UNIX

Install ZooKeeper as follows:

- Download ZooKeeper from the ZooKeeper Releases page (*http://bit.ly/2tmX0Rm*).

- Extract the TAR file from the GZipped file you downloaded (current/latest Zoo-Keeper download):

```
tar -zxf ZooKeeper-3.4.9.tar.gz
```

- Add system environment variables in ~/.bashrc:

```
export ZooKeeper_HOME = <Zookeeper-Install-Path>/zookeeper-3.4.9
export PATH=$PATH:$ZOOKEEPER_HOME/bin
```

Install Kafka as follows:

1. Download Kafka from the Kafka Downloads page (*http://kafka.apache.org/down loads.html*).

2. Extract the TAR file from the GZipped file you downloaded (current/latest Kafka download):

```
tar -zxf  kafka_2.11-0.10.1.1.tgz
```

3. Add system environment variables in *~/.bashrc*:

```
export KAFKA_HOME = <Kafka-Install-Path>/zookeeper-3.4.9
export PATH=$PATH:$KAFKA_HOME/bin
```

Credit for the Apache Kafka installation on UNIX instructions goes to TutorialsPoint (*https://www.tutorialspoint.com/apache_kafka/apache_kafka_installation_steps.htm*).

Install Kafka on Windows

Install ZooKeeper as follows:

1. Download ZooKeeper from the ZooKeeper Downloads page (*http://bit.ly/ 2tmX0Rm*).

2. Use your favorite zip tool to unzip the ZooKeeper file to the C: drive.

3. Add System Variables as follows:

   a. In Windows, navigate to Control Panel → System → Advanced System Set-tings → Environment Variables.

   b. Create the following new System Variable (current/latest ZooKeeper down-load):

   ```
   ZOOKEEPER_HOME = C:\zookeeper-3.4.9
   ```

   c. Add ZooKeeper to your PATH by editing that variable and adding this at the end:

   ```
   ;%ZOOKEEPER_HOME%\bin;
   ```

Install Kafka as follows:

1. Download Kafka from the Kafka Downloads page (*http://kafka.apache.org/down loads.html*).

2. Use your favorite zip tool to unzip the Kafka file to the C: drive.

3. Add System Variables as follows:

   a. In Windows, navigate to Control Panel → System → Advanced System Set-tings → Environment Variables.

   b. Create the following new System Variable (current/latest Kafka download):

```
KAFKA_HOME = C:\kafka_2.11-0.10.1.1
```

c. Add Kafka to your PATH by editing that variable and adding this at the end:

```
;%KAFKA_HOME%\bin;
```

Credit for the Apache Kafka installation on Windows instructions goes to Gopal Tiwari's article on DZone (*http://bit.ly/2rssBoa*).

References

- The AsciiDoc (*http://asciidoc.org*) version of Appendix A in the book was generated by Pandoc (*http://pandoc.org*) from the original Markdown in the *JSON at Work* GitHub examples repository (*https://github.com/tmarrs/json-at-work-examples/blob/master/appendix-a/README.md*).

JSON Community

JSON has an active and vibrant community. Visit the following groups and lists to get involved and learn more:

JSON.org (http://www.json.org)
  Douglas Crockford's JSON site where it all started.

JSON Yahoo! Group (https://groups.yahoo.com/neo/groups/json/info)
  This Yahoo Group is affiliated with the JSON.org site.

`json-ietf` *Mailing List (https://www.ietf.org/mailman/listinfo/json)*
  This list is for the JSON IETF (Internet Engineering Task Force) Working Group that maintains the JSON IETF specification.

JSONauts (http://jsonauts.github.io)
  Another great source of JSON tutorials, tools, and articles.

JSON Schema Specification Working Group (https://github.com/json-schema-org/json-schema-spec)
  The JSON Schema specification is maintained in this GitHub Repository.

JSON Schema Google Group (https://groups.google.com/forum/#!forum/json-schema)
  This Google group is associated with the JSON Schema Specification Working Group.

`api-craft` *Google Group (https://groups.google.com/forum/#!forum/api-craft)*
  This group focuses on API Design and development.

Index

About the Author

Tom Marrs is passionate about demonstrating the business value of technology. As an Enterprise Architect at TEKsystems Global Services, he leverages the enabling architectures and technologies that fuel the growing API Economy—REST, Microservices, and JSON. Tom has led enterprise-class API, Web, Mobile, Cloud, and SOA projects. An avid Agilist, Tom is a Certified Scrum Master and enjoys mentoring and coaching project teams.

In other JSON-related work, Tom wrote the Core JSON Refcard for DZone (the #1 downloaded Refcard in 2013). In a past life, Tom co-authored *JBoss at Work* for O'Reilly. Tom has also been a speaker at the O'Reilly Open Source Convention (OSCON), No Fluff Just Stuff (NFJS), and Great Indian Developer Summit (GIDS) conferences. He hopes to speak at these conferences again in the near future.

Colophon

The animal on the cover of *JSON at Work* is the Siberian jay (*Perisoreus infaustus*), a small bird native to northern Eurasia. Its habitat range is extremely large, stretching from Sweden in the west to China in the east. They make their nests in coniferous trees found in dense boreal forests (also known as taiga).

Siberian jays can grow to be 29 centimeters long and can weigh up to 79 grams. They have long tails and brown and gray coloring. Siberian jays are omnivorous, feeding on berries and seeds as well as insects, carrion, and small rodents. Females lay their eggs once a year in March or April, and raise their young before the winter arrives.

There is some evidence that the European population of Siberian jays is declining as a result of human-caused deforestation. However, because of their massive range across sparsely inhabited regions of Asia, the Siberian jay not currently listed as endangered or threatened.

Many of the animals on O'Reilly covers are endangered; all of them are important to the world. To learn more about how you can help, go to *animals.oreilly.com*.

The cover image is from *Riverside Natural History*. The cover fonts are URW Typewriter and Guardian Sans. The text font is Adobe Minion Pro; the heading font is Adobe Myriad Condensed; and the code font is Dalton Maag's Ubuntu Mono.

Learn from experts.
Find the answers you need.

Sign up for a **10-day free trial** to get **unlimited access** to all of the content on Safari, including Learning Paths, interactive tutorials, and curated playlists that draw from thousands of ebooks and training videos on a wide range of topics, including data, design, DevOps, management, business—and much more.

Start your free trial at:

oreilly.com/safari

Milton Keynes UK
Ingram Content Group UK Ltd.
UKHW052011300824
447620UK00007B/210